the New Diary

How to use a journal
for self-guidance and
expanded creativity.

Tristine Rainer

Preface by Anaïs Nin

JEREMY P. TARCHER, INC.
Los Angeles
Distributed by St. Martin's Press
New York

Library of Congress Catalog Card No. 76-062677
ISBN: 0-87477-061-0
Interior design by Tom Gould
Manufactured in the United States of America
Published by J. P. Tarcher, Inc.
9110 Sunset Blvd., Los Angeles, Calif. 90069
s 17 16 15 14 13

The author gratefully acknowledges the following publishers and copyright holders for permission to reprint or reproduce illustrations from copyrighted material (the rights on all unpublished excerpts are held by the contributors):

Chatto & Windus, for excerpts and illustrations from *A Life of One's Own* by Joanna Field, ©1936.

Clarke, Irwin & Company, Ltd., for excerpts from *Hundreds and Thousands: The Journals of Emily Carr,*©1966.

Doubleday & Company, Inc., for excerpts from *Anne Frank: The Diary of a Young Girl,* ©1952 by Otto H. Frank.

Harcourt Brace Jovanovich, Inc., for excerpts from *A Writer's Diary* by Virginia Woolf, © 1953; *The Diaries of Anaïs Nin* by Anaïs Nin, © 1966, 1967, 1969, 1971, 1974, and 1976; and "Professions for Women," in *The Death of the Moth and Other Essays* by Virginia Woolf, ©1974.

Alfred A. Knopf, Inc., for excerpts from *Journal of Katherine Mansfield* by Katherine Mansfield, ©1927; and *The Measure of My Days* by Florida Scott-Maxwell, ©1968.

Macmillan Publishing Co., Inc., for excerpts from *The Novel of the Future* by Anaïs Nin, © 1968 by Anaïs Nin.

Nichols, Susan Claire. *"The Personal Journal: A Mental Health Proposal,"* Ph.D. dissertation, Ann Arbor, Mich.: University Microfilms International, 1973.

Simon and Schuster, Inc., for excerpts from *The Golden Notebook* by Doris Lessing, ©1962.

Swallow Press Publications, with the permission of Rupert Pole, for excerpts from *A Woman Speaks* by Anaïs Nin, ©1975.

Universities Press, Inc., for excerpts from *on not being able to paint* by Marion Milner, ©1967.

I have been rich in mothers.
This book is dedicated to three of them:
   Marie, who gave me life
   Anaïs, through whom I found the second birth
   Tawney, a true godmother

Contents

Acknowledgments

I am grateful for:

Marion Milner's responses to my letters; Christina Baldwin's sisterhood; the continuous support of Lyndon Leavitt, Ph.D., and Paul Proehl at International College; the advice and encouragement of Anaïs Nin and Rupert Pole over the years; the support of Hal Stone, Ph.D., Ernest Rossi, Ph.D., and Esther Lurie; the commitment of my publisher, Jeremy Tarcher, and editor, Victoria Pasternack, and the assistance of Lucy Barajikian; the information and encouragement offered by Bob Rosen, Jennifer Easier, Earl Miner, Ph.D., John Espey, Howard Goldstein, Sharon Spencer, Ph.D., Deena Metzger, Richard Rosenthal, M.D., Susan Levin, Jane Moffat, and Charlotte Painter; the generous contributions of the diarists who have allowed me to read and freely use their work, including Paul Aratow, Linda Barnes, Ruthane Capus, Ricardo Cerni, Gina Chase, Wes Craven, Dean Echenberg, M.D., Phyllis Eisenberg, Jane Gray, Christine Grimm, Lois Henley, Nan Hunt, Donna Ippolito, Eve Kalani, Albert Kriennieder, Ph.D., Philomene Long, Shirley Marcoux, Piere Marton, Betty Lou Maybee, Caroline Pinkston, Jim Rogers, Al Ross, Ph.D., Nancy Schiffrin, Richard Watts, Debby White, Anne Wilder, M.D., Nancy Scholar Zee, and especially Linda Lehmann (whose diary will one day be famous).

Last, I wish to express my deep gratitude to the many unnamed diarists who shared their work with me. Each made an important contribution to the development of this book.

Preface

Diary writing has become an increasingly popular activity. To answer a need for more knowledge about it I taught a course with my friend Tristine Rainer, who had been studying the diary for many years. We taught the diary as an exercise in creative will; as an exercise in synthesis; as a means to create a world according to our wishes, not those of others; as a means of creating the self, of giving birth to ourselves. We taught diary writing as a way of reintegrating ourselves when experience shatters us, to help us out of the desperate loneliness of silence and the anxieties of alienation.

In the diary we discovered a voice for reaching the deep sources of metaphysical and numinous qualities contained in human beings. We found in it the ultimate instrument for explorations of new forms of consciousness and ecstasy. We practiced it as a way of opening vision into experience, deepening understanding of others; as a way to touch and reach the depths of human beings; as nourishment; as a means of linking the content of the dream to our actions so that they become harmonious and interactive. Now Tristine has written a perceptive and revolutionary work that will share the immense wealth of new knowledge she has learned from the diary with all those who are seeking inner harmony and creative freedom.

Anaïs Nin

December 1976

Foreword

The diary is the only form of writing that encourages total freedom of expression. Because of its very private nature, it has remained immune to any formal rules of content, structure, or style. As a result the diary can come closest to reproducing how people really think and how consciousness evolves.

It was this untamed freedom of the diary that first intrigued me eight years ago, when I was still a graduate student in literature. The diary represented a refuge from the literary expectations and restrictions that had been so much a part of my education. I felt a calling to become an environmentalist of the mind. I wanted above all to proclaim and defend the diary's wilderness beauty.

Yet with all my desire to preserve it as a private sanctuary, I have written a book that opens the diary's uncharted territory for all to enter. I have researched it with indiscriminate passion, read insatiably every published diary I could get my hands on, violated musty manuscripts lying quietly in libraries, and solicited and lured hundreds of private diaries coast to coast from friends and students, acquaintances and strangers. There were diaries in my mailbox and diaries on my doorstep, Xeroxed diaries pushing out of drawers and overflowing files.

While researching diaries for eight intense years, I also taught journal writing at International College in Los Angeles with my friend of many years, Anaïs Nin, at UCLA as part of the Women's Studies Program, in the English department at the University of Indiana, Bloomington, and I worked privately with diarists as a writing advisor.

In justification of my prying and treading in a once-secret province, I found that each diarist had a golden nugget of self-discovered knowledge to share. One had a new journal method for alleviating depression, another a means of contacting her real feelings, another a suggestion for developing a creative work. This was more than folk wisdom. Put together it represented a natural, collective psychology of the diary and a testament to the creative process.

In this book I present this accumulated knowledge distilled and conveniently arranged, and cite examples from over a hundred different diaries. In many cases I have not identified the writer, respecting the confidence in which the original material was entrusted to me. We had agreed that what was important here were the insights to be gained from each example, not its source. In all cases I have remained faithful to the original diary entries, merely altering a word or two if the sense was unclear or changing a name at the writer's request.

On occasion I have borrowed an example from my own diary to illustrate a particular device or process, just as a scientist would cite the results of her own laboratory experiments along with those of her colleagues.

I have broadened the scope of my rich discoveries from diaries by including an eclectic synthesis of concepts from philosophy, literature, creative expression, and especially from psychology. I draw on theories of Jung, Freud, Transactional Analysis, Gestalt therapy, reality therapy, creative dreaming, and other therapeutic and personal growth techniques, and combine these with concepts from surrealism, New Criticism, and contemporary art.

I also have the good fortune to be able to include many of the personal insights acquired through a lifetime of diary writing by Anaïs Nin, probably the most important diarist of this century. During our seven years of friendship we spent many afternoons together discussing, among other things, her diary writing—whom she wrote to, when she wrote, whether she rewrote, why she published, what and how she edited. She brought to our relationship the same intuitive wisdom, spontaneous creativity, intimacy, and joy that enliven her celebrated diary.

Yet I suspect that the rich legacy of insight and information that has contributed to this book merely begins to tap a great river of knowledge that has been submerged for centuries and is just beginning to surface. And we have only started to grasp the potential for the parts of the mind the diary helps to develop—memory, imagination, feelings, dream imagery, intuition, and other creative faculties. When these capacities are brought into an active relationship with the rational, practical part of oneself in the diary, the result is a mental fusion that releases tremendous creative energy into one's life.

A similar creative fusion resulted from the collective exchange of knowledge that went into making this book. Individually, we diarists had been limited by secrecy and isolation. But in sharing our secrets and openly admitting our need for private space in our lives, we recognized that we were part of a worldwide phenomenon I have come to call the New Diary. The New Diary is not a system of rules on journal writing; it is an expanding new field of knowledge to be shared.

Tristine Rainer
October 1977

1 | The New Diary

A recently divorced woman writes in a journal about her confused sexual feelings. She is helping herself learn what she wants and doesn't want in her next relationship. She is creating the New Diary.

A middle-aged advertising director sometimes talks into her tape recorder during the hour she drives on the freeway to and from work. She finds it helps her sort out thoughts about her job, her marriage, and her state of mind. She is creating the New Diary.

A movie studio grip handwrites his diary at lightning speed, allowing whatever enters his mind to go on paper. He writes on the backs of old filmscripts—while a scene is being shot and in the evenings when his girlfriend watches TV. He is creating the New Diary.

A woman in San Francisco rises an hour before her large family to capture her dreams, some lines of poetry, and a list of her joys and complaints.

A country-western singer writes on planes and in dressing rooms to stay intimate with the private person behind his public image.

An artist uses an oversized notebook to sketch images of her innermost thoughts, and some of them find their way into her paintings.

A businessman works in his leather-bound diary to examine the factors that complicate a major decision he must make.

A university student writes between classes to integrate what her professors teach with what she is learning from life.

A publisher clips quotes and photos from periodicals. He tapes them in a book and writes a personal comment next to each one.

A marriage and family counselor writes imaginary conversations in her diary with an inner advisor to counsel herself.

An elderly widower writes his diary as a practical prayer to invoke his own wisdom and inner strength.

A fashion executive goes to her diary when she needs to prepare for an important meeting. She imagines her client's point of view and rehearses what she wants to do and say.

A novelist accumulates material by posing questions to himself and jotting down hunches, snatches of conversation, and fantasies.

A young expectant mother writes about the sensations in her body and her conflicting thoughts to stay attuned with herself in a time of rapid transition.

All these people and many others, in myriad forms and styles, are creating the New Diary.

They are keeping a natural diary as an active, purposeful communication with self. They write, sketch, doodle, and play with their imaginations. They record whatever their immediate feelings, thoughts, interests, and intuitions dictate. They write whenever they wish—for pleasure and for self-guidance.

Later they reread what has accumulated from the simple act of satisfying the needs and desires of the moment. And all find in their hands a book that contains—in form, content, and style—a unique, unrepeatable story of self. From reflecting upon what has come from within they discover unrecognized parts of their personalities and interests of which they were unaware. They see patterns of meaning in their lives and secrets of self more interesting than any detective story.

Through this journal process of expression and reflection they discover new solutions to problems, enter into and appreciate the process of their lives, and exercise their creative capacities. They experience firsthand how the qualities they most enjoy in their writing—spontaneity, honesty, depth, clarity, ambiguity, humor, and feeling—are also the qualities of a mature, self-aware person. They develop their creativity simply by developing themselves.

This widespread use of the diary as a tool for personal growth and for realizing creative potential is a phenomenon of the twentieth century. It would not have been possible without modern psychology's recognition of the subconscious, the free experimentation of contemporary art and writing, and the recent popularization of certain psychological insights and concepts of personal responsibility. But thanks to these pervasive cultural changes it is now possible for anyone who can read and write to keep some form of New Diary—a personal book in which creativity, play, and self-therapy interweave, foster, and complement each other.

This new concept of journal writing has little to do with the rigid, daily calendar diary you may have kept as a child, nor the factual travel journal you may have written to recall the Grand Canyon or Notre Dame as you sat by the fire in later years. It has little to do with outdated notions and misconceptions of diary keeping as a self-discipline, a dutiful record of events, a narcissistic self-absorption, an escape from reality, or a nostalgic adherence to the past.

Instead, the New Diary is a practical psychological tool that enables you to express feelings without inhibition, recognize and alter self-defeating habits of mind, and come to know and accept that self which is you. It is a sanctuary where all the disparate elements of a life—feelings, thoughts, dreams, hopes, fears, fantasies, practicalities, worries, facts, and intuitions—can merge to give you a sense of wholeness and coherence." It can help you understand your past, discover joy in the present, and create your own future.

At the same time, the New Diary is a safe place to free the creative child within you and experience the full range of your imagination. It allows you to develop an ease with writing and the habit of writing simply from using what you already have—your own experience. As you discover your natural voice in the diary, you can also begin to focus on your genuine interests and to collect material for many creative uses.

The therapeutic and creative benefits of keeping the New Diary are, in fact, almost as numerous as the people who enjoy the pleasure of keeping it. Among the advantages most frequently mentioned are:

A healthful release for feelings and tensions ... a place to advise yourself, clarify goals, and make decisions ... a way to nourish yourself with friendship and self-acceptance ... a nonthreatening place to work out relationships with others and to develop your capacity for intimacy ... a path to self-awareness and self-knowledge ... a place to rehearse future behavior ... a technique for focusing your energies on what is immediately important ... a way to organize and expand your time ... a place to find creative solutions to problems ... a memory aid ... a means of achieving self-identity ... a way to enjoy and profit from solitude ... a guide to finding clarity in the midst of crisis or change ... a device for discovering your path and taking responsibility for the direction of your life ... a means of accelerating or concluding psychotherapy....

A place to develop skills of self-expression ... a method for turning negative mental habits into positive energy ... a way to gain perspective on your emotions and to resolve the past ... a means of keeping in touch with the continuity and rhythms of your life ... a place to record meaningful insights ... a way to preserve family and personal history ... a quiet place to relax and refresh yourself ... a device for freeing your intuition and imagination.....

A way to learn to trust life ... a means of experiencing the essential humanness that links all people ... a tool for recording and understanding dreams ... a way to become your own guide and guru ... a place to celebrate the process of living ... a path to spiritual peace ... a workbook for creative writing and drawing ... a safe place to take intellectual and creative risks ... a source book for future projects ... a means of discovering joy within the context of your life.

Of course, any tool with so many potential uses and advantages does not spring fully formed into existence. On the contrary, what I am calling the New Diary has evolved from centuries of experimentation by creative diarists and has a long and fascinating history. Journal writing has reflected the prevailing values, attitudes, and needs of each country, culture, and age in which it has been practiced. (Incidentally, I use the terms *diary* and *journal* interchangeably. For though some individuals ardently prefer one term to the other, both have exactly the same dictionary meaning, "a book of days," and both have referred throughout history to the same written form.)

The first diaries that were not essentially historical records were written by Japanese women in the tenth century. These ladies of the royal court developed the diary into a form of personal expression that explored subjective fantasies and fiction, not just external realities. Like the New Diary, Japanese diaries were kept according to the writer's inner calendar of feelings and events rather than every day. (In one classical Japanese diary the writer made an entry only once every seven years or so.)

Whereas in Japan the earliest diaries shine brightly as part of a literary Golden Age, a period of peace, prosperity, and cultural sophistication, in medieval Europe and England the roots of the diary are buried in mystery and magic. Diaries were kept by "witches" attempting to preserve pagan wisdom, which probably accounts for the taboo of silence and secrecy associated with them in Western tradition. If a witch's diary were discovered, not only would the book be burned, its writer might be burned as well.

From this common root of subversive pagan writing, the diary took on distinct national characteristics. For example, in seventeenth-century England Samuel Pepys and other Protestant gentlemen developed the diary as a place to confess and account for one's life to a watchful God. The American tradition of the diary came over on the *Mayflower* with the Puritans, who furthered the association of diary writing with self-discipline and self-judgment. Puritan ministers in the New World taught children to use it to keep tabs on their consciences. But there were also the philosophically religious journals of the Quakers, and later the diary of self-reliance developed by Emerson and Thoreau as an integral part of American transcendentalism.

Women's diaries in Europe and in the United States had their own independent tradition throughout the seventeenth, eighteenth, and nineteenth centuries. By the eighteenth century literally hundreds of American pioneer women had created a network of correspondence and mutual support that stretched from North Carolina to Massachusetts and was based on a shared interest in journal writing. In fact, so many women relied on the diary to preserve their history and culture that 200 years later, many people had come to think of the diary as primarily a woman's mode of expression.

This was particularly the attitude in the United States in the early 1950s, when there was widespread merchandising of one-year diaries with toy locks and keys designed for young girls. These diaries parodied the long tradition of women's secret diaries. They also represented the tail end of the Puritan tradition of diary keeping as a self-watching, daily discipline. These little calendar diaries were as relevant to the needs of the twentieth century as lace pantaloons were to piano legs. But they had a visibility that the New Diary—which had, in fact, been developing throughout the twentieth century—still lacked.

The New Diary is a widespread cultural phenomenon rather than a system or program of writing. No one individual or even group of individuals can be said to have created it. But four twentieth-century pioneers of psychology and literature played major roles in conceptualizing the principles of modern journal writing: Carl Jung, Marion Milner, Ira Progoff, and Anaïs Nin.

Each of them, in an individual way, pointed out how the diary permits its writer to tap valuable inner resources. And they developed techniques that aid this process. Jung emphasized the importance of recording dreams and inner imagery; Milner, the usefulness of intuitive writing and drawing; Progoff popularized techniques for uncovering an inner destiny; and Anaïs Nin demonstrated the creative fulfillment achieved through listening for and valuing one's feelings. All of them recognized a need in the modern world to reflect calmly upon knowledge that comes from within.

Psychoanalyst Carl Jung (1875–1961) used the diary to develop his theory of the collective unconscious. He recorded his dreams and fantasies of recurrent figures, images, and symbols in the Black Book, which eventually consisted of six small, leather-bound notebooks. He believed that many of these inner images and figures were not unique to him but observable in countless other people's dreams and fantasies and in the myths of all cultures—thus, part of a collective unconscious. In his journals Jung wrote frequent imaginary conversations with one of these inner figures, his "anima," which he understood to represent an unconscious "female" side of his mind. He also drew mandalas—circular geometric patterns—in his notebooks, observing that the patterns changed from day to day in correspondence with his moods and inner needs.

Jung's major psychological works evolved out of the intense self-study he pursued in his diaries. In his autobiography he wrote, "All my works, all my creative activity, have come from those initial fantasies and dreams which began in 1912, almost fifty years ago. Everything that I accomplished in later life was already contained in them, although at first only in the form of emotions and images."

Yet Jung recognized a potential danger in his method of diary keeping. The preponderance of images, symbols, and dream figures could, he felt, draw the writer too far down into the subconscious inner self—if not balanced with a strong base in external, day-to-day reality. Although Jung used the journal as a vehicle for a heroic journey into the sea of the unconscious, he concluded that an awareness of dreams and inner images always needs to be integrated with the pragmatic realities of everyday existence: "Particularly at this time, when I was working on the fantasies, I needed a point of support in 'this world.' It was most essential for me to have a normal life in the real world as a counterpoise to the strange inner world."

It was precisely this balance that Marion Milner (b. 1900), an English psychologist and later a psychoanalyst, emphasized in the first book about the process of diary writing, *A Life of One's Own*. Published by Milner in 1934 under the pen name Joanna Field, the book tells of her personal experience of eight years of diary keeping.

Milner used her journal as a practical tool for living as well as a means of self-insight. Her goal in keeping the diary was to learn what happiness meant for her. Among other experiments she made lists of what brought her personal joy to find out what she really wanted out of life, not what society or those around her had taught her she "should" want. She also explored free association in writing and drawing in addition to diary-related experiments in meditation, relaxation, body awareness, and a number of other techniques advanced by humanistic psychologists today.

Her work in the diary led her to important philosophical and psychological insights. For instance, she learned how to work with the principle of opposites in her own mind—distinguishing between the rational, narrow-focused, categorizing, analytical, "masculine" side of her mind and the intuitive, wide-focused, synthesizing, receptive "feminine" side. From this she developed a theory of what she called "psychic bisexuality," which anticipated by thirty years the scientific evidence now being provided by split-brain research.

Modern science indicates that so-called masculine and feminine ways of thinking are really different functions of the two sides of the brain. For the most part, the left hemisphere's function in both men and women is rational, verbal, linear, logical, and "conscious." The right hemisphere's product is communicated in images and symbols and is intuitive, nonlinear, creative, and "subconscious."

Through keeping a diary Milner learned how her happiness depended upon developing the skill to balance these two modes of thinking. She devised journal techniques to bring into play either her active, analytic capacities or her receptive, yielding capacities in response to life's changing demands.

A Life of One's Own was too far ahead of its time to gain popular recognition. And Milner's quiet, personal style and her ideas were easily quelled amidst the other psychological theories then being established. She wrote a sequel in 1939 called *An Experiment in Leisure,* which was blitzed out of print by World War II, and later another book entitled *on not being able to paint,* which explored free association in drawing as a technique for achieving self-understanding. Today she works quietly as a psychoanalyst in England.

It was the more systematic methods of psychologist Ira Progoff (b. 1921) that brought journal writing as a form of growth work to public attention. Although his system for keeping a journal is quite specific, his view of its benefits is consistent with that of the other pioneers. He describes the journal as "a continuing confrontation with oneself in the midst of life," and as a psychological laboratory in which personal growth is recorded and studied to bring the outer and inner parts of one's experience into harmony.

His system, called the INTENSIVE JOURNAL (Progoff's registered trademark), uses a three-ring binder partitioned with colored dividers. These designate preestablished sections for recording and working with daily activities, dreams, lists of decisive events in one's life, and various imaginary conversations or dialogues—with persons, works, events, one's body, society, or a figure of inner wisdom. The Progoff method is complex but can be learned by attending one of his journal workshops, in which he or one of his assistants leads participants through exercises in the various sections of the journal.

By popularizing the journal as a means of looking at one's life from many different perspectives, Progoff has made important contributions to a new concept of the diary. His work dispels the inhibiting attitude that journal keeping requires literary training or a special talent for writing. It provides a clearly structured method for those who feel uncomfortable with the total freedom of a natural diary.

Anaïs Nin (1903–1977) contributed to the formulation of the New Diary by example as well as by theory. Thousands of people have been inspired from reading her edited diary since its publication in 1966. She introduced a concept of diary writing that synthesized elements of psychology with literature. She countered the tradition of the Puritan self-disciplinary journal by replacing its motivation of guilt with liberating concepts of personal responsibility and maturity. Nin felt that society had placed a taboo on looking within, but

that everyone needed a spiritual island: "An inner life, culti-
vated, nourished, is a well of strength," she wrote, "the inner
structure we need to resist outer catastrophes and errors and
injustices."

Nin began keeping diaries at the age of eleven to see
herself through a difficult childhood. The first published volume, however, covers the years 1931–1934, when she had
already created for herself the exciting life she could only
imagine as a girl. Living in France Nin found herself among the
surrealist artists, who were playing with free association, automatic writing, and other spontaneous forms of self-expression.
The diary describes her friendships with three of the most
influential experimental writers of the time, Henry Miller,
Antonin Artaud, and Lawrence Durrell. With them she shared
a love of spontaneity, feeling, flow, and freedom in writing.

The second published volume of her diary recounts her
work as a lay therapist with psychoanalyst Otto Rank in New
York, whose view of neurosis as blocked creativity reinforced
her own belief in the benefits of writing. The later volumes of
her diary (III through VII) show clearly how the journal form
had become for her a marvelous way of grappling with and
growing with the major cultural changes of her lifetime. The
diary always kept her in sync with time and with the times.

For women, particularly, Nin provided a model for
finding creative solutions to internal conflicts. She emphasized
the importance of woman's articulateness at this moment in
history and demonstrated how the diary could help them find
their own expressive language. She recognized that the true
liberation of both women and men would mean a change in
thinking itself—to integrate what has been named the unconscious, the intuitive, the emotional, with the conscious, the
rational, the intellectual.

Nin's now-famous diaries are traditionally literary in a
way that most people's are not—and need not be. Yet they
helped create the New Diary by illustrating the same balance
between spontaneous emotional expression and active, objec-

tive analysis, which was found so necessary by the other pioneers of the New Diary. In her diaries one can observe how the outer woman—who perceives and acts in the world—becomes integrated with the inner woman—who feels and dreams. From this interaction a new self is constantly born, one with greater coherence and personal knowledge.

Nin celebrated creativity as a way of life. She advocated a concept of the creative person not as an alienated "artist" but as an alive, curious individual who is ever finding new ways to grow, expand, and enjoy the moment. She used the diary not to escape from life but to live it more fully and deeply.

For her, creativity and self-therapy were interrelated and interdependent. She described the overall movement within her own diary as a journey from "subjectivity and neurosis to objectivity, expansion, fulfillment." This harmony of personal growth and creativity may be considered the theme and guiding spirit of the New Diary.

This book, then, synthesizes the major contributions of these four pioneers of the New Diary with my own research and experience as a journal consultant. It applies centuries of experimentation in diary writing to the solution of familiar, contemporary life concerns. And it formulates a readily under-standable terminology of techniques and modes of expression relevant to all journals, no matter what their format.

In the chapters that follow I will present a great variety of writing devices for you to choose from, including games you can play with your inner consciousness to get to know it better. I will suggest scores of fruitful directions that may be pursued and indicate some unfruitful ones encountered by other diarists, which are easily avoided. In using the diary devices suggested for self-guidance, you will simultaneously be practicing a full range of creative techniques.

However, it is not my intent to present "the right way" to keep a journal. Although some may claim to know the right way, I simply wish to suggest the limitless range of possibilities to free your intuition to discover your own unique way. My experience has shown that each person intuitively develops methods and uses for a diary that suit his or her needs, and those methods alter as the life and the needs alter.

So flexibility, an openness to adventure, and a willingness to experiment, play, take imaginative chances, and follow your path are essential in this process. As you write in your own way you, too, will be creating the New Diary. More importantly, you will be re-creating yourself.

2 | Beginnings

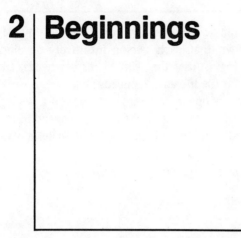

Paul Gauguin, the painter, began his intimate journal with the phrase, "This is not a book." He repeated the line frequently throughout the journal to remind himself that writing a diary is not like writing a book or any other form of literature. Gauguin wanted to write his diary as he painted his pictures, dabbing a few experimental colors at first, adding more as his intuition told him, following his fancy, "following the moon," discovering the pattern from what had occurred by chance.

To make full use of the diary you, too, need to forget all the requirements and restrictions you have probably been taught about writing. Most forms of writing have traditions that have been traced by literary critics, and agreed-upon conventions that can be learned and then accepted or rejected by writers.

Diary writing is free of such conventions and rules. Everything and anything goes. You cannot do it wrong. There are no mistakes. At any time you can change your point of view, your style, your book, the pen you write with, the direction you write on the pages, the language in which you write, the subjects you include, or the audience you write to. You can misspell, write ungrammatically, enter incorrect dates, exaggerate, curse, pray, brag, write poetically, eloquently, angrily, lovingly. You can paste in photographs, news paper clippings, cancelled checks, letters, quotes, drawings, doodles, dried flowers, business cards, or labels. You can write on lined paper or blank paper, violet paper or yellow, expensive bond or newsprint.

It's your book, yours alone. It can be neat or sloppy, big or little, carefully organized or as gravity-free as a Chagall skyscape. *Flow, spontaneity* and *intuition* are the key words. You don't have to plan what you are going to do. You discover what you have done once you have set it down.

Selecting Your Book

For some people learning to be free in their diaries is a way of learning to be free with themselves. Therefore, selecting a book that permits free flow, spontaneity, and experimentation can be especially important in the beginning. The structure and design of a book can actually influence what and how you write in it. For instance, small books, though they have the great convenience of portability, may produce a compressed writing style: controlled, cramped, or aphoristic. Large books, in contrast, may encourage expansion, ease, drawing as well as writing, experimentation, and elaboration.

The rigid design of those one- and five-year calendar diaries many of us kept as children certainly influenced how we wrote in them. I know now that the little diary I received on Christmas morning at age twelve had a profound influence on how I wrote the diary, an influence that lasted many years after I had destroyed the book itself.

My first diary, like many others, was a calendar book with one lined page for each day of the year. I assumed from its structure that every evening I had to fill a page with a summary of my day's activities. I came to despise that unnatural duty as I labored with stapled-in pages when I had too much to say one day and apologies when I'd forgotten to write for a whole week. One friend of mine says he solved the problem, at age nine, by writing the whole week in advance, repeating for each day, "Went to school..." "Went to school..." "Went to school...."

Like most of the diaries merchandised for children, mine had a tiny lock and key. This caused me to assume that only secrets belonged in diaries and that keeping secrets had something to do with being a girl entering puberty. But anyone knew that the flimsy lock could be jimmied with a bobby pin. So I never dared to write my deepest feelings there, which in time became a secret even from myself.

The cover design of my diary conveyed further messages about what and how I should write in it. The cover was a particularly common one in the late fifties, designed and signed by someone named Betty Betz. It was pale blue, dotted with a field of small flowers, over which floated two bees about to kiss. Next to the bees a pink cloud contained the words "My Wonderful Year," and beneath the cloud sat a girl with a pug nose, wearing a string of pearls and a pink dress. At her feet lounged a redheaded boy with the same nose. In one hand he held a yellow daisy, which he was offering the girl. The girl seemed to be reading to the boy out of her diary, and he was smiling.

I got the message, and that year I wrote about my crushes on boys, and only about boys. I felt ashamed at the end of the year that it hadn't fulfilled the promise of the pink cloud and even more ashamed that I didn't have a boyfriend to whom I could read my diary. Instead, my mother read it. And I, in outrage, burned it.

Yet thirteen years later when I began to write a diary again (this time in a blank bound book), I was still influenced by the subliminal message of that old Betty Betz diary cover. Now I had a boyfriend, and without realizing why, I wrote that diary to and for him. He never read a word of it, yet I continued to think "to" him whenever I wrote, long after our relationship had ended. One evening, without fully understanding what I was doing, I suddenly scribbled across the page in a large hand:

LET MY PAGE BE A WOMAN FOR THE FIRST TIME!

and then,

> There is nothing but blank before me. I don't know
> where to begin . . .

In that moment, on that page, I finally met myself as the audience of my own diary. In retrospect I consider it the single most important moment in my life.

The unstructured book I was then using actually encouraged the personal liberation I experienced. In the pages of that blank book, without divisions and without instructions, I began to discover and create the rules of my own being.

Today I feel strongly that even children would do best with blank diary books, which allow them to write as often or as infrequently, as much or as little as they wish. And I generally suggest to my adult students that they begin with a large, undated, bound book.

Some protest that writing on blank pages, without lines or dates or any other structure, would be intimidating for them. But there are no dates or sections within the self. There, time is continuous like a blank page, and subjectively long or short, fast or slow. Even on blank pages you still record the date when you write. In fact, if there is any rule in writing a diary, it is to record the date of each entry. Otherwise there are no guideposts to your personal history. No matter what you write or how often, the dates make the diary a useful reference tool.

Many people seem to feel comfortable with even less structure than a bound blank book provides. Without realizing it they keep diaries on scraps of paper they grab when an inspiration seizes them or the desire to record a thought or a dream or a fantasy takes hold. Frequently they date these scraps and keep them in boxes. Though this system has the advantage of total spontaneity, it has some disadvantages. Entries may be lost, continuity is forgotten, and the chaos of such scattered pieces of paper may discourage rereading or preserving what has been written. Actually, the advantage of writing in the heat of the moment—seizing an envelope or any available scrap of paper to capture a thought—can be combined with keeping a bound book. You can glue, tape, or staple onto the pages any loose scraps of paper you wish to preserve.

In choosing a book it is good to find a balance between "just any old thing," like scraps of paper or a pad that will fall apart, and a book so beautiful that it is intimidating to write in. It's the balance between respect for yourself, represented by your involvement in the diary process, and a consideration of the freedom you need to feel that you can do anything you wish on the pages.

Artist's diaries, sold at most stationers and art supply stores, seem to achieve this balance between an inexpensive bound volume that will last and total spontaneity. These diaries come in various sizes: a very small 5½-inch by 8½-inch book; an 8-inch by 11-inch book, which is what I usually recommend; and a very large 10½-inch by 14-inch version of the same black book with smooth white pages and a sturdy paper binding.

You might also want to look for imported Japanese diaries. They are beautifully made, come with cloth bindings, and are sometimes folded accordion fashion so that the pages open out like a long scroll.

A few people keep journals in three-ring binders. Binders are useful as organizers and creative source books (which will be discussed later). Ira Progoff's INTENSIVE JOURNAL is actually a binder with sixteen dividers. But unless you are keeping a journal according to his method, I do not recommend the notebook format for a personal, spontaneous, self-exploratory diary. Not only does a three-ring binder connote schoolwork, it may also influence the writer to become too concerned with filing, rearranging, rewriting, and even removing pages. Too many diaries are nipped in the bud by harsh self-criticism. In the initial stages of keeping the diary it's best to choose a book that encourages spontaneous, unretouched writing. And a prebound volume seems the best.

Some people keep different books for different purposes. They may use one book to record dreams, another to explore fantasies, another to jot down thoughts and experiences, and another for creative inspirations. The heroine of Doris Lessing's novel *The Golden Notebook* at first keeps four different colored notebooks that represent her personal fragmentation. Near the end of the novel she decides, "I'll pack away the four notebooks. I'll start a new notebook, all of myself in one book."

During one point in my life when I was under considerable stress I similarly kept three separate books simultaneously, and also felt fragmented with the use of so many diaries. The one large bound book I now use (other than a separate creative notebook for particular projects) allows me to integrate all my selves and all my forms of spontaneous expression into one book. When the dreams lie next to the fantasies, and political thoughts next to personal complaints, they all seem to learn from each other.

Though my large book has the disadvantage of not being very portable, its size and number of pages allow me to develop familiarity with it over a long period. With time the book seems to give back the energy I have put into it. When I pick it up and feel it in my hands, I immediately feel anchored, centered, at home. It has helped me find solutions to so many potentially shattering experiences, that now just touching the book gives me a sense of comfort, security, and well-being.

For some diarists the choice of a writing implement is as important as the choice of a book. They may develop an affection for a special fountain pen kept just for diary writing, and some people use several different colors of ink for different purposes. You may wish to experiment to find the writing implement that feels most comfortable and natural.

Other diarists alternately type and handwrite their diaries; a few type it entirely. I prefer to handwrite mine, for through the handwriting my body communicates directly to the page. Even though my scrawl may be awkward I appreciate its variations—sometimes cramped, sometimes neat, sometimes scribbled across the page, occasionally sideways. When I reread my diary the handwriting tells me as much as the actual words and helps me recall my emotions at the time I wrote an entry.

Whether your diary is handwritten or typed, in a handmade, custom-bound volume or a soft-cover, dime-store notebook, all that really matters is that it suits your needs. You can experiment to find what makes you feel most comfortable, and make changes at different times in your life.

Some Principles for Beginning

When asked how to write a diary by those just beginning, I generally respond: "Write fast, write everything, include everything, write from your feelings, write from your body, accept whatever comes." That is often all the guidance they need. From there the diary process seems to take care of itself. However, some of the principles that have proved most effective for diarists are worth describing. Please bear in mind that these *are not rules*. They are merely suggestions to help you get started.

Writing Spontaneously. Allow yourself to follow your intuition. Play. Experiment. Let the writing flow without making judgments about yourself. There are no "shoulds" or "should nots" in the diary process. You needn't write about something because you think you should, nor need you keep from writing things you think you shouldn't. Write quickly so that you don't know what will come next. Allow the unexpected to happen. Surprise yourself.

Allow yourself to write whenever you feel like it: when you need the emotional release, when you need to clarify your thoughts, or when the spirit moves you. Don't feel that you have to write when you don't want to or haven't the time. The diary allows you to make excellent use of time when you have it. It makes no demands when you haven't time for it. As it is in poetry, silence is part of the form. The blank time between entries speaks of great activity, or deserts of experiences, or absence for other reasons. The silence in diaries can speak as eloquently as the words.

Some diarists find when they go several weeks without writing they begin to feel off balance and take it as a signal that they are avoiding the inner self. So it is essential that you allow the ebb and flow of your own moods, your own life cycles, to dictate when you write. Your rhythms will create their own pattern. Eventually a structure, created by intuition and spontaneity, begins to emerge from what at first may seem chaotic.

Further, fear of being "boring" mustn't inhibit you. Attempts to avoid being boring may lead to exaggerated and distorted writing. Lack of intimacy with yourself creates boredom, so the solution is always to touch your true feelings and write from them. Diaries prove that any life can be interesting or boring, depending upon how deeply it is perceived. The life of a recluse can make a fascinating diary, while the diary of a celebrity can be superficial and dull. Therefore, don't judge your writing, just trust your process.

Writing Honestly. Honesty in a diary has less to do with the "truth" than the way you reveal your "real self" as distinguished from social roles you play and masks you wear to make an impression. It involves an openness about what you really feel, what you really want, what you really believe, what you really decide. Through diary writing this real self can become the vital center of your psychic life.

Few diarists actually lie to themselves in a diary, but many out of shyness with themselves avoid writing about the most intimate aspects of a situation. When you objectively report an experience it is easy to present the image of yourself you would like the world to see, rather than the less visible dimensions of your personality. For example, if you write something like, "Had dinner with Caroline. She has a new job as a fashion coordinator. Afterward I drove her home," you learn little about yourself that you didn't already know. You may be keeping secrets of omission from yourself out of shyness or fear of seeming "not nice," "unfeminine," or "unmasculine." But if you make a point later of including or adding your honest feelings and reactions, you may discover some unexpected dimensions or insights you wouldn't ordinarily admit. Ask yourself whether there's anything important you've avoided writing.

For instance, the diarist who wrote the above entry might ask, "How did I feel toward Caroline? What was my reaction when she told me about her new job? Was that what I really felt? How do I feel about it all now?" Such questions put to yourself in the diary encourage personally revealing statements to enter. Feeling very sensitized or vulnerable is a sign that you are writing honestly in a diary. When you feel, "*Dare* I really say this?" you are probably working honestly and well.

Many diarists, concerned over seeming too self-absorbed, actually avoid including their own perceptions, reactions, and feelings. They describe other people and events but forget to include themselves as observers with unique perceptions and feelings that are validly explored in a diary.

There is certainly a place for observations about other people in your personal diary, particularly those close to you. But if they are out of proportion with your self-revelations, it may be a symptom that you are too other-directed. As you write try always to ask yourself, "What did I feel? What did I think about what happened? How do I feel about him or her at this time? How did I respond? Was there anything I wanted to say that I didn't say? What did I really want to happen?

What do I want in this relationship? Did my actions correspond with my desires? Do I have any secrets I'm keeping from myself?" You can even write these questions directly in the diary and then respond to them. Such questions will keep you writing honestly and centered in your real self.

Writing Deeply. You will get as much out of diary writing as you bring to it. One of the major disappointments for diarists in rereading their old journals is the impression that they only stayed on the surface of a problem or on the surface of a life. They wonder, "Why didn't I write about the most important things that were happening to me?" Even Anaïs Nin felt disappointed when she prepared to edit her childhood diaries and found, upon rereading them, that she had neglected to write all the important things—her embarrassment over sexual propositions when she was working as an artist's model, her feelings toward her family, her inner thoughts.

Nin later developed the practice of sitting quietly for a few minutes before beginning to write. She would close her eyes and allow the most important incident or feeling of the day or of the period of time since she last wrote to surface in her mind. That incident or feeling became her first sentence. By using this approach you will at least have recorded what is of greatest significance to you, even if you don't have enough time to write everything that you wish to explore. You can imagine it as deep-sea fishing, casting the line as far and as deep as you can. Don't stay close to shore where the water is muddy. Cast for your deepest thought or emotion.

Did you have a dream you wish to remember? Did you meet someone who could prove significant in your life? Did you experience an important emotional encounter? Did you have an idea or a memory you wanted to preserve? Are you worried about something?

What is of deepest importance to you is most important to your diary. It does not need to interest anyone else.

Writing Correctly. Many people have serious inhibitions about writing because of the way they were taught in school.

There one's writing was always judged "good" or "bad," as if it were subject to an unchanging natural law, and grammatical errors were confused with moral judgments.

Actually there was no such thing as "correct" English spelling or grammar until the eighteenth century, when Samuel Johnson and a group of other British gentlemen decided that they could apply scientific rules to language. The result was an arbitrary codification of the English language, which had developed freely until that time.

There was no logic to most of the rules they established. Expressive language is not a science. By their "scientific" standards Shakespeare—who used double negatives and spelled his name three different ways—was a bad writer. But they managed to influence the way English has been taught in schools. Well-informed teachers now know that language changes and evolves just like everything else, and many common "mistakes" people now make will one day be accepted as the standard.

Diarists have traditionally written in the vernacular—as people actually speak—so linguists have always valued diaries as a historical record of the most colloquial, advanced stage of a language for that time. If you write a letter applying for a job as a proofreader, you would be wise to consider standard rules of punctuation, spelling, and grammar. But there are no rules when you write your own diary. You are writing for yourself, so self-expression is the key. Concern about correctness will only inhibit you and slow you down.

Beginning diarists also frequently feel concerned about writing style, but style takes care of itself in time. It is particularly important to be patient with yourself at the start and to accept whatever comes to you to write. In the unknown territory of self-expression many sophisticated people are like children just learning to speak. Their natural voice is still undeveloped and needs an opportunity to test its range. You will find that the longer you keep a diary, the more your natural voice and natural writing style will develop.

In the beginning the object is to learn to flow without stopping to correct yourself, to be spontaneous, to expand and develop. Try not to allow a desire for perfection to interfere with the real purpose of your writing—your own expansion, awareness, and growth. Many diarists have regretted crossing out what they have already written. It is more valuable to add new insights to an entry than to erase or cross out or rewrite. Spur-of-the-moment negative judgments may actually be resistance to an insight that might later prove invaluable.

It takes the perspective of time to know what has significance in a diary. Some misspellings or word accidents acquire meaning upon rereading. "Freudian slips" may give you a key to subconscious attitudes or feelings. And some are quite entertaining. I once accidentally wrote "spychiatrist" for "psychiatrist." In another entry I wrote "Was" for "Wes," the name of a man with whom I was about to end a relationship. Clearly my subconscious was ahead of me in considering it already past. The hand tells the truth, so write fast and trust your body.

Errors are part of the form of the diary, as they are part of life. As Anaïs Nin wrote, "It is a process of nature, and not of the ideal. The diary is a place where you don't have to worry about being perfect."

Choosing Your Audience. Some people have a particular plan in writing the diary. For example, it may be written for a grandchild as a means of creating family continuity. But in most cases the best audience is your future self. If you think of your reader as the person you will be in five or ten years, it will encourage you to write concretely and to include details that make the experience interesting to reread. In ten years you won't remember the situation unless you capture all its sensual vitality now.

Valuing Contradictions. If you are true to yourself within the present moment—that is, writing honestly—you are likely to contradict yourself frequently. Not only might you disparage on one day what you praised on another, you may even find yourself having divergent and contradictory attitudes about a topic in the same entry. What you do in the New Diary is not objective truth so much as a chosen way of looking at the moment and working toward understanding it in a larger context.

A diarist records multiple valid insights that at first seem to contradict each other, but that in time develop into a larger truth. This is not to say that everything is relative and equally true, but that there are many valid perspectives on the same subject. You will get the most benefits from keeping a diary by striving to understand your major concerns as completely as possible and from as many perspectives as possible.

Ambiguity means admitting more than one response to a situation and allowing yourself to be aware of those contradictory responses. You may want something and fear it at the same time. You may find it both beautiful and ugly. Ambiguity is one of the primary qualities of honest writing. It is also a quality of a deeply felt life.

If you allow ambiguity in your diary it can help you develop the maturity to tolerate the true complexity of a life, not a simple either/or vision but one that resolves contradictions because it contains them. Try not to deny any thought or feeling in the diary, even if it doesn't seem to fit or if it frightens you. The process is one of simple addition. You write one feeling, which leads you to another, which leads to another: "I don't like her," "No, I really do like her." The truth is the sum of them all, achieved simply by saying everything. Out of the contradictions and ambiguity a larger truth seems to emerge. By adding one piece at a time you develop a self large enough to contain all your perceptions. Your only concern while writing is being true to yourself within the moment.

Walt Whitman's bold claim in *A Song of Myself* applies well to the diarist:

> Do I contradict myself?
> Very well then I contradict myself,
> (I am large, I contain multitudes.)

Where to Begin

My main advice about beginning, then, is the same as my suggestion on how to write a diary: Write fast, write everything, include everything, write from your feelings, write from your body, accept whatever comes. It doesn't matter whether you have kept a diary in any form before. If you keep one long enough, all the important memories of the past will find their way into the story when it is appropriate for them to do so. You simply begin your diary now, in the middle of the ongoing action of your life.

You may know exactly how you want to begin or have already done so. If not, the few brief suggestions that follow may help.

Begin with the Present Moment or the Present Period. One way to begin might be with an expression of the present moment, whether in an image, a feeling, or a description. This approach will bring you in touch with the immediacy of your life. Where are you in your life now? How do you live? What are you feeling, thinking, experiencing? What do you desire? What do you fear? What do you value? Whom do you care about? What is the significance of the present moment in the context of your life? What is changing in your life? What is changing about you?

Or you might start with an image, a feeling, or a description of the most recent period of the past that has meaning in your present. Ira Progoff begins his INTENSIVE JOURNAL classes with this meditative exercise for drawing the most recent period of a life into focus. The recent period could be a month, five months, two years, or seven years. It might be the period of time since you married, got divorced, moved to another city, changed professions, were hospitalized, or came into an inheritance. The most meaningful recent period varies with each individual.

There is generally so much potential material to write about in this exercise that Progoff advises brevity. You merely indicate the main characteristics of the recent period, beginning with the decisive event that marks its inception and allow it to pass before you in images or feelings, until you reach the present. You might capture this recent period of your life in a simile. For example, "This period of my life has been like a narrow covered bridge," or "I feel as if I've been on a roller-coaster."

It may have been a period of anxiety or loneliness, of passivity or activity, a time of outstanding dreams or dream-lessness. Whatever it was, simply record the memories and facts without judging or censoring yourself. This is an effective way to bring yourself up to the present moment and help you understand how you came to be here.

Begin with a Self-Portrait. Another way to begin could be with a word-portrait of yourself or a description as you know yourself to be at the present time. Rather than writing a detailed autobiography this approach, too, can be brief and rely upon images or similes. The portrait you write of yourself now may differ radically from a portrait you write of yourself at a future time. It might include a description of the circumstances and influences that led to your present state. What recent or not-so-recent events of the past have contributed to the person you find yourself to be at this moment? And where do you feel your life is leading you now?

Begin with the Day. You might also like to begin with a more traditional sort of entry, a description of the day. This can be a valuable exercise if you have time to expand it as fully as possible, to push beyond an outline of the day's activities, to explore the feelings, nuances of emotion, thoughts and reactions you might ordinarily ignore. It could become exhausting and dull to do this kind of description every day. But occasionally a complete record of the day will give you a sense of the complex, detailed fabric of your life.

You might also begin with an outpouring of strong feelings if you are very angry or lonely or sad or exhilarated, or record a recent dream, a statement of purpose in keeping the journal, a photo, a drawing, a news clipping, or anything else that comes to you. Since each fresh entry in a sense begins the diary anew, the actual beginning is no different from any other part. My diary first began when I was twelve and received my Betty Betz diary. It also began when I started to write again in my twenties. It began again when I discovered myself as audience for the first time. And it begins anew each time I start another volume or write the date for a new entry.

When you face a blank page the excitement of the unknown always lies before you. And it is precisely this unpreconceived, unrestricted quality of the New Diary that encourages continuous self-creation. You choose and select and experiment. In so doing you begin to know your free, spontaneous, creative self.

3 | Privacy: To Share or Not to Share

Jane Carlyle, wife of the English essayist Thomas Carlyle, joked uneasily at the beginning of her journal that diarizing might be justifiable grounds for murder:

> [1855]
> I remember Charles Buller saying of the Duchess of Praslin's murder, "What could a poor fellow do with a wife who kept a journal but murder her." There was a certain truth hidden in this light remark.

The "certain truth" is that saying on paper what one has been barely willing to formulate in thought can be fearsome. Anaïs Nin had repeated nightmares that the inflammable material in her diaries would burn the house down. Eventually she realized that her fears were the result of guilt over her creative self-assertion.

These are obviously extreme cases. However, it is common for diarists to confuse the guilt of facing personal secrets or deep dissatisfaction about cultural assumptions with a fear of someone else's reaction. Such fear of censorship or criticism is an obstacle to self-discovery and can be dealt with effectively through many techniques suggested in Chapter 10 on overcoming writing blocks. In the meantime, you needn't blame others for your fears and blocks. Simply take responsibility for providing yourself with the privacy you need to open your heart to yourself.

Privacy

There is no rule that a diary has to be kept secret, though there are many good reasons for wanting to keep it private. For example, you may wish to write fantasy as well as fact and not distinguish between them for someone else's eyes, since the writing is meant for yours alone. You may tentatively consider ideas that you eventually reject, and that would be misunderstood if read by another. You might write delicate material that could hurt another.

People often begin diaries because they experience a block in communicating with a person important to them. In the diary you may write what you can't say to your mate or what your spouse doesn't seem to understand when you do try to say it. You may have negative feelings about one of your children or a parent, which you don't want to express to them for good and humane reasons. So you explore and work through these feelings in a diary, which represents your subjective process and may not include even your knowledge of the entire picture.

You may simply want the freedom to write sloppily, ungrammatically, profanely somewhere in your life, or you may want the freedom to explore your "lesser" selves without making explanations to others. Therefore, you may wish to keep the diary in a locked, safe place to protect others from misunderstanding, misinterpreting, or judging your writing.

For these reasons you may find yourself in a conflict between your own need for privacy and your family's feelings. In fact, it's not uncommon for members of a household to feel threatened by the diary at first, in part because the time you spend with yourself is time you cannot spend with them.

Discussions about your diary may also become the vehicle for more far-reaching issues in your relationships. The journal may come to represent your independence and individuality for you and those close to you. Helping threatened persons understand your need for private space may become a part of your growth as well as theirs. To a mate you might want to say, "I don't want my writing to be a threat to you. I'm not doing it to write unkindly about you or to hide things from you. I'm writing so that I won't hide from myself, so that I can become clear enough about myself to share with you what I really think and feel. My intimacy with myself can make our relationship even more open. But I would feel too self-conscious if you read the raw material. I need that place to be private, to work it through while it's still unformulated, mistaken, or confused."

I asked the husband of a diarist who worked with me to write down his feelings when his wife began to keep a journal. Here is a small part of his response:

> When she invested herself in her diary and it became obvious that my direct knowledge about its contents would contaminate its quality, I did experience a sense of threat: "What is she saying about me?" (an assumption about my inviolate omniscience), "Will she need me less now that she has the diary?" (fear of abandonment), "Will she really report the 'truth' about the various events in our marriage?" (fear of being wrong or misunderstood).
>
> It's evident that it is not the diary that is the threat but the fears that linger within us, which become manifest when partners deviate from the illusion of "togetherness."

If members of your household initially experience your writing as a threat to their relationship with you, the tension may have to be lived through. Eventually the journal will become normal and acceptable to all of you. But until that time comes, as the diarist's husband wisely suggested, "The diarist should take into account the discomfort that can be expected to arise and not treat fear or anxiety as a peculiar reaction that in any way poses a challenge to the diarist's integrity or desire."

Along with understanding and considering the feelings of family members, you still have to take care of your own needs for privacy. This may include privacy while you are writing and privacy for the book itself. Some writers are able simply to explain to their families or friends that time with the diary, like practicing a musical instrument, meditating, or reading, requires a certain amount of undisturbed concentration. For others, achieving privacy takes more creativity and ingenuity.

Fear of exposure needn't stop you from writing; just make sure that the diary won't be read. You can keep it in a cashbox with a secure lock. Accumulated volumes can be stored in a locked trunk, suitcase, or drawer.

One man kept his diary locked in the trunk of his car; another kept it locked in the vault in his office. One woman who keeps her diaries with her cookbooks in the kitchen says that no one in her family would ever look there. But in general, hiding a diary is impractical. And writing in a code or shorthand is likely to keep the entries a secret not only from readers but also from the writer in later years.

If locking it away doesn't satisfy your need for security, write the entries that cause you the greatest fear of exposure on separate sheets of paper and then destroy them. At least you will get the benefits of release and clarity by working out your "forbidden" thoughts on paper.

Some diarists, particularly those who have been writing for a long time, report that they really don't care who reads it. But you will need to decide for yourself what your privacy needs are. They vary from person to person and from time to time in the same person's life. To help yourself discover what your attitudes are, ask yourself if you need to keep the journal private, why, and from whom. Further, you may wish to ask yourself if you have taken sufficient responsibility in this matter. Have you, for example, made your standards of privacy clear in your relationships? Do you extend to others the respect for privacy they desire?

It is important to recognize that the responsibility for keeping your diary private is yours. Take precautions if you feel they are needed. It's unfair to present those you care about with the temptation of a diary left out in the open and expect them to resist their curiosity on the basis of good manners. The diary has its own body language which may belie its owner's stated wishes. If it is accessible, it seems to say "Read me!" If it is consistently locked out of sight, it is saying "Private."

Sharing

After you have been keeping a journal for awhile you may feel an urge to share it, as a way of having someone else understand something about you. Sharing a diary should be approached with caution. When, where, how, with whom, and how much to share are decisions so personal that, like most aspects of diary writing, no one can give you rules. But I do suggest that you ask yourself why you want that person to read it. For example, you might ask yourself whether there is unconscious hostility behind the desire to have the person read the diary, and what the results might be after the entries are read.

What are you hoping will be the result? Do you, for example, hope to change that person by opening everything to him or her? If the person has not been receptive to other attempts at intimacy, you can probably predict he or she will not be receptive to your diary. And in offering it to be read you might be setting yourself up for rejection. If you aren't willing to take responsibility for possibly unpleasant consequences keep your diary private and find alternative ways to communicate.

If someone offers you a journal to read, you needn't feel pressured to offer yours. And you don't have to read a diary offered to you, especially if you feel it implies a reciprocal exchange. Nor do you have to let a person who gives you a diary as a gift read it later. You may not wish to use the book if you feel such a claim is implied.

The greatest caution I wish to extend is to women who have unrealistic expectations about sharing their diaries with boyfriends or husbands. One must be prepared for any reaction. Ingmar Bergman's film *Scenes from a Marriage* illustrates the not-uncommon scenario. Marianne, the wife, has felt herself experiencing a profound inner rebirth, a discovery of her real self behind her mask of social conventionality. She reads a particularly meaningful passage from her diary to her husband, Johan, at his encouragement. When she has finished reading she looks up from the notebook. Johan has fallen asleep.

A talented young friend of mine reported her attempts to interest her boyfriend in her diary with results similar to Marianne's. Several years later I had the opportunity to ask the boyfriend why he had been apparently uninterested. He had grown in self-awareness during the intervening years and was now able to articulate what he was not even conscious of then. "I felt intimidated," he said. "Her inner life was so rich and I had none at all at the time. I ignored hers, the way I ignored my own."

Getting valid feedback from others on your writing is always a delicate matter, and especially so in the case of a diary. Since people rarely have the chance to read unpublished diaries, they don't know how to do it. Most often they look for references to themselves or to friends or for sexual entries and ignore the context of the references. They forget that the diary does not represent the "truth." It often contains fantasy, psychological projection, overdramatization, and overemphasis for its own reasons. They may expect the writing to have the quality of published prose, which it never does. All in all, they are likely to bring their own expectations and biases to the experience and miss the meaningful themes and individually evolved forms that truly communicate the writer's spirit.

In a personal relationship, then, if you wish to share your diary, it seems best to extract particular passages that apply to a specific issue rather than offering the entire volume for reading. Again, it is often better to communicate your thoughts directly. Of course, there will always be exceptions to this advice, times when sharing a diary can bring deep intimacy. And you may develop a relationship or correspondence with other diarists that will allow you to experience this intimacy.

But even if you never share a sentence of your diary with anyone else, you will share it through your life. Its existence will touch other people by the way it changes you and permits you to develop in self-awareness, directness, and honesty. As you acquire and refine the talent for helping yourself in the diary, you will also grow in your ability to understand and nourish others. While it permits you to take responsibility for your own emotional well-being, it also opens the way for a deep understanding of human nature. As Anaïs Nin has said, "The personal life deeply lived always expands into truths beyond itself."

4 | Basic Diary Devices

Diary devices are written modes of expression that diarists have found effective in the process of self-discovery. They were not invented by one person as a set of rules to be imposed on others but instead evolved within the books of innumerable diarists working independently over the centuries. These devices represent a collective practical psychology, an inheritance of personal, daily, inner wisdom preserved by one generation for another in diaries. They illustrate the limitless flexibility of the diary as a personal tool for entering the mystery of a life.

The diary devices are not intended to represent the "correct" or the "best" way to write a journal. There is no system to learn or memorize. Delineating them is meant only to stimulate your imagination.

In labeling and describing these devices I have simply tried to look at the diary as a literary critic looks at a novel. The critic might notice that some novelists use a particular literary device, which the critic then labels "religious symbolism." If you were a novelist it could be helpful for you to be aware of the technique of religious symbolism, but you wouldn't necessarily want to use it just because it had been defined. Novelists wrote successful novels for hundreds of years before critics described what they were doing. And people have been keeping diaries for at least a thousand years without anyone's telling them how. On the other hand, there is no reason for you to spend a lifetime of diary writing to rediscover the aids that other diarists have already discovered.

Simply to make you aware of the range of ways to write in a diary, this chapter and the next describe eleven possible diary devices, which I have divided for convenience into "four natural modes of expression" and "seven special techniques." In practice there are no clear boundaries between the devices. They often overlap or lead into one another.

Four Natural Modes of Expression	Seven Special Techniques
Catharsis	List
Description	Portrait
Free-Intuitive Writing	Map of Consciousness
Reflection	Guided Imagery
	Altered Point of View
	Unsent Letter
	Dialogue

The eleven devices are like possible moves in a game or steps in a dance. They become part of your repertoire, and your intuition becomes the choreographer. Each diarist can choose the device or devices that best suit his or her purposes at any particular time. Again, there is no "right way" to keep the New Diary other than the one you evolve for yourself.

The first four devices—catharsis, description, free-intuitive writing, and reflection—are basic to all writing. They correspond to the four basic modes of human perception—emotion, sensation, intuition, and intellect—which, according to ancient and modern psychologies and philosophies, characterize a "complete" person. *Catharsis* releases and expresses the emotions; *description* conveys the information perceived by the senses: sight, touch, smell, taste, and hearing. *Free-intuitive writing* is the language of intuition. And *reflection* is the contemplation of the intellect. All four varieties of expression may be found within one diary entry, and they often intermix. For the sake of illustration, however, I have separated them and excerpted diary entries in which one of these natural devices predominates. The diary excerpts in this chapter and throughout this book have been generously provided by students of mine, friends, and diarists around the country, and an occasional example is from my own diary—unless an excerpt is attributed to a published source.

Catharsis

Cathartic writing is done under the pressure of intense emotion that calls for immediate expression. It could be as simple a statement as, "I'm so angry!" or "I'm crazy about her!" It could be as elaborate as twenty pages of emotional outpouring.

The use of the diary for catharsis, or emotional release, may be so obvious that it seems not to warrant mention. Yet it is surprising how many people fail to take advantage of the opportunity offered for emotional purgation because they think of the diary as a product rather than a process. And if they use the diary for purging strong emotions through writing, the product may not be very pretty. The process, however, may allow the life to proceed more easily. One young man I know expressed it dramatically: "Instead of screaming or going to the window and shooting a gun wildly into the street, I put the scream in the diary, catch it between the pages, close the book tight, and go on."

Some people use catharsis so skillfully that they have made an art of it. After all, great literature has often served as a purgation for the writer. Most of us, though, just have to get it out in raw, primitive form. If you dump anger, greed, lust, and grief into your diary remember that the diary isn't you—it's all the things you've purged yourself of for your own well-being.

Many people observe that their diaries contain only "wailings and complainings." One famous novelist says he writes in his diary only when he is angry at someone, and therefore his journals are full of one-sided, self-justifying, negative portraits of his friends and acquaintances. Some people write in the diary only when they are confused, when they don't understand something about themselves or their lives. Upon rereading they find the passages seemingly incoherent and contradictory. Other people write only when they are hurt or grieving, and their diaries are pessimistic, heavy, and painful.

The importance of the diary in these cases is not as a product—a point I can't repeat too often—but in the life that is freed from excessive anger, confusion, and grief. Putting the pain in the diary keeps it from destroying a life. The life liberated from such destructive emotions is the true "product" of this purgative process.

Cathartic writing is often recognizable by the nature of the handwriting. No matter what the words, one can often feel the emotion from the script itself. It may be large and irregular or scrawled across the page. The physical energy that sometimes goes into cathartic writing is itself a release of emotion for the diarist. The page should not be judged as ugly or the writer, imbalanced. Instead such an entry should be seen as part of the process that reestablishes emotional balance.

Sometimes cathartic writing expresses itself in halting, laconic phrases, as if it is all the writer can do to name the emotion. The outbreak of World War II, for example, entered many personal diaries with the same elliptical, heavy-rhythmed voice, as in Anaïs Nin's *Diary II:* "The world in Chaos. Panic. Hysteria." Sometimes cathartic writing expresses itself as a disjointed list of seemingly unrelated thoughts or events: "I have problems with money, the damned stereo isn't working, I can't stand the intensity of this relationship, I hurt him, I feel overwhelmed." At other times catharsis takes the form of extended, repetitive emotional language: "Deep inside me it cries out. I don't want to go on by myself. I haven't got what it takes. I'm too little. I'm afraid I won't make it. I can't comfort the continual pain. Take care of me, love me, help me."

Cathartic writing may not represent reality at all. It uses exaggerations and distortions because realistic writing cannot contain the amount of emotion behind the words. It can be a curse to let off steam or a sudden outburst of harbored resentment:

> I feel so bitchy I can't believe it. I hope M. and D. think it's weariness but it isn't really. I feel bitchy and I'm acting tired because I don't want to have sex tonight after that long drive and I know C. would like to just because he's as tired as I am. He would spill all that exhaustion into me and call it love and me the good wife. Forget it!

Cathartic writing can be an expression of excitement: "I got the job! I can't believe it! I got the job!" It can also be a release for intense feelings of joy.

> Joy, effervescent happiness bubbles up in me day after day. I have no explanation for it. It's a physical well-being, an escape from worry, an escape from obsession, a release from the past, an experience of the moment, an acceptance of what is, a delight in detail, a delight in being.

Intimate diaries are characterized by spots of intense emotion, "that which is created when we are unable to suppress our feelings," as the first Japanese diarist wrote. Many diarists find that they need to allow an emotional, spontaneous, cathartic expression before they can understand or transform it through the use of other diary devices.

Description

Description, perhaps the most common and familiar form of expression in diaries, satisfies the universal creative urge to reproduce reality as it is, better than it is, or worse than it is. It can include any narrative account of events, feelings, dreams, people, places—anything that derives from your life experience. Description also satisfies the defiant human desire to preserve certain "unforgettable" perceptions against the annihilation of time. There are moments that, for the artist in all of us, seem too important to allow to pass into oblivion.

Description does not transcribe reality, it re-creates one person's view of experience. Diaries have less to do with objective observation than with individual perception. You record not what actually was, so much as how you perceived what was. For example, in the following journal entry the diarist is not just taking a verbal snapshot of Mount Fujiyama but recording her unique experience of Mount Fuji at a particular moment in her life. It is her personal relationship with the experience that she preserves:

> I woke suddenly at 5:25. I hurried silently through the cold, red-carpeted halls toward the front door. It was locked. I tried a service door down the hall and yet another side door before I found one that let me outside. On the frosty grass were a pair of workmen's clogs that keep one's feet up out of the mud. I stepped into them and clumsily picked my way through the bushes. I became part of a Japanese print in the beige, waist-high brush brittle with frost. I had entered the sunrise world of Mount Fuji, a perfect white cone

against a blue-white morning sky. Nobody has mentioned it, but I know the world stood still for a moment.

Though the diarist may have had many other experiences
which she did not describe on her tour of Japan, she perceived
this one in a highly personal way that made her want to
preserve it.

Many people labor under the misconception that description in a diary should be a running account of everything
that has happened to them during the day. They dutifully fill
their books with news of every person they meet, every party
they go to, when their children graduate from high school,
when they take the dog to the vet. When they reread their
diaries they are bored. So many pages have been written and it
all seems so futile.

The point is, you don't have to describe anything in a
diary that you don't feel compelled to write about. You don't
need to include all your daily experiences; select only what
you wish to describe. In that process of selection you are
creating your values and yourself. *The Secret Diary of William
Byrd of Westover* (1709-1712) records everything that that
Virginia gentleman ate at his prodigious meals. He regurgitated
every course in his diary in admirable detail. But with a whole
world of experiences to describe, you may find more significant subjects than breakfast. When you let go of the obsession
of recording the weather, the traffic, the news, or any other
seemingly appropriate journallike description, you will find
that more meaningful experiences will cry out for inclusion.

Because description captures the sensual details of experience, it can provide the most pleasurable diary passages to
reread. Diarists can describe people, places, aspects of nature,
human interactions, works of art, books they have read, or
films they have seen in a way that is more interesting than the
actual experience because they select the interesting details
and leave out the dull moments. Some of the most painfully
embarrassing moments in life also make the most amusing diary

entries to reread, since the diarist does not simply report the experience but transforms it through humor, insight, or irony.

Anaïs Nin's diaries show how individual perception—more than any other factor—transforms the quality of experience. Some of the incidents she turns into magic in her diary were actually everyday occurrences that another person might have overlooked. But she observes the immediate world around her and finds the significance or symbolism just beneath the surface of the mundane, as in this diary description written in 1943:

> In a Chinese shop I bought a Japanese paper parasol
> which I wear in my hair. So delicately made, with
> colored paper and fragile bamboo structure. It tore.
> I repaired it with tape.
>
> When Samuel Goldberg took us to Chinatown for
> dinner I went into a shop to ask for parasols. The woman
> who received me was very agitated: "No, of course I
> don't carry those. They are Japanese. You bought them
> in a Chinese shop? Well, that may be, but they're Jap-
> anese just the same. Tear it up and throw it away."
>
> I looked at the parasol in my hand, innocent and
> delicate, made in a moment of peace, outside of love
> and hatred, made by some skilled workman like a
> flower. I could not bring myself to throw it away. I
> folded it quietly, protectively. I folded up delicacy,
> peace, skill, humble work, I folded tender gardens, the
> fragile structure of human dreams. I folded the dream of
> peace, the frail paper shelter of peace.

The insignificant parasol becomes a vehicle for Nin to articulate her personal reverence for peace during the hatreds of wartime.

In her diaries Nin not only described her world as it was but also as it appeared to her, enlivened by her values and perceptions. She wrote because she had to, to create a world in which she could live. In so doing she didn't avoid reality but embraced it and transformed it. Though the actual experiences

are gone forever, the world she created still lives as she captured it. Such is the potential power of description.

Frequently a description follows naturally after a cathartic expression, explaining the source of the emotion and thus
putting the experience into clearer focus. At other times the
description itself is cathartic, simultaneously venting emotion
and beginning the process of distancing, which helps you
understand it. This process is what seems to be taking place in
the entry below, written by a doctor in a military hospital in
Vietnam:

> It seems that death brings me back to this book. Today I
> lost a patient. A six-year-old Vietnamese girl that I knew
> for less than twenty minutes. She opened her eyes
> once. She lay there and threw her arms and legs out
> while her father looked on uneasily. I had promised
> him that she would be all right. Then she died. I blew
> my breath into her lungs and it came out with a soft
> moan past a dead larynx. I was fooled for a moment.
>
> You hate to fail. Hate yourself even more for
> being upset at failing. You do your best, and yet through
> the world's eyes you judge yourself.

When the diarist unconsciously switches from "I" in the first
paragraph to "you" in the second, he has already begun to
distance himself from the experience.

Describing an experience can sometimes be frustrating
because of the inevitable gap between the perception of reality
and the ability to capture it in words. However, it is precisely
this frustration of trying to find the right expression that leads
you gradually to write descriptions to your satisfaction. Like
whittling shapes out of wood, you learn by doing it. Most
published writing, including most published diaries, are edited
so that you don't read the passages in which the writer wasn't
able to capture the magic of an experience.

The reward of trying to translate the immense complexity of reality into a satisfying description is that it pushes
you out of the narrow boundaries of the self and causes your

senses to interact with the environment—to see, hear, feel, touch, taste, smell, and develop sensual memory. Attempts at faithful description help you discover your own flexible, expressive prose style.

The key to writing satisfying descriptive entries is to include vivid details. When you reread an entry made ten years earlier, which includes specifics about an experience such as the color of a dress, the way a person sat down, the exact tune on the radio, perhaps even snatches of actual conversation, you reexperience the moment. Similarly, you can recapture memories if you search for concrete details with which to describe them. For example, one woman in her sixties recollected how, as a young girl, she had curled her hair into ringlets to try to win her father's approval:

> I opened the sliding door to the dining room and stuck my head in. Dad was already sitting at the table having his morning coffee and reading *The Chronicle*. He put his newspaper down, turned to look at me and let out a blood-curdling, unexpected guffaw. At first I couldn't believe his laughter was directed at me, but my puzzlement was cleared up immediately when he said, still howling with laughter, "If you don't look like a skinned rat! Go upstairs this instant and wash those silly ringlets out of your hair. Then come back down to breakfast. You're already late!" I could hear mother arguing with him in a placating kind of voice as I walked up to the bathroom and rinsed out, brushed out the curls, bawling.

In this journal entry details such as the sliding door, *The Chronicle* (rather than just the newspaper), the "placating" tone of the mother's voice, and the actual words of the father made the description come to life in the rereading.

Literary diaries have traditionally relied on description. But you needn't write with an intent to publish to find satisfaction from the technique. I don't write a literary diary. I even find that trying to do so takes most of the pleasure out of keeping the diary. But I do use description frequently both to preserve precious moments and to give me a sense of personal power. When I describe an experience, I no longer feel controlled by it but responsible for it in the overall context of my life. I affirm my own existence and validate my vision of the world. In describing my experience I am recording not what happened or what exists but how I perceive it. In so doing I define myself. As I create my diary I create myself.

Moreover, as a woman I feel that my power to describe my life is a gesture against powerlessness. I defy the "official" version of reality with my own version. As a result of my power to describe my experiences in the diary, I feel there is nothing that can really overwhelm me—not hunger or cruelty, success or poverty, loss or love, illness or disappointment, or even other people's manipulations. As long as I have the power of words to describe my experience, I have a bastion of personal control. The diary is not just a friend, a mother, a psychiatrist, and a home—it is also a weapon.

Free-Intuitive Writing

Catharsis is primarily an emotional language, an overflow of intense feeling. And description is primarily an intellectual and sensual language. But *free-intuitive writing* comes from a deeper place in the psyche. It is primarily an intuitive language, a message from the inner consciousness. Free-intuitive writing releases the voice of the subconscious by removing or putting aside the control of the conscious mind. Messages received from the subconscious through free-intuitive writing may sometimes contradict feelings expressed in cathartic or descriptive writing. More often free intuition can help explain the source of an intense emotional reaction that seems inappropriate or isn't sufficiently understood.

Free-intuitive writing also has important creative uses. Some people regularly loosen up or warm up for other work in the diary by first using this device, and some use it as a strategy against writing blocks. Since it gives you a direct line to the subconscious, it is also a vital source of fresh imagery and varied rhythms in writing.

There are many ways to do free-intuitive writing, and various schools of literature and psychology use different techniques and names for what is basically the same process. Free association, stream of consciousness, automatic writing, and active imagination are all varieties of free-intuitive writing. So I have grouped all spontaneous writing within this category.

No matter what you call it, the technique is simple. You relax and try to empty your mind. You don't think about anything. You simply wait for whatever comes into your mind, and you write it just as it comes, without worrying about whether it makes sense. You let your hand do the writing. You record what you hear from the back of your mind. Nothing is irrelevant. You try to capture every word and image that occurs to you. It may all seem silly, just nonsense, but you write it anyway. It may seem embarrassing, but you write anyway. You write fast, so fast that you don't have time to think about what you are doing. You don't take time to censor or make sense.

You may wish to experiment with free-intuitive writing just for the fun of it. You will marvel at the completely original, surrealistic narrative of your subconscious. This funny, nonlogical language is there all the time, and you can listen in whenever you choose. For example:

> night on bald mountain receding snow line fall line
> line backer gooble gooble gooble tubes eating
> tubes my dad had hair on his chest of drawers ports
> of call heat of hearts time of day out of the pool
> over the rainbow mars has two moons but the
> moon has no mars time waits for no one table
> chair and roomcat sprints into the myrtle tree if a
> doctor is a quack can a duck operate a gas station
> station station.

The surrealist artists who gathered in Paris in the 1920s and 1930s were avid enthusiasts of free-intuitive writing, which they called "automatic writing." They played games with it and wrote whole novels using the technique. André Breton, surrealism's principal theorist and leader, offered some helpful instructions on how to do it:

> Attain the most passive or receptive state of mind possible. Forget your genius, your talents, and those of everyone else. . . . Write quickly with no preconceived subject, so quickly that you retain nothing and are not tempted to reread. Continue as long as you please.

You may find it helpful to use some of the other techniques developed by the surrealists to do free-intuitive writing. You might avoid looking at the page entirely as you are writing or close your eyes. You can ignore all rules of punctuation, capitalization, grammar, and logical meaning. You can begin arbitrarily with any letter, such as "I" and then write quickly, in a semitrance-like state. If you find yourself thinking or trying to make sense, you can stop writing, try to relax completely, and wait for the conscious effort to subside. If you sense a break in the flow of intuitive writing you can repeat the last spontaneous word (for example, "station station station") until the nonlogical language reasserts itself.

Everyone can do free-intuitive writing, and everyone does it in a completely individual way. The rhythms and style vary from person to person. Some diarists write in different directions over the page. They treat the page as free space that can be divided in innumerable ways, not simply with imaginary lines that run from left to right and top to bottom. (See the example on page 64.)

Free-intuitive writing can be a liberating, fascinating game. It can also have a very valuable function in leading you to understand the existence, importance, and meaning of your subconscious feelings and motivations. It is a useful device when you sense that you are out of touch with your inner needs.

In the following example the writer wanted to understand more about the discontent and inner turmoil that were occurring at that point in her life:

> the thought leads to a circle it's so aggravating everything is its opposite the world of nightwood again I become you become the dream become macaroon mother kettle mother fear mother Jerry Mother mother home kitchen care infantile when will I grow up Jerry an overgrown child sweetmouse my child depend dependency immaturity no one wants me mother wants me married to my mother my mother

my mother this is Jerry's fault why am I unhappy?
Unhappy because Mother told you so What did she
tell me so? She said you should go to the store for
cookies and me right home you didn't. I didn't come
right home this is nonsense Why am I unhappy? can't
relax Fear of what? Internal life no good no more
Used it up time to change fear of failure fear of too late
fear fear rejection fear overweight fear dumb so dumb
so dull so sweet so crafty so so . . .

Though the entry may appear to make little sense, it uncovered for the diarist her anxiety over failure and problems with emotional dependency, a desire to be taken care of as though she were still a child.

Some people find that writing with the left hand frees their subconscious. If you normally write with your right hand you may discover a very different personality speaking through the awkward lefthanded script. The theory is this. Since the right hand is governed by the left brain—which is rational and logical—and the left hand is governed by the right brain—which is emotional and intuitive—the two hands may express different modes of perception. The left hand seems to know what the right hand doesn't. Some diarists who are sufficiently ambidextrous write alternately with the right or left hand as a means of keeping in tune with both sides of the self.

Many diarists who are familiar with Jungian psychology practice what they call "active imagination" in their journals. The intention is to establish a relationship between the conscious mind and the subconscious. Generally the diarist asks the subconscious a question, feels an audience listening from deep within the psyche, and allows that audience to respond in its nonlogical language. For example, you might consciously ask yourself in the diary, "What is bothering me?" and allow a voice of wisdom from deep inside to answer in its own imagistic language.

Experimenting with forms of free-intuitive writing will take different people to very different levels of consciousness and subconsciousness. What is deep into the hinterland for one explorer may be only on the outskirts for another. Though a few people have reported frightening experiences while practicing automatic writing—a sense of possession by another personality speaking through them—such experiences are extremely rare. The diarist may simply be in touch with a latent part of the self that is being mistaken for another's personality. But if the experience is too threatening, the diarist should discontinue it or seek professional psychological guidance.

Since free-intuitive writing covers many levels of the subconscious, like descriptive writing it may overlap with cathartic writing. Marion Milner practiced a particularly emotional variety of free-intuitive writing. She referred to her experiments as "butterfly catching" or the setting down of "blind thinking." From keeping a diary of all the "butterflies" she could catch, Milner developed the theory that she could evolve out of childish thinking into maturity only by recording, and hence becoming conscious of, how her mind really worked. She wanted to discover how one thought actually led to another at the subconscious level. Milner warned those who might try it that they should be prepared to find themselves a fool, since so much of what we ordinarily don't admit to consciousness is humiliating to our adult image of ourselves.

The following illustrations from her book *A Life of One's Own* fall somewhere between catharsis and free-intuitive writing. Included also are her own reflections upon these diary entries:

> Here is . . . a butterfly caught in a moment of acute emotion, remembered and written down later:
>> He won't do what I want, he doesn't care . . .
>> but I'll show him, he'll have to in the end. . . .
>> I could refuse to go and see him—that's no good,

> he wouldn't mind—I could run away somewhere,
> go wild about the streets, run amok, hurt myself,
> make him take notice, make him feel sorry, feel
> sorry how he's hurt me, make him help me, be
> nice to me ... I'll kill myself to punish him, so
> he'll have to be sorry. . . . That's no good, he'll
> guess, he'll see through it, shrug his shoulders, say,
> "If she wants to hurt herself ...

Here I was contemplating killing myself to make someone do as I wished, and sucking comfort from the
thought of the offender's remorse, quite oblivious of the
fact that I would not be there to see it. Actually this
particular train of thought continued, and in the later
part showed a tendency to emerge from such complete
irrationality, perhaps because I was observing it with
half an eye, even through my tears; for the next sentence
reads:

> that won't do, for I shall know that I'm doing it
> on purpose ... what can I do then to escape this
> thing in me that knows I'm doing it on purpose,
> that tells me I'll have to behave sensibly in the
> end? go mad, then I should not know ... then I
> could do things to make them care and there
> would be nothing to hold me back.

I suspect it was the thought expressed in this final sentence which actually brought me to myself again. . . . I
remember "coming to" with a flash of understanding
which dissipated all my impotent rage in a moment, for
I was delighted at having caught myself out in such a
flagrant piece of absurdity and pinned down such a
super-butterfly.

By giving us both the examples of her diary entries and her
later reflections about them. Milner demonstrates the usefulness of free-intuitive writing. Beyond bringing a calming effect
from releasing pent-up thoughts and emotions, such entries
provide a basis for self-knowledge at a deep level. Upon rereading them in a less passionate mood the writer can see how

childish thinking takes over at certain times and in certain situations. Working in the diary can help the writer recognize and then rechannel the energy of such childish emotion into more mature and constructive modes of thinking and behaving.

Reflection

Reflection as a mode of expression in the New Diary is an observation of the process of one's life and writing. It seems to occur when you stand back, even if only momentarily, and see connections or significances that you had not noticed before. Reflection can also be called musing, self-observation, or contemplation.

Diarists frequently reflect upon why they write in their journals. For example, Anaïs Nin muses:

> The false persona I had created for the enjoyment of my friends, the gaiety, the buoyant, the receptive, the healing person, always on call, always ready with sympathy, had to have its other existence somewhere. In the diary I could reestablish the balance. Here I could be depressed, angry, despairing, discouraged. I could let out my demons.

Reflection often follows a cathartic entry, after an emotion has spent itself and the diarist is ready to look at the situation more objectively. For example, after releasing a tirade of complaints one diarist reflected:

> Now that I've let it all out, none of it seems so important. Strange how turning the anger into words allows me to get past it.

Reflection also frequently records insights gained from allowing the inner voice to speak in free-intuitive writing. It often precedes, leads into, concludes, or summarizes many of the other diary devices.

Through self-reflection you create, piece by piece, a personal philosophy of life based on your experiences and feelings. But reflection need not always apply to yourself. It can be the free play of the intellect on any subject—on a film, a book, or on any concept or principle. One diarist reflected on fame:

> There must be a frustration in fame, if the motivation
> is to be loved. Because you want to be loved for who you
> are, but instead, you are loved for who you are not, or
> for who you seem to be, or for a small part of you, and
> the rest is ignored, still unloved.

Notice that the diarist uses the abstract "you," indicating distance and depersonalization that frequently characterizes reflective writing, as it did in the cathartic-descriptive excerpt used earlier.

Sometimes reflection takes the form of speaking directly to the self, of giving advice, encouragement, or bits of philosophic wisdom. I call this self-helping, healing, guiding voice the Silver-Lining Voice of the diary, since it often appears in times of stress as a voice of hope. At first it may speak in adages, such as "Keep on trying. Don't give up," or "You have to believe in yourself." As it is allowed to be heard and to develop, it can expand into the most important guide in your life—your voice of inner wisdom.

The Silver-Lining Voice seems to enter a diary spontaneously and of its own accord, without any conscious effort on the part of the writer. One diarist found that it offered her advice about her current relationship with a man who did not satisfy her desires. It said:

> He is a beautiful person, but he doesn't know who or
> what you are. Your belief in love with this person has
> distorted your perception of him. He is not your fantasm.
> He is what he is and where he has come to. His life
> confusion with women is his own construct. Only he
> can get out of it. Your business is to fulfill your own
> goals.

This message from the Silver-Lining Voice was a truth that the diarist had resisted when other people had suggested it. When it came from the self during a moment of quiet reflection she was finally able to hear and accept it.

The quiet reflections of the Silver-Lining Voice can be a comfort in illness, in the midst of emotional turmoil, in the contemplation of death and aging. Florida Scott-Maxwell, an actress and later a psychologist, listened to its wisdom in a diary she kept at the age of eighty-two. After a full life the Silver-Lining Voice seemed to have become the reflection of her cumulative experiences. When she had recalled a childhood memory in her diary it approved, observing:

> You need only claim the events of your life to make yourself yours. When you truly possess all you have been and done, which may take some time, you are fierce with reality. When at last age has assembled you together, will it not be easy to let it all go, lived, balanced, over?

In this entry the reflective passage ends with a question. Such self-questioning is another characteristic of the reflective mood in writing. You might even begin a diary entry with an incisive self-reflective question: "What is the secret I am keeping from myself?" or "What is really bothering me?" The reflective voice can thus encourage the feeling, interior self to speak.

Self-directing questions push you forward in the midst of writing when you wish to look at an experience or feeling. The short-story writer Katherine Mansfield frequently used reflective questions in her journal to focus her desires:

> Now, Katherine, what do you mean by health? And what do you want it for? Answer: By health I mean the power to live a full, adult, living, breathing life in close contact with what I love—the earth and the wonders thereof—the sea—the sun. . . .
> Then I want to *work*. At what? I want so to live that I work with my hands and my feeling and my brain. I want a garden, a small house, grass, animals, books, pictures, music. And out of this, the expression of this, I want to be writing. . . .

Sometimes the reflective voice is willing to ask a question and wait for the answers to accumulate over an extended period of time. Questions such as, "I wonder what I really want?" can be posed to the self in the diary to give direction to your search. If you are patient, the answers will inevitably appear in the diary, piece by piece.

Reflection, then, is characterized by the perspective, or psychological distance, it provides. Through it the diarist addresses the self as "you," asks the self a question, or looks at personal experience from a universal point of view.

Reflection tends to deal with the general and the overall perspective, unlike description which concentrates on the physical and the specific. Because it is the province of the abstract intellect, a diary that is all reflection may lack emotional depth. In contrast, a diary that contains no reflective writing may feel emotionally chaotic and intellectually unfulfilling for its writer.

Reflection and description give voice to your more objective, rational adult-self, while catharsis and free-intuitive writing give voice to your more subjective, emotional, intuitive self. The interrelationships in the diary among the various faculties of perception lead to self-knowledge and underlie all creativity. Together the four natural modes of expression can convey the full range of human experience. They permit release of emotion, confirmation of your relationship with the physical world, access to your inner consciousness, and contemplation of experience from a detached perspective. These traditional devices form a familiar base for the more experimental special techniques described in the next chapter.

5 | Seven Special Techniques

By searching in the diary for ways to help themselves, diarists have sometimes purposely invented and sometimes simply stumbled across certain tricks and techniques that brought desired results. Some of these special techniques are insights from the human potential movement that have been incorporated into private diary keeping; others come from literary sources. Having access to a broad range of diary devices permits the writer to select a special way of proceeding when expressing an event, feeling, or thought using the four basic devices, described in the previous chapter, seems insufficient. When you can't get to a problem through the front door with one of the more traditional forms of expression, the special techniques may be used as side entrances.

Lists, portraits, maps of consciousness, guided imagery, altered point of view, unsent letters, and dialogues make up the seven special diary devices. You may never use some of them. A diarist who uses all of the techniques isn't a better or even a more versatile diarist than someone who uses only one or two. Like the diarists who discovered these techniques, you have to find what works for you.

Lists

A *list* can perform any of the functions of the four natural modes of expression. It can enumerate feelings, sense impressions, intuitions, or thoughts without using complete sentences. Lists are time-savers and time-condensers. For example, if you haven't written in the diary for a long time, a list allows you to summarize all that has happened. Anaïs Nin uses lists in this way in *Diary III* to give a sense of the pace of her life at the time: "Friends, Dinners. Visitors. Hans Boeb, a German painter. Elie Agnnides, Greek engineer...." Lists are also particularly useful when you feel overwhelmed by the magnitude of something you wish to describe. Here is a characteristic diary entry that includes list making:

> Feeling overwhelmed. Too much to do. How can I ever get it all done? An avalanche has fallen on me.

do list:
laundry
write bills
call Sharon

upset list:
Charles saying my last article was tacky
not enough time for my own work
mother losing her job once again

things I'm afraid of:
If I get too absorbed in my own writing—
the dusting won't get done (it doesn't anyway)
I won't eat properly (I don't anyway)
No one will love me (a lot of people already do)
No one will want to marry such a poor housekeeper
   (no one does anyway)

Even when nothing is resolved lists help focus problems and make them finite. When your head is swimming with unresolved issues they seem infinite. On paper they become focused and concrete. You can do something about each item on a list if you want to.

Personal uses of lists for making plans or decisions have become so common that people often don't think of them as diary writing. But lists have always been an integral part of the diary form, created for self-enjoyment and for mastering parts of one's personal reality. One of the most famous classical Japanese diaries, the twelfth-century *Pillow Book of Sei Shōnagon,* is a random collage of poems, nature descriptions, character sketches, anecdotes, and lists of awkward things, things that give one an uncomfortable feeling, pretty things, and embarrassing things, for example.

The Puritans frequently made lists of their moral transgressions in their diaries, adding up at the end of the week, the month, and the year all their failings. Benjamin Franklin made lists of the thirteen virtues he resolved to acquire—such as temperance, frugality, cleanliness, tranquility, and humility—and he kept a graph of his poor progress on each virtue. Such lists of resolutions and failings never seem to bring satisfactory results; they are only a way of nagging at oneself.

On the other hand, Marion Milner had remarkably positive results when she decided to keep ongoing lists of all the things she desired and all the things she observed that made her genuinely happy. For seven years she made lists of her desires and joys, gradually teaching herself about her own happiness and the ways she could achieve it.

By the same token some diarists have developed self-knowledge by listing things that irritate them. Mary MacLane, a young diarist who lived in Butte, Montana, at the turn of the century, wrote an amusing list of such irritations:

> *March 8, 1901*
> the kind of people who call a woman's figure her
>   "shape"
> hips that wobble as one walks
> persons with fishy eyes
> tight garters
> insipid sweet wine
> men who wear moustaches
> unripe bananas
> wax flowers off a wedding cake
> fools who tell me what I "want" to do

some paintings of the old masters which I am unable
   to appreciate
people who don't wash their hair often enough
a bed that sinks in the middle

Similarly, a list of fears can get them out of your head and onto paper so that you don't have to dwell on them any longer. When you are overwhelmed with negative feelings it can be a cathartic release simply to list all the possible causes.

One diarist, who felt that his strict Baptist upbringing not only limited his development as a young man but also gave him a predisposition to cling to arbitrary beliefs, found it helpful to write a list that he titled "Beliefs I have discarded, or believe I have":

1. Mama loves me. Daddy will always be there.
2. Jesus loves me, this I know, for the Bible tells me so.
3. Christ died for my sins.
4. Mama loves me. Daddy will come back soon.
5. God is an American white male.
6. The Lone Ranger really lives.
7. You'd better not shout, you'd better not cry, you'd better not pout, I'm telling you why . . .
8. I'm an angel. I'm going to live forever.
9. If I do this, I'll go blind.
10. If I do this, I'll go insane.
11. If I keep doing this, I'll die of a heart attack, like my father.
12. If I go to college I'll be smarter than anybody else.
13. If I learn to play the guitar, I'll have my pick of the girls.
14. If I study trigonometry, I'll be able to be a pilot.
15. This paralysis was God's judgment on me.
16. This paralysis ruined my body forever.
17. If I stay up all night, I'll write a good poem.
18. I'll die before thirty.
19. If we bomb the Vietcong in Hanoi, they'll quit.
20. If I march down South, blacks will love me.
21. We are a generation of vipers.
22. God is dead.
23. If I get married, I'll be happy.

24. I'll be able to realize everything in my son that I haven't realized in myself.
25. The Beatles are perfect.
26. If I swallow this pill, I'll be enlightened.
27. If I smoke this number, I'll be hip.
28. If I snort this stuff, I'll write a great script.
29. All cops are pigs.
30. We've got to get back to the garden, I believe we can.
31. If I get divorced, my mother will be crushed.
32. If I get divorced, I'll be punished.
33. This therapy will restore me.
34. All belief is sleep, the lowest form of consciousness.
35. If I make a hundred thousand on this film, I'll never have to worry about money again.
36. If I take this consciousness-raising training, I'll be high.
37. This whole spiritual trip is just Fundamentalism in drag.
38. I'm an outsider.
39. This anger will never go away.

This list was more than a humorous debunking of previous beliefs. It was also the outline of his life, with its seasons and transitions. From making it he saw the ingenuousness and disillusionment that had become a pattern for him.

Another kind of list that can help you perceive the pattern or plot of your life is a "table of contents" for the autobiography of the person you are at this moment. In other words, in your diary you write the chapter headings for your life. Such a list is likely to suggest some of life's predictable passages—the twenties as a search for individuation, the thirties as alterations of previous commitments, the forties as a summersault to recapture values set aside in the thirties, and so on. Yet these chapter headings will, at the same time, point out your uniqueness and may even reveal a hidden destiny. The precise form, sequence, and content of such self-reflective lists will vary, but it is the process that is important.

For example, one diarist wrote the following chapter headings for the stages of her life:

1-7	Recipient
7-12	Sure Knowledge, Alienation
12-18	The Virgin, the Actress, and the Whore
18-22	Copping Out to Be In
22-26	Scholars Are Made, Not Born
26-28	Revolution
28-30	Discovery of the Self and Being Loved
30	Losing It All and Starting Over

Four months later she again wrote a set of chapter headings:

WW II Ends and I Am Born
Daddy Left
My Period
Mother and Daughter in Struggle
From Mother to USC, a Poor Kind of Freedom
On the Track, the Grad Student
The Commune, We Tried
Danny, a Dream Come True
Remember Death?
Independence and Struggle

Some of the chapter headings have changed and many of them would have meaning to no one but the diarist. But the movement and continuity of the life come through in both lists. Each tells the writer about herself at the present moment. What at one time seemed unimportant suddenly becomes important at another time, and chapter headings appear and disappear according to the writer's present perspective.

Ira Progoff in his INTENSIVE JOURNAL uses a very similar device. He instructs his journal writers to list the major events, or "stepping-stones" in their lives. He recommends that they try to limit these stepping-stones to approximately twelve entries so that the most significant ones will rise to the surface—a helpful suggestion. Here is an example of how one diarist looked at the movement of his life in stepping-stones:

1. I was born.
2. Around six my first real pain and scare in the hospital. I

woke up during a tonsillectomy—inadequate anesthesia.

3. My first love—I was 15, Rose was 14.
4. College and an awareness of class distinctions, money, real competition.
5. Graduate school, the development of aesthetic sophistication and effete elitism.
6. Marriage to Corinne—it seemed a perfect idea at the time.
7. Bought a movie camera and deemphasized graduate school. I began to make experimental films.
8. Divorce—Corinne left me in a way that I could not fail to get the message.
9. Marriage to Leah—this one really felt right!
10. Made a film in Greece and realization that my marriage was not right.
11. Boy born in London—so many complex emotions and conflicting desires.
12. Directed first feature-length film—low budget schlock, but I did it!
13. A beautiful daughter born—she had me from the moment I saw her.
14. Started commuting to Hollywood, made my first studio deal.
15. Second marriage breaks up.

When he had assembled his stepping-stones the diarist was able to see a continuity in his career aspirations, which he had thought of as always shifting. And he was able to see an element of emotional growth through his cycles of marriage and divorce.

Progoff also has a journal exercise for listing the stepping-stones or significant events of another person's life—someone who is important to you—in an effort to understand that person as if you had written his life story. In so doing you can suddenly see another's ongoing life in context. You gain a sense of him in motion, moving from one phase of life to another. You can perceive the other as autonomous and separate from you, rather than seeing him as the object of your needs and desires.

One diarist wrote the stepping-stones of his father's life:

1. Mother ran away.
2. Assumption of responsibility for siblings.
3. Youthful professional success.
4. Romance and marriage.
5. Children.
6. Growing success and the rewards.
7. Disillusionment and the search for meaning.
8. Attempted escape into charity work.
9. Failure at attempt to give it all up and start again.
10. Sickness and dying.

When the list had completed itself the diarist could understand the relatively minor part he inevitably played in the total context of his father's life. He could feel the movement and integrity of his father's journey as separate from his own.

Lists in the form of stepping-stones can be used to look at your life in many different ways. You could write the stepping-stones of abandonment, rage, walls you've built around yourself, secrets, loves, fears, expectations, successes, giving your power away to others, taking your power back, goodbyes, self-definition, learning to nurture yourself, the psychological hooks you have allowed others to grasp you with, self-awareness, your career, your attitudes about death, your philosophic or religious beliefs. The possible ways of looking at your life and feeling its movement through writing lists is infinite.

A list will help you focus, tame, and comprehend wayward parts of your experience. A list you particularly like may lead to further creative work. You may transform it into a poem or use it as an outline for a longer work. And lists frequently lead you to further journal writing. You will often discover elements on a list that you wish to explore more intensively through other diary devices.

Portraits

The *portrait* is generally a form of description, and like all descriptions it is a particularly enjoyable device to reread. Anaïs Nin is the master of the descriptive portrait in the diary, and much of what I will have to say about it I learned from her. Nin made a special effort to be fair and free of malice in her word-portraits of friends and acquaintances, though she was aware of the weaknesses as well as the talents of those she described. In writing portraits she always tried to include as many details as possible about herself and about the other person. "If you include enough," she said, "you cannot be unfair."

Portraits in the diary evolve as a relationship with another person evolves. They are often as much a device for self-discovery as for discovery of another, because they reveal as much about the writer as about the person described. From writing a portrait you learn what qualities you notice and what you value in others.

A portrait in the diary is never really finished; you can always recolor it, revise it, contradict it, and add to it in later entries. You record the beginning of a fascination with another person, its development, and what you learn about yourself in relation to that person.

This mobile, evolving quality of the portrait makes it a useful tool in recognizing the psychological process of projection. When you "project" you see your own unrecognized qualities in another person. Rather than seeing the person on his or her own terms you see a mirror reflection of yourself. Projections change the world into the replica of your unknown face. Through writing portraits in the diary you begin to see if the face you are describing is also your own.

For example, one diarist wrote an unflattering portrait of a woman she disliked and realized in the process that she herself was trying to overcome the qualities that irritated her in the other woman:

Portrait of Julia

Julia is fairly tall, with lots of crinkly dark hair. She falls in love all the time. Right now she is in love with someone she met on the crew.

I don't quite understand why I dislike her so much. I think of her as always in heat, desperate for love, hungry. There's something obscene about her, an odor of fertility, but not the sort that leads to children or family, the sort that leads to nights of passion, intense brief affairs, tears, and the search again. She's extremely female without being feminine.

Do I see something of myself in her? There's a part of me that, like her, wants to take my pleasure now, heedless of the patterns and what I should have learned from them, that is pure passionate woman, willful woman, ego woman. And the part of me that now wants commitment, structure, peace, and integrity is threatened by that willful self in Julia.

In this example the projection caused negative feelings, but in other cases it is the root of an intense attraction characterized by an obsessive need to think about the other person. Marion Milner observed that her wandering thoughts perpetually strayed to some special person when she felt the other's qualities to be missing in herself. "Like a cannibal eating his enemy's heart in order to partake of his courage," she wrote, "I was impelled towards someone whose qualities I felt the need of." Psychologists often point out that you actually have the qualities, at least in embryo, that fascinate you in another.

By writing diary portraits of people who intrigue you, you enter their qualities in your book, in your space, and begin the process of recognizing and taking possession of those qualities.

Portraits can also work in an opposite way, to help you recognize another's separateness from you. Like listing the stepping-stones of other people's lives, objective portraits help you see them on their own terms. You begin to see their patterns and complexes as an outside observer would, and to understand why they act as they do. Writing objective portraits of parents, mates, or children is particularly valuable because it helps you understand them as autonomous individuals rather than in their role in relation to you.

Like all descriptions, a portrait in the diary can also be a private weapon that helps you reaffirm your power when you feel overwhelmed. For example, one woman wrote the portrait of a man whom she felt had treated her condescendingly:

> Willy, though only thirty, lives like a retired gentleman. When we walk to the heated pool and the sauna at his condominium, I see only gray-haired men with flabby stomachs and gold watches. Willy exudes masculinity, wealth, and power. He speaks in elegant silken tapestries, creating a complex pattern of lies, contradictions, spiritual truths, psychological wisdom, elitist assumptions, defensive jokes, clever repartee, sincere self-revelation, eloquent flattery, cruel criticism, astute observation, and irrelevant chatter. I am caught in his weaving and quickly spun through the woof of his life, only to be pulled out at the end and discarded.
>
> He has the expansiveness of wealth and I the limitations of genteel poverty. He is a gambler who has all the cards and he plays to win. He does not know that with women, a man who wins this way can actually be the loser. The essence of the woman slips away and he is left with empty booty, a body without its dignity, a mind without resiliency, and desire without joy.

The portrait helped the diarist fight back in a situation where she felt powerless. Describing this unsatisfying relationship helped give her a perspective from which to reassert her own worth.

Portraits don't have to take the form of description; they can be done as lists of qualities or as free-intuitive writing. They can also be developed as comparisons whereby you discover how different people represent and satisfy different sides of yourself, and why you may be drawn alternately to one person and then to another. For example, Nin repeatedly compared Henry Miller with his wife, June, in the first volume of her diary to understand the polarities they created in her own mind. She projected her own ambitions as a writer onto Henry and her desire to be an archetypal femme fatale onto June:

> I am trapped between the beauty of June and the talent of Henry. In a different way, I am devoted to both, a part of me goes out to each one, the writer in me is interested in Henry, Henry gives me a world of writing. June gives me danger. I must choose and I cannot.

Part of Anaïs wanted to become June, to melt into being woman as society has defined her; part of her wanted to become Henry, the iconoclastic thinker and writer. By comparing, studying, weighing, and evaluating their qualities again and again in the diary, Nin was able to synthesize and resolve her own identity as both woman and artist.

Portraits written in the diary when one is working out feelings may have many creative uses at a later time—as character sketches for stories, articles, drawings, or other works. Nin's portraits of Henry and June were transformed into the fictional characters of Jay and Sabina in her novels.

Maps of Consciousness

Some diarists use free drawings as they would free-intuitive writing to tap their inner consciousness. Such drawings might be called *maps of consciousness*—graphic images of what's in your mind. The process is like meditation. You relax and without intent allow the pen to move where it will on the page. You let your hand lead the drawing and see what it makes as it goes.

Marion Milner described the process of free-intuitive drawing in her book *on not being able to paint*. One day after a quarrel she began by drawing a thick line on paper:

> Now that's only a scribble, what's the good of that? It
> looks like a snake, now it's a serpent coiled around a
> tree, yes, like the serpent of the Garden of Eden, but I
> don't want to draw that, oh, it's turning into a head,
> goodness, what a horrid creature it is, a sort of Mrs.
> Punch or the Duchess in *Alice*. How hateful she is with
> that hunched back and deformed hand and all that
> swank of jewelry.

Without any conscious intent the drawing of a hunchbacked
matron had created itself. And when the drawing was finished
Milner realized that her anger had disappeared, having found
expression on the page.

It requires no artistic talent to make maps of consciousness. They can be stick figures or shapeless blobs. Their purpose is your own enjoyment and self-awareness, not accuracy
or beauty. Sometimes when I am particularly confused I draw
a map of all my conflicting parts. Often friends and family
members will appear, my work, my ambitions, the house I live
in or wish to live in. I try to put them on the page to represent
graphically my relative psychic distance to each element and
their relationships to each other in my mind.

Sometimes I am floating in my drawing, sometimes
firmly grounded. Sometimes fragments of myself line up on
opposite sides of the page, demonstrating the nature of an
inner conflict, and I look for a common denominator to link
the two sides. Sometimes I am in the center of a harmonious
circle of my needs, sometimes isolated in a tower of my own
making. Sometimes I make free line drawings that reveal
meaningful shapes to me only when they have been completed—a figure seven, or an initial, or an astrological sign.

Sometimes the character of the lines themselves carries
the meaning and the emotion, as in Chinese calligraphy. In all
these cases the map of consciousness allows me to express my
state of mind in a whole, rather than a partial, way.

Some diarists use "found images" that become maps of
consciousness. One woman pastes into her diary pictures from

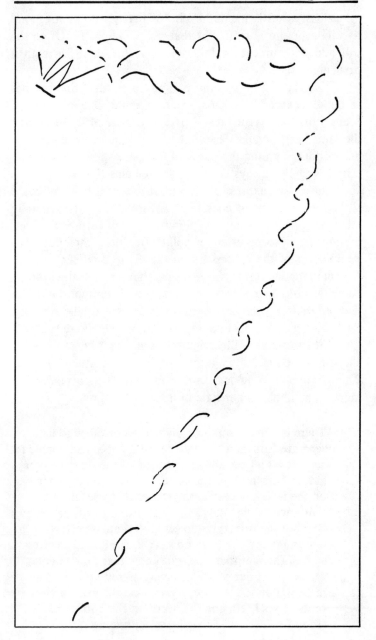

magazines, advertisements, or photos that seem to correspond to whatever she is feeling at that point in her life. Often she will add a comment to indicate why she identifies with a particular image.

A diary can be all drawing and no words if the sketches or doodles capture the diarist's state of mind. One man, Pierre, keeps a primarily visual diary, page after page of self-portrait— the same long, angular face in its evolving moods and developing wisdom. Turning the pages of his diary shows him graphically how he is always changing yet remains the same person.

Surrealist, expressionist, and visionary art works could all be seen as maps of consciousness. But the diarist generally takes the process of inner exploration a step further by interpreting the drawing at some point after its completion. The significance of the process lies in the diarist's reflection upon the spontaneous images from the psyche. Whether the drawing actually looks like a tree or a dust mop is unimportant. Nor does it matter what anyone else might see in the drawing. What does matter is its meaning for the diarist who draws it.

For example, Milner interprets a free-intuitive drawing she calls "Young lady wanting to get the most out of life." Though the drawing may not mean much to a reader, for Milner it symbolized her state of mind at the time:

> There is a figure on the right at the bottom who is separate from all the confusion and noise, and unable to achieve either the absorbed action of the sharpshooter girl on horseback or the swooning abandon of the lady on the left. The drawing shows what the separated figure wants, but she cannot get. Her attitude also shows the way she was trying to get it—by intense effort, determination . . . I can now see it as a graphic expression of the fact that I did not know that I could only get the most out of life by giving myself up to it. The markings on the left seem to express the general clash of impulses I felt, and the horses at the bottom probably stood for feelings of the energy within me.

Maps of consciousness can take you into the dynamics of your personality. Making images of the self and coming to understand them may signal the beginning of release from confusion and conflict. Free-intuitive drawings come to the rescue to express feelings when words have failed. With a map to your own inner wilderness you can explore the future with a greater sense of direction. Maps of consciousness also have value simply as creative fun and amusement, and they may inspire further creative work—paintings, drawings, cartoons, or animated films.

Guided Imagery

Guided imagery, like catharsis, free-intuitive writing, and maps of consciousness, taps the right side of the brain—the feeling, intuitive, imaging side. Doing guided imagery is very much like daydreaming and simply recording in your diary what images appear on the screen of your mind. Some people see distinct images, as if they were watching a movie on the insides of their eyelids. But many people have much less distinct visual impressions and seem to hear an inner storyteller describing the fantasy.

Like free-intuitive writing and drawing, guided imagery is an intuitive process that depends upon relaxing and trying to clear your mind of daily concerns and conscious controls. But in guided imagery you choose to visualize self-nurturing images.

In its simplest form guided imagery may be a meditation upon an ideal setting—any physical space that represents tranquility and beauty for you. You might visualize and then describe yourself lying on the sand by the sea, feeling the sun beating down on you, hearing the rhythmic sound of the waves. Or you might imagine yourself in a grassy meadow surrounded by protective mountains, in a forest full of exotic birds and friendly animals, floating in a kayak on a clear blue lake—whatever would be relaxing and pleasant.

Once you have created and made yourself comfortable in your private spot you can populate it with people or animals of your choice. You might contact a fantasy figure of wisdom, a fairy tale character, or even a sympathetic animal who will offer you advice, teach you how to accomplish a particular task, or help you heal an illness.

Guided imagery used in this positive way is one of the highest forms of self-nourishment. It is actually a written form of meditation, with all the benefits generally associated with meditation—relaxation, clarity, elevation of mental outlook, heightened consciousness, and sensory awareness. Experimenters have documented the success of guided imagery for inducing mental and physical relaxation, and the effectiveness of imaging a nurturing fantasy figure for helping with creative problem solving. Biofeedback machines have shown that guided imagery can reduce muscle tension and even correct blood pressure, body temperature, and other supposedly "involuntary" physical functions. The diarist who visualizes and then records guided imagery has the added advantage of being able to return to the self-nurturing fantasy again and again for solace and meditative peace, by rereading it in the diary.

Once you have imagined an interior landscape, you can further guide the flow of inner imagery in a narrative structure. Efforts at recording guided imagery may result in a poem, play, short story, song, fairy tale, myth, utopian vision, or fantasy journey.

Deena Metzger, who teaches a diary workshop in Los Angeles, encourages participants to practice guided imagery in the form of a fantasy journey. She suggests the framework, which the participants complete in their own imaginations and then record in their diaries. She begins with a guided meditation, which is condensed and paraphrased in the following excerpt:

> Imagine yourself in a physical space that represents tranquility, solitude, and beauty for you. Begin your journey here.
> You find yourself walking along the road.
> Suddenly in your path you see an object that catches your eye. You're not sure what you will do with this object, but it's important to you and you take it with you.
> In the distance you see an animal. You and the animal confront each other. There is a recognition and the animal decides to accompany you.
> You go on with your totem object, and your animal, and your sense of purpose, and your sense of joy.
> You see an impediment ahead. You don't know how to surmount it. But suddenly it is clear how you will surmount it. After overcoming the impediment you seem to know something you didn't know before. And you begin: "Once upon a time . . ."

Metzger's outline was simply a bare loom upon which one diarist spun the story of her inner imagery:

> Once upon a time there was a woman who had only herself. She knew all there was to know (but she did not know that). She lived on the sand surrounded by sandcastles she built with her own two hands and her imagination and her love for the child in herself. Until one morning, for no reason she could think of, she wondered if there was another place for her to be. And so she arose and left her home behind and began on a journey. . . .
>
> On the way to the other place she saw shining in the sun a wondrous seashell, large as her belly and wise as God. She lifted it to her ear and knew that the power of its roar would never betray her.
>
> A little further on . . . stood a small pony whose size might have deceived her had she not known what there is to know about strength. She looked into his eyes and said . . . "Let us move on together." And so they did, the woman holding her shell over her belly and the pony nuzzling the woman's strong shoulders.
>
> But a little further on . . . a mountain appeared in their path and there seemed to be no way to get beyond it. . . . Then the pony . . . told her to climb upon his back. And the woman did.
>
> The path that they took was very narrow and quite dark and the woman forgot that the shell held shimmering sunshine in it and would have helped to light the way. . . . they moved on . . . until finally they thought they got to the mountain top. The woman laughed and the pony laughed and she climbed off of his back . . . but just as she did so a terrible and frightening sound happened that made her close her hands over her ears and the pony's ears. . . . Later . . . but still not too late, she saw something shining on the ground and it was the shell she had dropped. . . . She picked it up and saw that its brightness was not from the sun after all, but from her very own eyes. She put it to her ears and the

power of its roar told her that the terrible sound she had heard was called . . . Silence.

And so she got to the mountain top and people gathered around and she told them to be alive and to speak to one another and listen to one another and love one another and to not let Silence destroy them.

And the people heard her and they began to move mountains. Their name was Women.

Such fantasy stories written in the diary allow you to create the psychological nourishment and sense of wonder and purpose that myth and ritual once gave to people. Masters and Houston's *Mind Games* provides the format for many meditations and fantasy journeys that may inspire you to record your own guided imagery.

Or you may simply wish to continue the images from a sleeping dream in a guided waking dream. You might transform the night dream into a positive story or a poem. (Although poetry can perform the functions of any of the four natural modes of expression, I include it in guided imagery because it so frequently depends upon the communication of feelings, sensations, intuitions, and thoughts condensed as images. The careful arrangement of images, along with a sense of rhythmic balance in poetry, allows the writer to create order out of what may have seemed chaotic in experience.)

For example, transforming her dream into a poem helped one diarist take charge of the confusing feelings it had evoked:

Nightmare
I dream that you are close to me
I dream of soldiers in a row
I dream of laughter, ecstasy
I dream you will not let me go.

Once she had ordered the images in this way she was able to appreciate how clearly they expressed the complexity of her relationship with her husband. She valued their closeness yet

she felt trapped by her love. She felt a rigidity and regimenta-
tion in their life together, "soldiers in a row," yet the relationship was simultaneously a source of laughter and ecstasy. Her
ambivalence had caused a confusion that felt nightmarish. But
arranging the contradictions into poetry transformed the
negative energy into creative expression, which in turn gave
the writer a clue to the inner harmony she could achieve
through accepting and embracing her contradictory feelings.

Poetry has for ten centuries been an integral part of
diary writing. Traditional Japanese diaries contain a prose
narrative that is regularly heightened with a poem that expresses an intense feeling or moment of acute perception. The
fantasy element of guided imagery within these poems adds a
level of lyricism and metaphor to the diary.

For example, Murasaki Shikibu, an eleventh-century
Japanese diarist, first described in prose the situation in which
she came to write this poem. Then she allowed the poem to
express her feelings:

> I wish I could be more adaptable and live more gaily
> in the present world—had I not an extraordinary
> sorrow . . . So I was musing one morning when I saw
> waterfowl playing heedlessly in the pond.
>> Waterfowl floating on the water—
>> They seem so gay,
>> But in truth
>> It is not gay to live anxiously seeking means
>> of existence.
> I sympathized with them who outwardly have no other
> thought but amusement, yet in reality are seeking a
> livelihood in great anxiety.

The prose describes the situation, and the poem is an example
of guided imagery in which the waterfowl represent the
writer's anxiety over financial insecurity. Murasaki was a mem-
ber of the Japanese royal court, and her own life appeared to
be lighthearted. But she was, like the waterfowl, "anxiously
seeking means of existence."

Songs, too, can be considered a form of guided imagery, since they, like poetry, are a heightened language of images and rhythms. In recent times many songwriters have used the journal to evolve a repertoire of lyrics. The rock musician Leo Sayer wrote the lyrics for his first three albums in a journal that he kept by his side while working in a factory.

But songs and poems written in a diary don't need to have critical or commercial acclaim to be of help to the writer. Some people record verse in a diary in an antiquated, highly stylized language. They use inverted syntax and biblical terms such as "thee" and "thou." Perhaps they associate all poetry with this antiquated style, or perhaps there is a voice in them that seems to come from the past. Regardless of whether the verse seems dated to another reader, the use of guided imagery within it may greatly benefit the diarist.

Guided imagery also has many practical uses as behavioral rehearsal, wherein you visualize yourself behaving in desirable ways. For example, it can be written as a Second Chance. You can take an experience from your immediate or distant past in which you were dissatisfied with your reactions or behavior and rewrite the incident to your satisfaction. It is a wonderful technique for learning from past mistakes. It is a self-strengthening form of guided imagery, for in it you reinforce desirable forms of behavior.

For example, a diarist had a phobic reaction to cockroaches, which on one occasion made her leave New York City quite abruptly. She had seen a very large roach and had been so terrified that she acted irrationally, packing her bags and leaving immediately without finishing her business. She was so embarrassed by her reaction that she rewrote the incident as a Second Chance in her diary. She entered the date of the actual incident, and through guided imagery, reexperienced the episode differently:

> I was walking over to the sink when I saw it, a three-inch cockroach. I was terrified. I got a broom and tried to hit him but he scuttled under some boxes. That made

me angry. I found the lye and the ant poison and made a mixture of it.

Then I waited, like a cat for its prey. I got as close as I could, then threw the poison. He shot away like a hot rod and took cover again.

Now I was really mad. I found a board and waited. He ventured forth and I told myself now or never, hit him hard! I threw the board on him and stepped on it. I could hear his shell crack.

When I looked at the board, he was a brown paste. I took it down to the garbage immediately, swept the poison into the trash, and wiped it up with paper towels. Then I took a shower and dressed for dinner. I was shaken, but I had won out over my fear.

After writing this Second Chance, the diarist reflected:

While I was writing this, I wanted to give up and run out again. But after my triumph, I felt like a different person. My running weakened me, but I feel strengthened now.

Writing the experience certainly can't be as good as actually smashing the thing, yet I seem to be getting half the benefits anyway. I chartered a new way for myself and countered my bad conditioning.

By visualizing herself acting aggressively instead of fleeing, the diarist began to change her self-image.

Just as free-intuitive writing and drawing can be employed when more traditional modes of expression seem insufficient, guided imagery can be very effective for approaching problems in a calm, fresh, creative way. Ordering your thoughts and feelings as guided imagery may enable you to maintain emotional equilibrium. It allows you to develop an inner landscape where you can go for amusement, advice, refreshment, support, and growth. Through it you may discover the inner myths and metaphors that convey the underlying significance of your experience.

Guided imagery can also be used to loosen up when you begin to write and for simply relaxing and enjoying the delights of your imagination. It may eventually lead to further creative products—children's stories, poems, science fiction tales, or other imaginative writing.

Altered Point of View

The technique of *altering point of view* as you write in the diary can give you a different perspective on yourself or certain aspects of your experience. Altering point of view means that you write about yourself objectively as "he" or "she" or you try to understand someone else's motivations by writing about them as "I." Altered point of view is central to all fiction writing, and you can practice it in the diary to distance yourself emotionally from a situation to see it more objectively or to look at it from "the other guy's" point of view.

Writing about yourself as "she" or "he" rather than "I" in the diary is like tracking back, back, back with a camera to give you a wide-angle view of an entire situation. Once "outside yourself" you are better able to see everyone in context pursuing his or her needs, and thus you can observe yourself more objectively. This third-person point of view allows you to perceive things that otherwise would be missing from the close-up perspective of "I."

There are also times when a diarist finds certain feelings so difficult to own up to that the only way to face them is by writing as if they had happened to someone else. For example, in the following entry the diarist was writing about herself but felt so uncomfortable with the feelings that she spontaneously assigned them to "she."

> She had turned thirty that summer. She could both feel it and see it—something was gone, some glow which she recognized from old photographs, the glow that the college students swarming all over town still had— pure youth, nothing more, but a natural juice, the energy of children which would dissipate sooner than hers had. She felt it happening as she stared at them

waiting for an answer to a meaningless question, chalk
covering her hand with white dust, the other one forgotten, holding her long cigarette which had gone out.

These feelings of stagnation passed and the diarist returned to
herself as "I," but the temporary change in point of view
allowed her to record an unhappiness that was difficult for her
to own up to. Similarly, the doctor in Vietnam who wrote his
diary in the midst of war frequently used the third-person
point of view, "he," needing to maintain psychological distance from the violence around him in order to cope with it.

The diarist might want to consider a caution, however,
that altered point of view can be a way of distancing you from
yourself and seeing your life as a fiction. It can be a very
helpful technique at times, but practiced to the exclusion of
other forms it might tend to alienate you from your own
experience.

Keeping this in mind you can take advantage of altered
point of view to open a new world of perceptions. For example, when you are having difficulty understanding another
you can write from his point of view as "I." Like listing the
stepping-stones of another's life or writing his portrait, altered
point of view allows you to understand the other's motivations
and perceptions. In fact, one diarist I know finds it helpful to
assume the body postures and gestures of the other person
when she writes from his point of view. Like an actress, she
feels where that person's body tension lies, and she sits as that
person would sit as she writes.

Altering point of view has other practical uses. It could
be used to imagine yourself in another geographic location.
Say you were thinking about moving to another part of the
country. In your diary you could write as if you were already
there to discover your assumptions about that place and what
inner changes the move might bring about in you.

Similarly, you can imaginatively travel into the past or
future by altering your point of view. The device can help you

recall or foresee certain things that elude you from your immediate perspective in time. For example, having burned the Betty Betz diary I kept at age thirteen, I have since longed to recall what I then felt and thought about. One evening in 1974 at a local movie theater I happened to see one of the episodes from the original Flash Gordon serials I had watched regularly at Saturday matinées when I was thirteen.

That night I entered the date June 27, 1957, as if I were writing in my old Betty Betz diary. I allowed myself to use the unsure, childish script I had written in fourteen years before. These alterations in point of view permitted me to re-create an entry from my old diary, which I think must be very close to the original:

> *June 27, 1957*
> Dear Diary,
>   Went to the show with Marcia. We met two guys, one named Butch and one named Bruce. Two b's.
>   Marcia made out with the big one and I made out with his friend. At first he said his name was Tony, but then he changed it.
>   He had dark hair and hazil eyes. He tried to touch my breast but I kept taking his hand away. I got really hot.
>   Marcia wanted to change. I didn't want to cause I wondered why she wanted to. I found out! Butch bites your lip when he kisses you.
>   So I made him stop and told Marcia we had to go. She wanted to give them our numbers but I said no.

I was so excited by the accuracy of tone achieved through changing the date and my handwriting that I have subsequently written other entries from the perspective of my thirteen-year-old self. Gradually, through altered point of view, I have been able to reconstruct much of the diary I destroyed in my childhood.

Using this technique you can enter the future to anticipate the course of your life based on your present attitudes or foresee the possible consequences of certain decisions. You can rehearse in the diary for anticipated situations. For example, if you were going on a job interview or asking for a raise you could write out what you might say and do (or avoid saying and doing). The potential for personal insight through altering your perspective in time is so great that I have devoted an entire later chapter to it, "The Diary as Time Machine."

Unsent Letters

People frequently write letters in the journal to those who have emotional significance in their lives. Just as a diary doesn't have to be a record of activities, a letter doesn't have to be a report of the weather and the news since you last wrote. It can be an exploration of whatever a particular person evokes when you think *to* them. The letter you actually send may differ substantially from the first draft written in the diary, or you may never send the diary letter in any form. It can simply remain in the journal as your record of spontaneous thoughts to a particular person at a particular time.

Sometimes diarists write *unsent letters,* with no intention of ever sending or showing them to the people addressed. You may begin to write unintentionally to the person with whom you need contact. For example in her *Diary VI* Anaïs Nin suddenly breaks from a narrative style and writes as if to her therapist: "Dr. Bogner, today I bring you only a curtain, just a curtain. Nothing else. There must be something behind this curtain." In the rest of the entry Nin talks to Bogner about the childhood memories behind "the curtain" in her dream. By evoking her therapist as the audience for this introspective entry Nin feels safe, as if she were in her doctor's office. Actually her unsent letter is a way for Nin to evoke her own inner therapist in a time of emotional need.

A diarist might also write an unsent letter to express thoughts to a certain person when actually doing so would be rude or inappropriate, when actual articulation could cause irreparable harm to a relationship, when one isn't sure if she really feels the way she thinks she feels at the moment, or when the audience is unavailable for deep communication.

For example, a friend of mine, Eve, went to the wedding of a man for whom she had had deep feelings. There was no opportunity at the wedding to tell him her thoughts, and they would have been inappropriate anyway. Instead she wrote them in her diary as an unsent letter:

> Addressed to you, Ron, in diary, for I doubt it could ever happen waking for these intimacies necessitate privacy and your lovely Diane is always so close, I do not wish to intrude. Today at the wedding, I lost so much of the picture in fantasy I'd created of you. My moving image was a great deal sexual, not concrete idea or wish, but just a longing to share with your flow. I still do yearn for some kind of give and take that originated in my imagination for you do attract me . . . but now I see it will fade. You didn't attract me at the wedding, you repulsed me. Your overpoliteness, and maybe it was your new haircut or that you were walking particularly stiffly. That politeness, so blatant and abhorrent to me; dangling, meaningless conversations.

As a result of writing this unsent letter the diarist was able to ease her mind and go on with her life, feeling that she had completed her side of the relationship.

The unsent letter doesn't have to begin with a salutation such as "Dr. Bogner" or "Addressed to you, Ron." Frequently you unconsciously write to a "you," who is the person to whom you are thinking. Similarly, you sometimes find yourself "thinking to" a particular person in your head—as you drive the car or take a shower or try to concentrate on something else. On a barely conscious level your mind is chattering away about all the things you would like to say to that person, especially if some aspect of the relationship is unresolved. Using the unsent letter technique can help make conscious such "thinking to" or "writing to" another person.

Women have had a historical tendency to "think to" men, and it reveals itself in diaries that are little more than a series of unsent letters to a lover, a husband, or a brother. For example, Eugénie de Guérin, a nineteenth-century French diarist, dedicated her journal to her brother, Maurice de Guérin. But in contrast, Maurice's famous diary was written to himself; it was an echo chamber in which he listened to the reverberations of his own voice. While nearly every passage in Eugénie's diary was addressed to Maurice, the only woman he ever addressed was an abstract personification of Nature. One can observe from reading both diaries how Maurice achieved a strong sense of self, while Eugénie felt increasingly diminished until she suffered from a sense of nonexistence. At one point she wrote: "I on my part, find myself alone, solitary, but half-alive; as though it seems to me, I had only half a soul."

Overuse of the unsent letter has the same potential for self-avoidance as overuse of altered point of view. Both can defeat the purposes of the New Diary—to encourage self-communication and self-awareness. It is important to resolve a preoccupation in the diary with an external audience because the direction of thoughts outward can implement a tendency to lose oneself in, or live through, another—and limit or even discourage intimacy with self. Nevertheless, if kept conscious the technique can be a means of deepening and extending self-awareness and self-knowledge.

The unsent letter can be an important tool, too, for self-definition, since who you are is partly defined by whom you reach out to and include as audience in your inner life. The diary offers an alternative to conventional laws of time and space: you can write to anyone, living or dead, within it. Some people write the diary as a continuing unsent letter with the eventual intention of giving it to a particular person when and if the time ever becomes appropriate.

One young mother I know, Gina, writes her diary as an unsent letter to her daughter, Lisa, who is still too young to share all of her mother's thoughts. The "letters" to Lisa, recording the child's development and the mother's responses, are mixed with Gina's current feelings about her adult life, memories of the time she was Lisa's age, entries addressed to different men in her life, and lists of things to do. This form of the diary escapes the potential for being completely other-directed by permitting Gina to be centered in her ongoing life while maintaining a continuous, timeless communication with her growing daughter. These are some excerpts from her diary:

> *Dec. 4, 1969*
> Last night we talked a long time and you talked about a
> fear of yours that you remembered having in "the little
> house where you had to walk through my bedroom to
> get to the bathroom." A feeling you couldn't get into
> words, and you cried trying to explain your fear. A fear
> of nonbeing, of nothingness; you kept saying "this is this
> and that's all there is—no! I can't explain." A fear of the
> void? We talked a long time about the universe, about
> fear, love, and friendship.

> *Jan. 22, 1970*
> Last night you said that it pained you to think nothing
> will ever happen again in just the same way but is gone
> forever (we were watching the cats fighting and playing).

> *April 1, 1970*
> Tonight you were perplexed: which kind of fairy to
> believe in? The small ones that live in buttercups or the
> medium-sized ones about a foot tall, or the ones that
> floated? With a sudden oh! you realized "There are all
> different kinds of fairies. I believe in all of them."

> *Oct. 20, 1970*
> Yesterday, sweet Lisa, you told me that when you think
> of making love, you get a "funny feeling" there . . . "not
> a tickle, but like when I have to go to the bathroom."
> Sweet growing girl-woman! Can I remember the first
> soft lappings of desire? Yes, I think: imagining (in
> bedcovers over head) being in an igloo with Gene—not

doing anything (did I know yet there was something to
do?) but a feeling, a tug . . . how old was I?
I told you making love was just great.

August 12, 1971
Lisa, I love you *now* wherever your *now* is,
because the stream of love I drank from has no
no beginning and no end.

These unsent letters, which Lisa will one day read, prove that
love recorded in the diary transcends time and space.

Unsent letters can also be written to any thing as well as
any one: to any part of your body or aspect of yourself. Some
diaries contain a series of unsent letters written over the years
to a parent, sister, brother, or spouse, that have allowed the
diarist to articulate and clarify what he or she needed to say to
that person.

The possibilities for audiences of unsent letters are as
infinite as your imagination. You could write to a future child
or grandchild, whom you wanted to know some important
truths about your life, to a particular trade or ambition, to
your hair or your wrinkles. Frequently unsent letters seem to
develop into dialogues, which give the audience of the letter an
opportunity to respond.

Dialogues

In the 1960s Gestalt therapists began using the technique of the
imaginary dialogue to help people become aware of various
aspects of their personalities. But a hundred years earlier
French novelist Aurore Dupin, known by her pen name
George Sand, intuitively wrote such imaginary inner dialogues
in her diary. She carried on regular imaginary conversations
with "Dr. Piffoel," whom she understood to be the efficient
"male" side of herself. In these dialogues Piffoel would give
Aurore rational, clear-headed advice about her relationships
with men. Sand's feminine self, in turn, reminded Piffoel,

when he became obsessed with his writing, that he should not forget to appreciate her deep feelings and human needs. As a result of these diary dialogues Sand's "male" and "female" selves (or rather the modes of thinking they represented) came to establish a friendly, mutually supportive relationship that helped Sand, the diarist, to feel more whole, balanced, and complete.

The diary *dialogue* is a conversation carried on with yourself to help you gain insight into a person, event, or subject you wish to understand better. The dialogue helps you deal with a situation you feel confused about and which you cannot seem to penetrate using any of the four basic diary devices. You can dialogue with aspects of your personality, people you know, or people you have never met, historical personages, dream figures, animals, inanimate objects, images, symbols, parts of your body, your religious or racial or cultural heritage, events, or institutions. You can even use the device with nameless voices that seem to be arguing in your head and sending insistent messages. In the dialogue you address the subject, whatever it may be, and simply allow it to speak to you in response.

Dialogues may often evolve out of other diary devices. For example, the diarist who found many references to her mother in her free-intuitive writing might follow that entry by dialoguing with her mother. Or the diarist who wrote the "Portrait of Julia," in which she saw aspects of herself, might dialogue with the "Julia" part of herself. You will know intuitively if one device has not been sufficient to release and explore a particular issue fully.

The Gestalt dialogue appears frequently in diaries when the writer senses the need to reintegrate parts of the self from which he or she feels separated or threatened. For example, one man in business, who was also a father and a husband, felt cut off from the poetic side of his personality, which he had known in college. He felt as if he had betrayed and lost forever his "self" that had read novels and written short stories. So he wrote a dialogue in the diary to evoke this neglected other self:

Me

Other self, do you still exist?

Other self

Of course I do. When you went to Monterey, you thought about Steinbeck's novels and you wished you had become a writer. That was me.

Me

But now it's too late for me to pursue literary interests.

Other self

It's not too late.

Me

I haven't the time.

Other self

You never say that when it comes to taking on a new building contract.

Me

That pays money.

Other self

You have enough money. But you don't have me and you want me.

Me

To do it right, I'd have to leave my family, give up everything.

Other self

I'm not asking that. You are so simple-minded, which has always been the problem. Just start giving me some time. I'm not asking for all your time. I'll enrich your life.

Me

I've been afraid you'd be angry at me for ignoring you.

Other self

I am a little, but I also understand. You were afraid I'd want to take over everything in your life, so you wouldn't acknowledge me at all.

Me

That's true. Well it sure is nice to have you with me again.

The dialogue helped the diarist give himself permission to be more than one thing, to play more than one role in his life. Dialogues are particularly useful in keeping yourself aware of all sides of your personality that deserve acknowledgment, consideration, and time—when you have it.

Diarists frequently find it helpful to write out imaginary conversations with people in their lives with whom they have had trouble communicating. Sometimes these dialogues are a rehearsal for an actual conversation, sometimes not. Writing a constructive, positive dialogue can help prepare you for talking things out in the same constructive manner. You may also notice that several days after writing a dialogue the relationship changes without the actual conversation's having taken place. There is a subliminal level within relationships that can be improved by writing dialogues and coming to know how much of the conflict or harmony is determined in your own mind.

Diary dialogue with people in your life can help you come to terms with a particular issue, which you feel involves that person. For example, one woman who had recently had an abortion and did not want to tell her mother, did want to dialogue with her in the diary about it:

Me
Hi mom. Well, I got pregnant and I got an abortion. I still don't believe it.
Mother
I'm relieved it's all over.
Me
Yes. Neither of us had to live with the problem for long.
Mother
I'm glad you did it safely.
Me
I still don't believe I was really pregnant.
Mother
When I was pregnant with you I went for five months not believing it. Even after that, when I went to the

doctor's and she told me I was, I still didn't believe it.
Me
But you didn't abort me.
Mother
I couldn't.
Me
I keep wondering how much I might have liked the
little life that was growing inside me.
Mother
Don't torture yourself. You did what was right for you.
Me
If you really feel that way, why am I afraid to
actually tell you?
Mother
You don't want to evoke my own memory and my
embarrassment. I'm from another generation. My
options and my values were different.
Me
I'm afraid you'll make me feel guilty, and I don't
want to feel guilty.
Mother
You're a woman, and you're on your own. My adult-
hood came with having you. Yours has come from
not making the same choice.

The dialogue clarified for its writer both why she wanted to talk with her mother about her abortion and why she had chosen not to at the time.

The greatest advantages of writing dialogues with another person or with aspects of yourself are derived when each side states its position clearly and with conviction and then listens to the other side carefully and with an open mind. The benefits are gained when each side manifests a willingness to grow and change through the process of interaction.

One man, named Richard, wrote a series of dialogues between "Dick," his businessman self, and "Ricardo," the dropout who had left his job as an engineer and experimented with every kind of therapy and "alternative lifestyle" imaginable. At the time of the dialogues "Dick" had taken a job in real estate to support "Ricardo's" expenses for classes, therapies, and consciousness-raising weekends. At first "Dick" and "Ricardo" were mutually antagonistic in the dialogues. Each felt threatened that the other would take over Richard, the diarist's, life completely. But gradually, through the diary dialogues the businessman self and the dropout self began to realize their interdependence. "Ricardo" needed "Dick" to support him financially, and "Dick" needed "Ricardo" to make life interesting enough to keep working. Eventually the dialogues ceased to appear in the diary when Richard came to understand that his personality could contain multiple aspects that could all get along quite well.

Richard was not a schizophrenic. He was a very normal man with several conflicting dimensions to his personality. The inner synthesis he achieved would not have been possible without getting the two sides of himself to speak with, listen to, and teach each other. He divided the self in the dialogue to bring it together again in greater harmony. His dialogues moved ultimately toward wholeness and oneness.

Dialogues occasionally seem unable to move beyond the level of argument. For example, a husband and wife in the process of a bitter divorce, or a child who is very angry at a parent, or a very strict religious self and a very sensuous natural self might argue with each other through many dialogues without coming to a resolution. An argument with an aspect of the self or with another person in the diary now and then can help clarify things and raise important issues to be worked on. But too much arguing, even in a diary, is unsettling. If the argument remains unresolved for long the diarist might want to assess whether the dialoguing is as constructive as it could be. For example, are the two sides being given equal consideration? If one side is top dog or underdog for too long, try to equalize the relationship so that each side may hear what the other has to say. Or the diarist might try another device for getting at the issues underlying these arguments.

Ira Progoff uses the dialogue device extensively in his INTENSIVE JOURNAL workshops. In the section called "Dialogue with Persons" he points out a number of audiences with whom to dialogue. For example, you might wish to dialogue with people who have been significant in your life but are no longer living, people with whom you have a current relationship, or people who have played a significant role in your life but with whom you are not now in contact. One diarist explored his roots by writing dialogues with his grandparents, his great-grandparents, and his great-great-grandparents. Any of these dialogues can be written into an ongoing, organic diary.

Another man ("J.") wrote a dialogue to establish a relationship with his father ("P."), who had died when his son was only seven:

J. Hi Dad.

P. Hello Jim. Good to feel you.

J. What's it like where you are?

P. I'm in you. That's the only place I am; so what's on your mind?

J. Well, you're the only person I really cared for that's passed out of this life. I wanted to ask you what it was like after.

P. That's not information you need.

J. I mean, are you wise now, are things clear? I always feel like I'm asleep down here.

P. Forget that down/up business. You're on a planet, not in an elevator. As for my being wise, I don't know. Death doesn't teach you more than you already know. Life has seasons and it ends.

J. Is there anything to believe in?

P. Death and Taxes.

J. I'm not trying to be funny.

P. Neither death nor taxes is funny. You're familiar with deadlines, and you're familiar with dues. You pay your dues, write music, love your kids, take your knocks, like everybody else. Beyond that, you're just torturing yourself looking for answers. You'd be better off if you looked around for more accurate questions. Forget about answers.

You've been crippled by beliefs; just experience and note what you feel.

The father's somewhat whimsical personality comes through in the writing. The diarist has used it to give himself the very down-to-earth advice his father would have offered, were he still alive.

Progoff's section "Dialogue with Works" suggests dialogues with projects or goals from earlier years, projects in which you are actively engaged, completed projects, or a particular painting, book, poem, musical composition, craft, or career. Diarists have always found it helpful to sort out their thoughts on a specific project by writing about it in their journals, and the dialogue device is particularly valuable if you feel stuck or blocked on a project. The dialogue technique of alternate questions and answers divides a subject into understandable segments and helps push the mind forward toward a solution.

Progoff's section "Dialogue with the Body" suggests conversations with the body as a whole, including its particular history and sensory memories. The same diarist who had written a dialogue with her mother about her abortion (excerpted earlier) also felt the need to communicate directly with her body about it:

Me
Well, body. How do you feel?
Body
Weak, shaky. I hurt a bit. I feel open and vulnerable. I can't trust my environment yet.
Me
But you'll mend?

Body
Yes, I'll mend well. I don't know how soon I'll want to
make love again, though.
Me
Maybe when you're feeling better it won't sound so
awful.
Body
Maybe. I just don't ever want to go through this again.
I'm strong—and I can take it, but I don't want it to
happen again.
Me
Are you kidding? I'll never make that mistake again. It's
not worth it. I was surprised at your strength while it
was happening, though. It hurt a lot—yet you didn't
flinch. You were calm and just let it pass. I'm pleased
to know how strong you really are.

This dialogue helped the diarist learn to listen to her body's
messages—which she considered especially appropriate because
she recognized her tendency to feel alienated from her body.

In the same way you can dialogue with any part of the
body that you think may have a message for you. An aching
neck, your hands, the circles under your eyes may all have
information to reveal. In these dialogues it is important for
both speakers to work toward mutual understanding. A sense
of humor and a constructive attitude can lead you to significant insights into how your mind and body interact.

Progoff's "Inner-Wisdom Dialogue" suggests conversations with the diarist's image of God, Christ, the Buddha, a
guru, a great philosopher, a political or literary figure, a
teacher. You can dialogue with any person or image that has
represented wisdom for you—through literature, words, music,
art, life, or legend. Even diarists with no formal religious or
spiritual beliefs may find themselves consulting an abstract
sense of inner wisdom in their diaries. One woman had regular
dialogues with a part of herself she calls her "guru woman."

Me
Guru woman, help me. Give me some advice.
Guru Woman
Feel, go through this sorrow, but remain calm with my
calm. You can celebrate life, even in your sorrow.
Me
Yes, but I feel I have been in this place of pain so many
times before. I make the same mistakes again and again.
Guru Woman
You are stubborn. You are afraid to risk genuine
change. But you have also learned. Your circles are
actually spirals. You will make the same mistakes until
finally you see them so clearly that the patterns be-
come separate from you. Then you will be able to
choose the old pattern or not to choose it.
Me
I want to be able to free myself this instant.
Guru Woman
It is a process, and you are inside that process. . . .

The benefits of such dialogues with images of inner wisdom
are inestimable. They can help you discover your own truths
and inner destiny.

The "Dialogue with Events" may be Progoff's greatest
and most unique contribution to journal work. He observes
that we tend to respond to the events of our lives with pain or
pleasure, but that there is a significance beyond our immediate
emotional reaction. To reveal and understand this further
significance you can converse with any important event in
your life—a sudden illness or a car accident, a sudden job change,
a political event or natural catastrophe that has touched your
life, a sudden success, an intense religious experience, a significant coincidence, a marriage, a friendship, a divorce, an important business relationship, or your feelings about your present
social and economic circumstances.

One man who had lost his job wrote a dialogue with the
event:

Me
Event, I want to know your significance in the context
of my life. I know your pain. Do you have anything
else to teach me?
Event
Lessons about your own bad temper. You have
learned those pretty well.
Me
Yes, but are you the beginning of anything other than
embarrassment and pain?
Event
Of course I am. I am part of your process of growth.
You try to turn me into a trauma, but I am only some-
thing that happened in your life.
Me
Not a very pleasant thing.
Event
I helped to create you.
Me
You have given me fear.
Event
You provide the fear. I provide access to self-knowledge.
Me
I'm humiliated, though. A man without a full-time job
isn't a man.
Event
I signify the beginning of new ways of looking at that
attitude.

By conversing with past events or with events as they occur
you can come to understand the unseen meaning beneath their
apparent meaning in your life.

Progoff's dialogue sections are a valuable contribution to
the possibilities for using the dialogue device. But it would be
unnecessarily limiting for people who are familiar with his
system to think that the dialogues he has included in the
INTENSIVE JOURNAL are the only dialogues they can write
or even the best dialogues for them. You might find it worth-

while to write a dialogue with an important pet, with money, with an image from a dream, or with various characters that you recognize as elements of your personality: the "playboy" or the "seductress," the "wailing brat," or you at an earlier or a later age. In a spontaneous diary each person finds individual uses for the dialogue device whenever the need arises.

Writing imaginary conversations gives you practice in writing dialogues, which could be useful later in other forms of creative writing. And Gestalt dialogues help you develop sophisticated thinking, in which things are not black and white but complementary. The whole of the self contains both sides of a Gestalt dialogue, and both sides can be "true" and "right." Often people want to be married and single at the same time, to live in New York and Los Angeles at the same time, to quit school and finish a degree at the same time. Being divided by conflict makes it difficult to move forward in life. The inner dialogue encourages the development of a self large enough to contain all its contradictions. Through the dialogue you tap your own inner resources to find original solutions that recognize all parts of the self and often promote inner synthesis, compromise, or reconciliation.

Using one of the special diary techniques described in this chapter to the exclusion of the more natural forms of expression could become an interruption to the continuity of your inner life. They can be used creatively to unblock a problem that seems to defy other approaches and to achieve greater self-understanding. But if you try to manipulate your psyche with some of these techniques or if you overuse them, you may find that they lose their effectiveness.

All the diary devices are meant to give you access to your inner consciousness. But the key is to listen receptively to what a device can release. You cannot "order" the psyche around: Sternly demanding in an unsent letter that your aching back stop bothering you will probably not yield results. But if you dialogue with your back, allowing the unexpected to happen, it might tell you why it aches. It is helpful to remember that if you can't open up a personal mystery with one device, you may be able to gain access to it with another. You should realize, however, that you might have to wait patiently until you are ready to hear what your back has to teach you.

If you never use most of the devices illustrated in this chapter it doesn't mean you aren't actively solving your problems through diary writing. Many diarists rarely use the kinds of psychological processes illustrated here. Instead they search for ways to express in descriptive, narrative prose every nuance of their feelings. Some diarists keep books that include only a few doodles and lists. But they are using journal keeping in a way that serves their purposes.

After you have been keeping the diary for a time you may begin to develop your own devices. Confronted with a situation in your life you may begin to look for new ways to approach it. Your intuition will tell you to try a certain dialogue, to free associate, or to make up an entirely new device to open up that particular issue. In this way you begin to take an active, adventurous attitude toward life's challenges as they arise. As Anaïs Nin said in *A Woman Speaks:*

> There is the whole mystery of growth, of expansion, of
> deliverance from the traps which life sets us, because
> life loves the drama of entrapping us and seeing whether
> we can get out. It's a game, a game of magic. Every
> difficult situation into which you are sometimes thrown
> has some kind of opening somewhere, even if it is
> only by way of the dream.

Using the diary effectively depends only upon the degree to which you trust your intuition and your process. The very act of sitting down with the diary signifies a readiness to commune with the self; and the very act of writing may place you inside the mystery of self-healing and self-re-creation, no matter what is written or how it is expressed.

6 | Transforming Personal Problems

The New Diary is a powerful tool for self-healing and self-guidance. Rather than standing outside problems and cursing them as enemies, the diary allows you to enter and explore them as personal mysteries containing messages of inner meaning for your life. When you treat problems as mysteries you don't try to understand them with your intellect. Rather you admit them on a feeling level and accept them into your life by including them in your book. You allow the new aspects of personal growth and courage they require from you to surface through the diary process.

Problems become stressful when you feel powerless to do something about them. Writing out problems in the diary allows you to take immediate action by focusing the real issues and evoking possible solutions. When you avoid confronting problems or postpone them in your mind they continue to call out silently for attention and bottle up energy. You obsessively retread the same unhoed mental ground.

Problems released and confronted in a diary allow you to transform their negative energy into constructive energy that moves you forward in your life. Every time you work through an issue in the diary you develop a talent for dealing immediately and independently with life's challenges as they arise.

The diary is not a substitute for good friendships or a replacement for the emotional support others can give. But neither is the counsel of others a replacement for the self-guidance the diary can offer. The feedback you give yourself in contacting your own inner wisdom may be more valid than the advice others can provide. And the better able you are to deal with many of your problems on your own, the more positive energy you will have to share with those you love.

You may find the following catalog of common problems—and suggestions for using the diary to move through them—particularly helpful when you are experiencing a particular problem. If you are suffering pain or anxiety, grieving over a loss, feeling lonely or jealous, or struggling with an addiction or an illness you may wish to turn to the section in this chapter that directly addresses the problem. Rather than reading through all the topics at once, you may prefer to overview the beginning and end of the chapter, scan its categories, read those of immediate interest to you, and return to the others at a time of need.

Psychological Pain (Loss and Grief)

Whether it is the result of a breach in a close relationship, the departure or death of a loved one, an onslaught of painful realizations or memories, or a case of disappointed expectations, psychological pain is often a mix of feelings. Grief, anger, and self-pity may all be part of it. Before your feelings can be understood and worked through in the diary, you often need to release them with the device called catharsis. One diarist's cathartic writing describes well the need for release:

> I feel the pain which has been forcing itself to the
> surface for the past four months. It swells inside me
> like a huge egg pushing its way out of my throat. I
> gag on it. The pain pushes and pushes. I am pregnant
> with it. I am in labor with it. A stranger to me, but
> inside me, pushing, pushing. I am exhausted with it. I
> lie on my small bed, exhausted with the pain I have

carried so long, the egg of pain with its yolk of guilt.
I write here in the diary, hoping that I will be
delivered of this pain.

Psychological pain sometimes needs to be expressed again and again because it may come, as the diarist describes, like the intermittent waves of labor. Repetition of the same pain or the same anger or the same sorrow in the diary indicates only that the pain is great. It must come out until it is all out.

Articulate as much as you can, even your barely formulated thoughts and fears. Allow yourself to cry as you write, if you feel the need. Write until you can write no more; write until you are exhausted. The more deeply you can express your pain, the sooner you will work it through.

Don't make judgments about yourself or your writing when you are feeling intensely. Don't be afraid that you will uncover more pain than you are able to cope with. You will go only as deeply as you can at any one time, because people working on their own in the diary have natural resistances and defenses beyond which they will not push themselves. You also need not fear that confronting and expressing the pain will create more pain. If you have pain inside, the articulation and the accompanying emotion help you to move through it. The only suffering that does not move from pain to ease is suffering that is blocked in some way.

Expressing your pain in the diary makes sure it is recognized and acknowledged. Putting it into words begins the natural process of distancing yourself from it that finally brings relief. Distancing cannot occur until you are ready for it, when the emotion has been released as fully as possible through cathartic writing. Then you can begin to work with a problem within the overall context of your life.

An effective means of seeing the pain in context is to write a dialogue with the event or the sorrow or with your inner wisdom about it. Another means is to try to write a description of the movement and growth in your life brought about by a painful incident. One woman tried to capture a sense of this movement in her life by writing about a separation from the man she had loved, both as an ending of one phase and the beginning of a new phase of her life. She chose to describe two scenes—in the first they were together and in the second she was beginning to live her life without him:

> We are in bed. It has taken months to settle into a comfortable position, his right arm circling me, my head on his left shoulder, my right knee over his right leg, my arm over his stomach. We have found a satisfactory temperature for the electric blanket; the tiny light glows between five and six. His left leg lies over the blanket so he won't be too warm.
>
> We have learned to breathe together. As I inhale his smell I am at peace with the world. His saliva is mixed with mine in my mouth.
>
> We breathe together a downy bridge to sleep. We fall into each other's dreams.
>
> The first night alone. I press my breasts against the mattress. I am listening for his breath, his heartbeat. I wonder where he is. No, I must not wonder where he is. I must wonder where I am.
>
> It is cold now. I turn the blanket up to 10.
>
> I hear things that I did not hear before, the buzz from the aquarium, the cars angrily swiping by the house on the highway, the drone of the refrigerator.
>
> I curl into a foetal position. I curl into myself. I search for that silent stream that I have always had, the life that flowed to me from my mother. I block out the sounds outside and search for the sound of my stream, the almost silent, continuous stream of self which has gone on and on from the beginning that will take me to tomorrow, to the next week and to the year when I will have forgotten to miss him. I become a cell of myself and ride my stream into sleep. The stream widens into a landscape of dreams, a landscape of all time in one, all days within one, all selves within one, all loves within one, the land of opposites and transformations, the

land where endings and beginnings exchange masks and meanings, where my own future kneels within me.

One could similarly describe the loss of a beloved to death as a beginning as well as an ending. The diary can be particularly consoling in helping individuals move through grief. Funerals and wakes provide a public structure for mourning, but one needs a place for one's private mourning song as well. Grief that would interrupt an ongoing life of responsibility can be saved up and put into the diary at the end of the day. Cathartic writing can help one to express the pain of the loss, and certain kinds of description and imaginary dialogues can help one to accept it.

One diarist used the diary to help her mourn when a friend died suddenly. She was shocked and upset that their relationship had not completed itself; there were still things to be said to one another. In needing to find her peace with him, she found herself writing a brief portrait of the man, which then led into a dialogue:

> Larry died in the hospital of a heart seizure. He was a dear, sweet man, too sweet it seemed. He was good to everybody, but himself—to his students, to all aspiring writers, to anyone who needed help or advice. In his case virtue was not its own reward.
>
> The last time he called I was writing. I had to tell him I would call him back. He sounded disappointed. . . .
>
> He's dead.
> I keep thinking I'll call him back.
> I want to call you back, Larry.

M: Larry, I'm sorry I didn't talk to you when you called. I'm sorry I didn't help more. I don't want you to be dead.

L: I understand. I just want you to learn from my mistakes.

M: Larry, how can we give to you what you deserve now?

I want to wish you an afterlife, a heaven as your reward.

Larry, I feel afraid of what your mortality says to me. You were a giving, self-sacrificing person. An elegant person. A handsome, intelligent man. A compassionate man.

It brought you nothing but pain. You seemed to have had so much pain. . . .

I was afraid to let you close, because I couldn't carry your emotional problems.

I should have helped, though.

L: I'm past caring now. It no longer hurts. I feel nothing. I have no consciousness. Your words, your guilt, your life mean nothing to me. I am on the other side.

M: I'll miss you, Larry. I wish I could call you.

L: I don't mind becoming your lines. You can talk with me here any time.

Writing this portrait and dialogue helped her express guilt and grief and accept closure in the relationship. When a relationship has been very deep, as in the death of a child, a husband, a wife, or a parent, one dialogue will probably not be enough. There may be many times over weeks and years when you want to converse with a loved one who is no longer present. In the diary your relationship with that person may continue.

Sometimes diaries seem to expand into a continuing dialogue with those we have loved. My relationship with Anaïs Nin, for example, continues to develop within my diary, and there I can write out the advice I knew she would have given me were she still alive. Death ends a life, but not a relationship. And through dialogues we can keep alive the spirit of the other that now dwells within us as the result of love.

Oversensitivity, Hurt Feelings, and Loneliness

Many people think that hurt feelings and loneliness are the principal content of diaries. It is true that the child-self, who seems to be responsible for these feelings, seems to speak more freely in the diary than elsewhere. But, as in the case of other negative feelings, oversensitivity expressed in the diary provides a basis for increased self-understanding and maturity.

Most oversensitivity and hurt feelings come from that part of the self that tends to respond as we did when we were powerless children. To this child-self all personal affronts seem disproportionately large. You can get in touch with this helpless child's voice in your own personality through free-intuitive writing or cathartic writing, as Marion Milner did in her diary:

> I must make a scene, must be miserable, when he says
> that, I'll cry, I mustn't let him know it's better, I
> won't say I'm happy. . . .

This free-intuitive writing allows the hurt-child voice expression. But there is generally a further step in dealing with oversensitivity. You also need to gain perspective on the feelings by writing objectively from an adult point of view. The adult-self must try to understand the cosmic comedy, to see the personalities of all involved. It often helps to write from an altered point of view of the self—as "she" or "he"—to see that rarely is a hurt intentional, and rarely is the other person even conscious of having done it.

You can also try to enter the other person's point of view. For example, one diarist named Marguerite was offended that her friend Janet hadn't had time to talk to her when she called. She decided to write about the incident from her friend's point of view:

Janet's POV
> Marguerite called me this afternoon just as I was in the
> middle of figuring the budget. She sounded hurt when
> I told her I'd talk with her later. I'm sorry about that,
> but she has to understand that I can't have energy
> for her until I get this off my mind.

After writing this entry from her friend's point of view the diarist recognized that her hurt feelings had disappeared. In cases of oversensitivity it is always helpful to see the problem from as many perspectives as possible.

You also need an expanded adult perspective to deal with loneliness. For the helpless child-self loneliness is as terrifying as the dark. For the adult-self loneliness is simply a warning signal, an almost visceral sensation that calls for analysis and action. To explore and understand feelings of loneliness you might dialogue with a figure of inner wisdom, with your inner child, or with a neglected creative aspect of your personality. Of course, the diary is not a substitute for human contact. If, after communicating with yourself in the diary you still feel lonely, the adult-self should take action to make contact with others.

However, loneliness frequently indicates a division within the self, a loneliness for union with the true self. If you are lonely for personal completion, surrounding yourself with people may only be an avoidance of the solitude necessary for self-confrontation. Diary writing can be a great aid to people who are afraid of being alone because it helps them experience solitude as an opportunity for communion with the self. Many people enthusiastically report that keeping a journal has made living alone an adventure of intimacy with parts of themselves they never knew before. Diarists often say they begin to miss themselves if they fail to write in the diary for a long time.

Most frequently loneliness indicates the need for self-love and self-nourishment. One diarist records her entire journal as a dialogue between her active, feeling self ("Me") and a nurturing, listening self (whom she calls simply "Other"). She finds that the love she gives herself in the diary reverberates in her relationships beyond the diary.

Me
You're getting to feel like my very best friend.
We'll never be parted, you'll never move away to
another town, never die even, until I die, too. It's
what everyone looks for in another person. And we've
found it right here.
Other
It feels good, it's very relaxed. I like being with you this
way.

Me
Thank you. I feel like I. . . . I really love you. Very much.
And, I know how important it is for us to be together.
It has an effect on all my loving, and on all the people
I love, too.

With self-affirmation you can feel complete, fulfilled, and
loved when entirely alone.

Envy and Jealousy

Envy—wanting what another person has—and jealousy—fear of
losing another's exclusive devotion—seem to be two of the
most difficult emotions to deal with because they focus your
energy outside yourself rather than in yourself. However, the
diary can help you bring your energy home.

The first step is to express the feelings of envy and
jealousy as fully as possible. You can't deal with any strong
emotions until you have let them spill out. Permit them to
take as outrageous a form as they will. Remember that negative feelings expressed in the diary are simply raw material for
the alchemical process that allows them to be transformed into
self-knowledge. Because envy and jealousy are really cover
emotions that hide a truth you don't want to see, it's important to allow the unexpected to happen. Don't censor anything at the stage of spilling out your feelings.

Since both are frequently forms of projection, you may
find it helpful to write a portrait of the person whom you
seem to envy or of whom you feel jealous. Generally such
portraits represent an image of an unfulfilled part of yourself
idealized in another.

You only envy people who have something you want.
You only envy people who represent one of your potential,
unsatisfied selves. Envy is a masquerader. As long as you
believe the disguised emotion, you will be unable to recognize
the truth that lies behind it.

But envy is an extremely helpful emotion if you can
take hold of its energy and employ it to your advantage. For

example, a friend of yours may have taken up photography with great enthusiasm and success. You go to look at his pictures and you admire them. But instead of feeling pleased that your friend has found a hobby that brings him satisfaction, you feel envious, your smile freezes on your face, and you find yourself wishing that his good fortune were not so great. You may be unable or unwilling to discuss these feelings with him at the time, but you can certainly dialogue with him in the diary about it.

Through the dialogue you can focus on just which elements set off your envy. It may be that you want a hobby or a job that will concentrate your energies in a satisfying way, and you have yet to find that for yourself. It may be that your envy has just revealed that you have an intense interest in photography which you have never acknowledged. What you discover through the dialogue can lead you to further action— to go out and buy a camera or to work in the diary to determine your goals. As long as the energy stays invested in your friend as envy, it will deplete you. When you can take possession of it as desire, you can use it.

Jealousy is more complicated to deal with because it often involves sexual feelings, and it catches us in the middle of changing cultural values. Traditional assumptions about marriage and monogamy encourage jealousy of our partners, while ideas about open marriage and free sex—which became popular in the sixties—tend to make people feel guilty about jealousy. It seems there are only individual solutions, and the diary may be able to help you find them—even if it is only a matter of calming yourself by using guided imagery or speaking with a nourishing figure of inner wisdom.

You may have to work very hard, perhaps using nearly all the diary devices you have at hand, to turn a problem of jealousy into a personal mystery from which you can grow. One diarist found it helpful to write a dialogue with her lover, who had had a secret affair with another woman. The dialogue

allowed a cathartic release of her anger and then helped her see
how she could grow from the incident that had caused her
jealousy:

Me: I remember finding out about your affair with Sarah
and I'm still really mad about it!

B: There's no point in being mad any longer. It's finished.
Let's continue in our life together.

Me: I still remember finding the letter from her to you.
I'd suspected it so long—and there it was facing me. I
couldn't deny it any longer. I was so stupid to have
believed in you.

B: I was always constant in our relationship, but that
was a trying time. I got what I needed from someone
else for awhile, because you weren't accepting me.

Me: You bastard! She fell in love with you—and she didn't
know about me—you were a sham with both of us—
nothing was real.

B: My feelings were real.

Me: Half the time with her—half the time with me. Kissing
her, kissing me—what a life you made for yourself.
God, it kills me to imagine the two of you together.
You can't be denied an inch of your pleasure, or you
go off in search of it somewhere else.

B: Well, maybe I did think of myself. I was frustrated that
you didn't want me. I need someone in my life who
wants me. So I did what I had to, to get those feelings.

Me: Then whenever there are periods of darkness in my life
or in our relationship, and I'm not able to give fully to
you—you'll just go out and get it somewhere else? I'll
have no credit built up? Nothing to hold you except
what I give you?

B: You hold me for what you are. I'll never abandon you.
But I have needs—and they will be filled—somewhere.

Me: I might be able to accept that if you would not constantly remind me of what I'm not giving you. By
choosing to be myself, I choose not to give you everything you need—and I can feel comfortable with the

fact you will search for this in others. I can accept this
of you and the part of my life you are now, but I need
you to accept me, too.

After completing this imaginary conversation the diarist wrote
a reflective entry on how the dialogue had altered her feelings:

As I depend more on myself, I am less dependent on
others. As I grow stronger in myself and my own life,
so will I let others be in theirs. This feels very good. I
celebrate this beginning of letting go in myself.

By fully entering the experience of her jealousy the writer
was able to discover an important truth about her own freedom. The challenge is great, but if you can turn jealousy and
envy around from self-punishing energy into self-affirming
energy, you will be able to expand that much faster toward
personal wholeness.

Anger and Fear

Anger and fear are vital emotions that can provide deep
self-knowledge when worked with in a diary. The tendency in
occasions of anger, resentment, or fear is to become so concerned with "the other guy" who may be the object of the
emotions that you lose touch with the power of your own
resources. Confronting these emotions in the diary gives you
the advantage of staying centered within yourself and aware
that you are the source of your feelings.

By spilling out your anger or fear through cathartic
writing you may be able to distinguish the real issues and your
genuine needs from the scramble of feelings. For example, one
diarist felt resentment toward Anaïs Nin though she had never
met her. The diarist allowed her angry feelings to flow out,
until the true source of her resentment surfaced:

I often become embittered when I'm exposed to a life
like Anaïs Nin's. Quiet, with order. I am drawn to
that life but daily must face the hectic, the loud, the

demands of my children for my time, my thoughts. My life is not my own. I'm tired of picking up other people's messes when my standard for cleanliness is that of a nun. When I experience the atmosphere in which Anaïs lived I'm filled with anger and jealousy. I cannot imagine ever becoming an accomplished artist at the rate I go about dabbling into the source, only to be yanked out at my children's whim.

A curse on all udderless men and bratless women!

Writing this entry focused the problem. The diarist reflected that the anger was not really at Nin or even at her children. It was at her inability to make private time for herself and her art. Once she realized this she decided to take action on the problem and the anger dissipated.

Sometimes the entire cathartic entry takes the form of an angry unsent letter, an extended curse directed at the object of the anger:

Daggers! Bah! Phooey! Crap! Norforms! Your mother's ass! Your brother's nostrils! Your sister buggers her pet mouse!

The humor mixed with the anger in this curse helped the diarist move out of intense anger and into an exploration of her fears behind the anger—just as emotional and irrational but closer to the real source of her feelings:

I'm going to be poor and pathetic and alone and old, with a wart on my foot!

Soon the helpless-child voice in herself emerged:

Nobody loves me . . .

and then the entry moved to a spontaneous dialogue when a more adult voice responded:

That must be the child-self. She always says that. Why do you feel so threatened?

> This reminds me of the time I got fired from my first job. . . .
>
> Is the situation the same?
>
> Well, not actually. . . .

The dialogue between the emotional child-self and the more objective adult-self began to reveal the real emotion behind her anger—a fear of being unloved, fired, rejected.

It may also be helpful to write a dialogue with the person toward whom you feel angry. Heated discussions sometimes arise because you need to clarify your own point of view. It may very often be preferable to do that in an imaginary diary dialogue to avoid the chance of misunderstanding or hasty words. When the source of your feelings is unclear to you, it is easy for someone else to misinterpret your meaning. You can get lost in dealing with the other person's reactions and never discover what you really wanted to say.

Practicing an encounter in the diary can help you know what you want and how you want to go about getting it—calmly, without getting angry or confused. In the diary you can rehearse until you feel ready for a confrontation; you can prepare a strategy for difficult situations in your life. As a result the diary has become an essential tool in Assertiveness Training: Before asserting your needs, desires, or objections you need to be clear about what they are.

Uncovering the real issues in your anger—through dialogue, catharsis, free-intuitive writing, guided imagery, or some other diary device—prepares the adult-self to take action without childish name calling, blaming, or fearfulness. In this way mature, adult assertiveness, which is motivated by self-respect and self-understanding, replaces inappropriate anger and hostility.

For people who are habitually passive the diary provides a safe place to visualize themselves taking active, direct responsibility for their needs and desires. Rehearsing an encounter in the diary is a reprogramming so that you have a new pattern to follow, rather than just the old habits of withdrawal and avoidance of confrontation. Of course, taking care of your needs does not end with writing a behavioral rehearsal in which you visualize yourself telling your neighbor that you want him to stop revving his motorcycle at six o'clock in the morning. Unless you take the risk of action in your life, unless you actually say something to the neighbor, the cause of the anger will remain.

At the same time, not all problems that evoke anger or fear can be dealt with directly. In some cases discovering alternative options for yourself may be the best plan, if direct assertion of your feelings and desires has failed to bring results. One woman who was in an extremely difficult situation was able to find a creative solution that only a diarist could discover. Her husband was an alcoholic, and several times a week he would not appear for dinner nor for the rest of the night. She was full of anger and fear on those occasions, yet she was not ready to give up the relationship.

In searching for a creative solution in the diary she hit upon what she called the Alternative Plan. She prepared a list of activities she enjoyed, which would be ready and waiting for her in the diary on the nights her husband did not come home by dinner time. The list included simple items such as reading a mystery novel, writing to a friend, taking a long bath, dancing alone in the living room with the shades drawn, and singing nursery rhymes to her baby. Within the obvious limitations of her situation, the diarist discovered creative options that freed her from unprepared nights of anger and fear. The diary helped her engage her own resources to deal with her problem.

Most fear, and the anger that often stems from fear, comes from a sense of impotence, a feeling of being out of touch with your own power to create options for yourself and take care of your own needs in a situation. As a diarist you have a means of countering that sense of impotence with the power of your own creativity.

Transforming Guilt into Responsibility

Diaries reveal that people often feel excessive guilt when it is inappropriate or, as an overreaction in the opposite direction, no moral responsibility when it would be appropriate. However, you can learn to distinguish between inappropriate guilt, which immobilizes you, and personal responsibility, which energizes you. If you are feeling guilty you are not yet taking responsibility for yourself. Guilt punishes, exaggerates, and oversimplifies. Guilt may actually function as an avoidance of responsibility because it makes you passive. Responsibility demands action.

Guilt is generally the punishing voice of an authority figure, or "the parent" within, long after parental warnings have relevance in one's life. A child caught in the act of being "bad" or simply adventurous will sometimes slap his own hand and say, "No, no, naughty baby." By administering his own punishment before the eyes of his mother, the child hopes to ward off any further slaps from her. The child has internalized parental authority. This form of self-punishment can be observed clearly in children's diaries. Children who most carefully guard their diaries from their parents often write to a self that is more judgmental and mature than the diarist.

For example, in her famous diary Anne Frank writes to "Dear Kitty," who is supposed to be comforting and supportive but who often turns out to be quite critical of Anne. The first entry that Anne writes to Kitty is, "I hope I shall be able to confide in you completely, as I have never been able to do in anyone before, and I hope that you will be a great support and comfort to me." But soon she is pleading, "Don't condemn me! Remember rather that sometimes I too can reach bursting-point"; and, "I expect you will be rather surprised at the fact that I should talk of boy friends at my age." The audience she has chosen to address in her diary has become a critical and judgmental projection of the parent.

Adults, too, can fall victim to an internalized, repressive, parental guardian and administer their own punishment in the form of unconstructive self-criticism. (This self-punishing voice can appear in the diary as the Internal Censor or the Internal Critic, and as such is discussed at further length in the chapter on overcoming writing blocks.) Perhaps because the New Diary offers an opportunity for the writer to explore a totally uninhibited, sensual, and imaginative playground the mechanisms of guilt and self-repression seem to awaken to criticize the writing and even the fact of keeping a journal. After a spontaneous cathartic or reflective entry, for example, the voice of guilt may intervene: "What drivel!" or "Have you nothing better to do than waste your life talking to yourself?" It is essential to answer this voice in firm self-defense: "Well, I can tear this up if I decide to later, but I want to see if I can come up with a new place from which to view my life. I don't want to see everything in your repressive, negative way."

Let the voice of guilt speak its piece and listen carefully to its words and tone. Sometimes it can be recognized as the voice of a father, mother, husband, wife, a stern teacher, employer, or a religious figure. Become alert to guilt as a false accuser. The standards it throws up to the self in judgment are often destructive and inhuman and should themselves be put on trial.

The process by which guilt inhibits and punishes, and the process by which you free yourself from its repression, are mysteries that gradually unfold on the pages of the diary. But the diarist must be persistent, for it may take some time to learn to recognize all the devilish masks guilt can assume— depleted energy, loss of confidence, self-sabotage, and self-loathing. For example, in many diaries guilt appears as self-doubt and insecurity:

> I feel so regressed, so retarded like I never have grown up and I never will. I never will be fulfilled. I never will be whole. I'm not an artist. I'm a pretentious fool. An empty-headed dilettante. I have nothing to say, nothing to share. No one wants to hear what a child has to say. Everyone knows more than me.

The diarist who wrote this writes beautifully and meaningfully except when the voice of guilt takes over. To see how this self-criticism is really an example of guilt, simply change the "I" to "you," and you will hear the exaggerated voice of a repressive parent:

> You are so regressed, so retarded like you never have grown up and you never will. You never will be fulfilled. You never will be whole. You're not an artist. You're a pretentious fool. An empty-headed dilettante. ...

In giving her self-criticism a voice and then distinguishing it from her own "I," the diarist who wrote those entries has taken a first step toward exposing the masquerade of guilt. Guilt can be dealt with, put into context, made fun of, rejected, or understood—only once it is identified and made conscious. It is better to express it, even as self-recrimination in the diary, than to allow it to stay at the level of a gnawing, unspecific anxiety in your life. Once the guilt is expressed and recognized you can begin to work through it.

After giving self-recrimination its own voice and distinguishing it from the "I," as in the example above, it is important to answer it in a dialogue:

> ... No one wants to hear what a child has to say. Everyone knows more than you.
>
> **Me**
> I want to hear what I have to say. And that is a ridiculous statement that everyone knows more than me. What do you hope to accomplish with that statement?
> **Guilt**
> To put you in your place.
> **Me**
> I don't think you know or can tell me where my place is. You just try to inhibit me. I think I'm alright. I like me. And I think you're puffed-up, old-fashioned, and sour-tempered.

Guilt
Hmmf!
Me
And hmmf to you. You're like Rumplestilskin. Once
I've recognized you, you don't have much power.

The repressive voice of guilt in this dialogue is something of a bully. But if the diarist recognizes it and continues to work with it, she will become more and more alert to the mechanism of guilt in her life and increasingly adept at circumscribing its power.

Once identified, controlled, and reeducated in the diary, the voice of guilt has the capacity to perform constructively as a voice of responsibility. That voice reminds you if you have deviated from your goals, if you are engaging in self-defeating behavior, or if you are needlessly hurting another person. It will be at your service for your true well-being, rather than bullying, depressing, or intimidating you as guilt. This transformation may take time and patience, but the reward is genuine inner freedom.

Apathy, Anxiety, and Depression

Apathy, or depleted energy, and "free-floating" anxiety are generally caused by suppressed emotion—envy, jealousy, anger, fear, or guilt that has not yet become conscious or focused. Depression is often considered to be the result of anger turned inward. The best diary devices for dealing with depression are those that tap the intuitive, feeling, right side of the brain: catharsis, free-intuitive writing, maps of consciousness, and guided imagery. These devices bypass the rational, intellectual mind control that is often responsible for keeping the root causes of apathy and depression from conscious recognition.

In some cases simply finding an image that manifests the suppressed feelings is sufficient to release you from depression. Relax in a quiet place, close your eyes, and allow an image to surface in your mind. Imagery comes directly from the right side of the brain and seems to have the power to cut through the intellectual censors that screen out emotions you have resistance to facing. Virginia Woolf intuitively searched for an image to express her anxiety in the following diary entry and found that after writing it out, she felt released from the feeling:

> *Mon., Oct. 25th (First day of wintertime)*
> Why is life so tragic, so like a little strip of pavement
> over an abyss. I look down; I feel dizzy; I wonder how
> I am ever to walk to the end. But why do I feel this:
> Now that I say it I don't feel it.

It is a common experience among diarists to find that anxiety or depression disappears once they have found an image to express it in writing.

In some cases, however, you may wish to carry further the image that has come to mind by using guided imagery or a map of consciousness. One diarist describes the circumstances and manner in which she transforms her maps of consciousness:

> I was going through a period in my life where I was
> experiencing a lot of emotional pain but trying to
> block it in order to maintain my responsibilities with
> school and the outside world. I came to a point where
> I could no longer hold my emotions down and every-
> thing started to surface. At this point I drew a picture
> of a lead pipe with water bursting out of it, which is
> where I was at but also where I did not want to be. I
> looked at the picture—decided how I wanted to change
> and then drew a stream teeming with fish which came
> out as a result of the pipe breaking—so that the burst-
> ing pipe was not seen as something destructive but as
> something necessary to free the stream and the wild-
> life within it. I meditated on this picture and called it
> back as an image in my mind whenever I felt pressure
> of the bursting pipe.

The diarist resolved the psychological pain from her internal conflicts by giving shape to them in a drawing and then transforming the drawing into a more positive, self-affirming image of her life.

When you are anxious or depressed, most of your energy goes into resisting conscious awareness of your emotions, and so you feel depleted and listless. Once you acknowledge the feelings in the diary you can redirect the freed energy back into your life.

One of the best ways to do this is with an exercise I call "speeding up into the future." Actually it's just a list of things you want and need to do, but which you've been putting off because of apathy or depression. After you have opened up the roots of your feelings in the diary, you can push yourself into the future by listing on the next page—quickly and without pondering—the things that need to be done. Select from the list one item you can accomplish immediately and do it without hesitation. Get out of the house, go to the exhibit at the museum, make a phone call, go see a movie, repot your plants, hang a picture, wash your car. Do whatever is on the list, but get going. Speed things up. Jump into the flow.

People tend to slow down in times of distress or discouragement. Their life energy flags, and they find themselves grounded like a kite without wind. This simple exercise helps you get unstuck from the past and into constructive activity in the future. Once life's energy has lifted you, you can begin flowing again and writing the ongoing story of your life."

Seeing Your Hidden Face in the Diary

Projection means seeing your own positive or negative qualities in another without realizing that what you perceive may have more to say about you than about the other person. As I suggested in discussing the portrait device in Chapter 5, you may be strongly attracted to, or strongly repelled by, certain people because you project a part of your personality onto them. For example, you may be constantly irritated by a co-worker and not understand why, until you realize that the other is extremely inefficient—a quality that disturbs you about yourself. Or a woman may repeatedly fall in love with artists, not realizing that she is falling in love with the potential artist in herself. Certain people in your life may represent an unappealing past self for you; others may represent your potential future self. Transforming such projections into self-awareness and personal expansion is one of the major functions of the New Diary.

The reason that projections are included under the general heading of "personal problems" is that, left unconscious they can easily take the form of envy, intimidation, slavish infatuation, or obsessive irritation. They can blind you to the reality of another person. Rather than seeing someone as the complex person she or he is, you see only a mirror reflection of a fragment of your own mind. And at least equally important is the fact that as long as you relate to others as projections of parts of yourself, you remain divided from yourself and blocked from realizing your full potential.

In the diary you can discover that aspect of the self you have projected onto another and take possession of it. Once projections are recognized, self-awareness and personal growth are freed to follow. One way to transform projections into self-recognition is through writing descriptive portraits, as in the "Julia" portrait in the last chapter. Another good example was provided by a diarist who felt unreasonably disturbed by her impressions of another woman in whose home she was staying as an overnight guest. The diarist decided to let it all out in a cathartic portrait in her diary:

> I have had many strong feelings today, but the strongest is my reaction to Mrs. Buchanan, who has provided supper and beds for all five of us, but who seems such a bore and whose house is so littered with things in the wrong places. The house is quiet and comfortable, hospitality has been given in unstinting measure, and

yet I am vividly conscious of the piles of papers beside the piano, the shoes on the cellar steps, the cluttered piano top, the garish and uninteresting duck vases displayed in the living room.

It must be that this arouses some quality of untidiness in me that I dislike. I am troubled by all the things I still have in drawers and chests and my inability to get rid of them.

Strange, now that I recognize that, I don't feel so controlled by my feelings. I can now feel the genuine hospitality of the family. It is as though I am looking back a long time ago to supper tonight, when I felt so uncomfortable and critical.

From this single entry the diarist was able to work through her feelings, transforming them from distress to self-recognition. She saw that her criticisms of the hostess were actually reflections of her own problem—her great fear of messiness and untidiness in her life. By releasing her secret feelings in the diary and coming to self-recognition through doing so she avoided taking her annoyance out on her hostess. The diary, rather than the other woman, became the reflecting glass for her projection.

There is nothing inherently wrong with the process of projection. It is a way your psyche enlivens and gives personal meaning to your world. It can create empathy with others, offer clues to positive aspects of yourself, and provide role-models who act as positive guideposts for personal growth. For example, a talented young pianist might project his desire to become an accomplished musician onto an older acquaintance who has already achieved success as a concert pianist. But unless the younger person recognizes that his slavish admiration is a projection of his own ambitions onto the other, he could easily feel intimidated and fail to realize his own potential.

If you ask yourself in the diary as you write about another, "Why do I fear, love, admire, resent, or envy this person? Does she/he reflect a part of me or my desires?"—the answers will push you past projection into self-recognition.

And once you have become conscious of a projection it can give you important insights into your personality, as well as release you from the uncomfortable feelings frequently associated with it.

The Diary's Role in Overcoming Illness

Diary writing can help you discover the psychological causes of an illness and sometimes even change its course, understand your role and responsibility in an injury, give fear and pain an outlet, and help the aged or terminally ill find meaning in suffering and in the journey toward death.

Recently, diary writing has been used to provide a means of discovering, understanding, and possibly altering the psychological causes of many physical disorders. Psychological self-therapy can sometimes be as significant in curing an ailment as the necessary medical treatment of the physical symptoms. Many individuals are now taking responsibility for finding a holistic approach to their own illness. This implies a growing awareness that emotional and psychological factors are as much a part of illness as the biological forces that may have generated it. In the New Diary one can function as self-healer through such techniques as the dialogue, free-intuitive writing, the unsent letter, guided imagery, reflection, and the list.

Since so many common illnesses are caused by viruses or bacteria always present in the environment, it is reasonable to ask yourself in a diary entry why a particular illness has taken hold at a particular time. You may discover stresses in your life that you have been ignoring, and from which the illness is an escape. The illness may have come as an order from mind and body to withdraw temporarily from the world and your regular routine to reestablish inner balance. Many people have found that when they get the message of an illness through working in the diary, the ailment goes away very quickly.

Different parts of the body seem to reveal different messages, so it can be helpful to write a dialogue with the specific part of the body or the specific illness that is giving you trouble. For example, one woman told me about using the diary to accelerate her cure from chronic bronchitis. She felt persecuted by the disease, as if it were a spirit that had unfairly attacked and possessed her. At night her lungs were so congested and her coughing so violent that she couldn't sleep. Finally, in desperation at four o'clock one morning, she decided to dialogue with the bronchitis in her diary. When she gave "bronchitis" a voice, it seemed as angry and violent as her symptoms.

> **Bronchitis**
> You bitch! I'm going to get you!
> **Me**
> Why me?
> **Bronchitis**
> Because you don't deserve to be well. You don't care about yourself.
> **Me**
> What do you mean? I've been eating right and getting regular sleep.
> **Bronchitis**
> Yes, and you've been smoking.
> **Me**
> But I've quit now.
> **Bronchitis**
> And you let S. take the car and smash it and you took all the responsibility for having it repaired. You told N. he could stay here for a week and you know you won't get anything done when he's here. . . .

By speaking to the bronchitis she was able to get it to explain its anger. As the dialogue progressed it became apparent that the bronchitis was the voice of her anger at other people in her life, which she had not been expressing. Her illness was trying to give her the message in a very forceful way that if she didn't use her anger to protect herself, if she shoved her words of self-defense back down her throat, they would hurt her. By refusing to express anger at people whom she felt were taking advantage of her, she had turned the anger against herself in the form of illness. When the diarist recognized the cause of her illness, she promised to take action about it, and the bronchitis, in turn, promised to go away when she had done so.

If you have neglected to listen to a message from part of the self, it may well choose expression through the body. For this reason working in a diary can be preventive medicine, helpful at the first signs of a cold or other familiar ailment. If you could get the messages of the self sooner, if you could keep the channels of inner communication open and the sense of responsibility for preserving your own well-being active through diary writing, then psychosomatic expression wouldn't be necessary. The diarist above followed a good procedure: Ask the symptom to reveal its message, listen to and accept its message, and then make a deal with the illness to go away.

In a similar way diarists have found that they can learn important messages from the "accidents" in their lives. Many of the personal-growth philosophies of the seventies teach an extreme version of personal responsibility: If you see a traffic accident it's your responsibility, you have chosen it; if you have an illness or an injury you have chosen it. In other words, these new growth philosophies teach that you are totally responsible for your own reality, since all the parts of your life are you. The value of these approaches is that through over-emphasis they tip the balance from passivity, conformity, and avoidance of personal responsibility to active control over your own subconscious expectations and beliefs.

With this sense of personal responsibility a diarist reported trying to understand why she had "chosen" a particular "accident" in her life. One day as she was running on the beach she injured her right toe badly, so that it required stitches. Later she decided to write a dialogue with her throbbing right foot and discovered that it had a peculiarly conservative personality:

Me
Hey, right foot, what's all the trouble about?

Right Foot
Put your right foot forward.

Me
Are you trying to say that I have trouble getting ahead?

Right Foot
You got it.

Me
But what does that really mean?

Right Foot
It has to do with foresight. You step where you shouldn't, you leap without looking; you put your foot in it. You're careless.

Me
Gee, you're very reprimanding.

Right Foot
I'm a right foot.

Me
You sure are. Listen, I also have a left foot. It doesn't seem to give me trouble.

Right Foot
He's a follower. I'm a leader. You're having trouble with leadership. You're afraid to take a stand. You don't have a sure step.

Me
Well how am I supposed to get all those things?

Right Foot
Start thinking. Look and consider before you act. Slow down. Think carefully about your life. Plan carefully. You have no time for mistakes. I want to lead you in the right direction.

Me
That's all pretty clear. Will you heal now?

Right Foot
You bet. I'm good at that, though I'll be sore for awhile as a reminder.

Me
Aw, give me a break.

Right Foot
That's exactly what I'm doing.

The dialogue seems to illustrate the relationship between "accidents" and the development of psychic balance. Her right foot was, in this case, a voice of inner wisdom cautioning her to slow down and take responsibility for herself, since her impulsive side seemed to be outrunning the rational and mature self. She recognized from this experience the importance of being receptive to messages from her feelings, dreams, and intuitions, before they had to do damage to get attention.

Using another approach a middle-aged man who had had a coronary decided to look at the possible psychological factors behind his heart attack. He asked himself in the diary, "Why do I want another heart attack?" and he made a list:

> to end this struggle to succeed
> to give up
> to hide
> to lay back, a failure

Then he asked himself, "Why do I *not* want another heart attack?" and listed:

> to discover my life
> to feel the process of my life
> to love
> to share
> to learn
> to be proud

Seeing the reasons for his first coronary and his very powerful reasons not to have another, he grew in confidence that he could influence the future of his health.

Diarists are only beginning to explore the journal's potential for self-healing. Every diarist who uses self-therapy to help herself or himself with physical disorders can make important contributions to the new field of holistic medicine. Some diarists write dialogues with "Health," inviting its curative power into their lives, and some imagine and describe themselves vibrant and well through guided imagery. Some women have told me that the diary helped them alleviate the psychosomatic elements of premenstrual tension and cramping when they explored in writing memories of their first period and the attitudes they had been taught about it. Other diarists have said that writing humorously about a congenital defect has helped them accept it.

Even those who have accepted the probability of terminal illness may be able to create an alternative world in the diary. Alice James (sister of the psychologist and philosopher William James and the novelist Henry James) used her diary to keep her mind free while her body was confined. Though she was bedridden most of her life, her consciousness was global. Her diaries are full of newspaper clippings from around the world and intense accounts of the everyday lives of the people near her. The diary was an outlet for Alice James's intellect as well as a private place to express her fear and physical pain when death approached. It permitted her to find a pattern of meaning in her difficult life, and to accept her death knowingly and profoundly.

Overcoming Compulsive Behavior

A special study deserves to be done on the usefulness of diary keeping in treating all kinds of compulsive behavior: cigarette smoking, overeating, alcoholism, drug addiction, and other obsessions. Many techniques of behavioral psychology are dependent on record keeping and what it reveals. Addicts— meaning obsessives of all varieties—develop selective blindness in their lives. They avoid full consciousness of their actions, of what cues their behavior, and of its frequency in order to continue their addictions. Keeping a record of one's thoughts and actions reverses that process, replacing blindness with self-awareness.

For example, I used the diary to help me quit smoking. Every time I wanted a cigarette I wrote about it instead. Here is what some of those entries looked like:

2:00 P.M.
I am trying to quit smoking cigarettes. I am dying to go
to George's market to buy a pack. I know that the relief
that a cigarette would bring would only be temporary.
There is a down after that initial drag. It is the first
drag, lighting the cigarette, taking a puff that I crave.
Somehow it says to me "You'll survive. You can always
smoke a cigarette to get through."
4:00 P.M.
I have almost grabbed my keys and driven to George's
many times. But I am feeling better. I know at this
moment that I will feel dreadful again. The craving will
return, but I have to remember this relief from the
need. It will also return.
Next day
I want a cigarette, a comfort stick. I want to kiss it with
my mouth. I want to feel the smoke tickle inside my
lungs, a place I can't reach any other way. Even if I
succeed in quitting smoking, I will always want a
cigarette. I will want to feel it between the second and
third fingers of my right hand, a friend, a companion.

Making such entries allowed me to fill the gap in my life that
living without smoking left. It gave me a substitute activity
and some satisfaction and relief in imagining and describing
the sensory and psychological rewards of smoking. I also
found it helpful to write dialogues with the part of me that
wanted to be joyously free of addictions.

Eater's Anonymous, an organization for compulsive
overeaters, has its members keep ongoing diaries as part of the
program. They believe that by recording everything you eat,
you become conscious of your eating habits. And self-awareness is the first step in breaking the habit.

One overweight woman I know used her diary to explore
the motivation underlying her weight problem. She began with
free-intuitive writing, which transformed itself into an unsent
letter to her own fat:

Rat. Cat. Mat. Slat. Fat.

Fat?

Me?

I'm not fat.

I'm an amazon.

I'm big boned.

I'm a whole lot of woman.

I'm fat.

Fat. Dr. Rubin calls you a tumor. A Weight Watcher lecturer brought a pound of chicken fat to class once so we could see what we were trying to lose. Yellow. Dead, vaguely evil.

Somewhere in our society's list of sacred commandments is: Thou shalt be slender. Graven in stone.

I hate you.

But I've applied you carefully all over my body— breasts, thighs, arms, chin, even my feet would be a half-size smaller without you. A lot of work has gone into acquiring such munificence—plotting, planning, eating. I'm better larded than Julia Child's roast.

You are my prison and my protection. You repulse people—sometimes the very people I long to attract.

You give me substance—so much substance that you slow me down. You keep me out of tennis, swimming (in public), the sexual Olympics. You give me a means of immediate gratification, comfort, and celebration. I pile you on top of the pain and anger I don't want to feel.

Without you I will be minus my magic shield, vulnerable to being rejected because someone simply doesn't like *me*, having no cushion between my soul and reality, forced to seek pleasure in things more complicated than food, having no glib excuse for being alone.

I don't like you. For a long time I thought you were a signal that I am morally insufficient, but I'm

> growing to a new realization now. I have chosen you.
> You make life safer, easier. How would I define myself
> if I got rid of you? I would have to reacquaint myself
> with me.
>
> Right now I am in the middle of a struggle. Stay
> safe and somewhat happy? Or reveal myself and
> risk . . . what?

Personal growth rises out of this diary excerpt. The diarist realizes that overcoming her addiction to food ultimately depends upon coming to know and accept her true self and becoming responsible for finding other forms of satisfaction in her life.

The diary can also be an aid in dealing with serious forms of drug addiction. One young woman used diary writing to help her kick an addiction to barbiturates. During the period of withdrawal she couldn't relate to anyone. She was irritable, she hated everyone; but she was terribly needful at the same time. The diary as an "absent presence" provided the best company and most comfort in dealing with the agonies of withdrawal.

Diary writing can also help you judge the effect of any drug on your thinking and perception. If you write under the influence of marijuana, alcohol, hashish, cocaine, or another drug you can later see just how the drug alters your consciousness and writing. Memory can be very deceptive when it comes to assessing the effects of a drug. Some drugs offer an elevation that seems to heighten the quality of an activity. Rereading and comparing entries made when you are under the influence of a drug with entries made when you are not can help you determine when a particular drug is not functioning as a mind-expander but as an inner con artist.

Recent theories on addiction broaden its definition to include any repeated experiences in which one seeks to lose the self. With this in mind I asked a friend who calls her journal "Diary of a Love Addict" to write about her progress in using the diary to cure her addiction:

I am a love addict. Like an alcoholic, I have a predis-position to be a love addict for life, even when I am not directly engaged with a lover. . . .

I think that the diary has helped me to make slow progress towards being able to deal with my addiction. . . .

I used to be completely subsumed by love when-ever I could get it. My work stopped or suffered. I felt incomplete, existentially nonexistent away from my lover, and I went through severe withdrawal symp-toms after a relationship was over.

Romance gave me a "kick" and without it, life seemed unbearably dull. . . . I wanted a free, auton-omous, self-fulfilling life. But my addiction worked on a physiological level that my thinking could not touch. Once I was sexually turned onto a man, I was hooked, often against my own will. The man's needs—whoever he might be at the time—began to override all other priorities in my life. . . .

I am less of an addict than I used to be, or at least my periods of addiction are less frequent and of shorter duration than they once were. I am now like the businessman who takes an occasional drunk vaca-tion in the bowery and then manages to dry up to go back to the path of his life. . . .

This progress is because I've begun to recognize the kinds of entries I make in the diary when I am hooked. Other themes that have a place in my diary when I am truly centered disappear. My focus narrows, and I write in the diary only when I am separated from "my man" and then only as a means of replacing him. . . .

It is always humiliating for me to read repeatedly in my diary: "I am in love with _____." The names change, but the adolescent quality of the writing at these times is always the same. I have a sense of waste after rereading these entries, which later have no value except as indicators of my addiction. In this, however, they have great value. . . .

The greatest help the diary has given me has been in reminding me that "I've been through this before." My addiction tends to obscure my memory By rereading the diary while in the throes of a new infatuation I am reminded that the imbalance and excitement I feel is exactly like my addictive love in the past.

I am also reminded of my other selves as they have accumulated in the diary. I can remember, at least, that I once had other interests, other friends, other needs, than just the man with whom I am currently obsessed.

Perceiving the pattern of her love addiction in the context of her life over time diminishes the power of the addiction. And the obsessive "adolescent quality" that the diarist notices in her writing defines areas for further growth. She might benefit from developing in the diary a personal concept of love that is more mature than temporary infatuation or sexual attraction. Or she might try to write about her affairs in a more adult, reflective manner. But even if she just continues to record the problem, she can gradually gain control of it through self-awareness.

Diary writing itself might be called an addiction, for it does become a habit upon which you depend. Anaïs Nin referred to it as her "Kief, hashish, and opium." Jane Carlyle compared her diarizing to the whiskey drinking of a Scotch professor, continued "because I like it and because it is cheap." But diary writing can be a positive addiction that, like regular exercise, encourages the enlargement of your capacities. William Glasser, in his book *Positive Addiction,* says that certain kinds of habitual behavior enhance a person's competence and contentment in other areas of life.

If diary writing were used as an escape from confronting important issues in your life, it might acquire some of the characteristics of a negative addiction. But instead the New Diary presents an opportunity to work through problems rather than avoid them. Negative feelings are a plea to pay attention to yourself. Rather than fearing, freezing up, or avoiding problems you can explore them in the diary like a detective tracking down clues to your inner resources.

There is no formula that can be given for working through personal problems in a diary. Each person and each situation is unique. You must simply follow your intuition. There is, however, a general pattern that you may wish to keep in mind. First give full expression to the problem in cathartic writing or allow the feelings to surface through the use of the subjective, intuitive diary devices—free-intuitive writing, guided imagery, or maps of consciousness. This approach works because you cannot think through problems; you must first feel them through. After you have released the feelings, which may appear to be rather childish and immature when you see them in writing, you can gain a more adult, objective perspective by using reflection, description, altered point of view, or dialogue.

However, the particular device you use is always less important than the trust you put in your own process of self-discovery. Simply writing about a problem as it arises allows the most important issues to surface and indicates the growing edge of your personality.

Some problems require persistent and repeated transformation, since personal growth is a gradual process and cannot be forced. Each time you work through a particular problem your progress toward inner freedom is expanded. Diarists, on rereading, sometimes interpret the reappearances of a problem as lack of growth. But once you have acquired the habit of unblocking and moving the negative energy of a particular problem forward, transforming it into constructive energy through your work in the diary, you will begin to see a long-term pattern of change. And when you deal with problems immediately and maturely, you free psychic space for joyful experiences.

7 | Discovering Joy

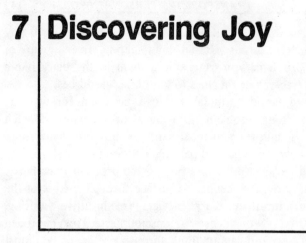

Happiness within a diary has less to do with the events you encounter in life than with the way you experience the process of living. I have noticed in my own diary writing and in all the diaries I have read that happiness, while influenced by external factors, depends upon internal capacities. It includes the ability to feel deeply and to perceive vividly through your senses, to be receptive to new experiences and to marvel, appreciate, understand, enjoy, imagine, create, synthesize, accept yourself, and embrace your growth and evolution.

Because the diary mirrors your habits of mind and the way you perceive and deal with events, it can become a tool for developing these internal capacities. In the diary you can consciously look for positive, creative, sensitizing, and life-enhancing experiences to record. The expression of these experiences becomes tied to the creation of your own happiness. Simply by writing of times of happiness you can learn how to use positive energy creatively; and when you get used to writing out of feelings of well-being and joy, you will be more likely to enter these states in order to create.

Recording happiness after you have lived it brings it back to life and is doubly rewarding. And giving power to positive perceptions and modes of thinking eventually becomes a habitual way of perceiving and thinking in your life.

You are more likely to discover the essence of your individuality by studying the unique composition of your happiness as it appears in the diary than you are by focusing on worries or disappointments. Negative ways of thinking are often an internalized punishing "parent" or other destructive mental habits acquired during childhood. But to find what brings you genuine happiness is to discover who you really are. Marion Milner concluded from her diary writing that "happiness not only needs no justification, but that it is also the only final test of whether what I am doing is right for me."

Diarists are fortunate in having a tool that allows them to make personal sense out of all the platitudes, theories, philosophies, and cultural conditioning about happiness. They have a means of defining abstract ideas like happiness, love, and freedom within the context of their individual lives. Diarists discover happiness inductively; the evidence is drawn from their feelings and experiences. Because the diary is always becoming, because there is no goal or end to it but only the ongoing process, diarists begin to perceive their lives, as Milner further observed, "not as the slow shaping of achievement to fit my preconceived purposes, but as the gradual discovery and growth of a purpose which I did not know." The meaning of a life is discovered from the life itself; and the ingredients of personal happiness are realized as you record your unique experiences of it.

No one can claim that keeping a diary will bring you happiness. Nevertheless, in reading through many lifetime diaries I have observed how men and women on very different paths have discovered happiness for themselves and used the diary for that purpose. Numerous diarists with unhappy childhoods have altered their ways of seeing the world and even their temperaments through diary work. The lifetime diaries of the French writer H. F. Amiel, for example, trace a path from guilt and self-condemnation to a growing maturity and happiness. In his later years Amiel attested to the journal's cathartic and curative powers: "The chief utility of the *journal intime* is to restore the integrity of the mind and the equilibrium of the conscience, that is, inner health."

Inner health is what the process of the New Diary is all about. It comes from the happiness of an integrated life, which includes loss, love, pain, pleasure, error, success, disappointment, and joy. It comes from the ability to stay in touch with your true feelings, needs, and desires within the rhythm and movement of the ever-changing present, to be alternately active or receptive as the tidal conditions of life demand. It is found in the continuous excitement of living experimentally, in accepting life itself as the goal of life. It is a sense of intimacy with the mysterious movement and process of life, a feeling of "being life."

These attitudes are all accessible through the process of keeping a diary. Yet people often associate the content of diaries—and the creative process generally—primarily with pain and sorrow. Many diarists admit that they write only when they are confused, unhappy, or full of self-pity. Some journals even contain a disclaimer stating that the writer is not really as unhappy as the book would indicate, but that the journal gives a slanted self-portrait. This distortion probably comes about from a Western misconception about creativity as the product of pain and frustration. The Eastern concept of creativity is more inclusive. According to Lady Murasaki, an eleventh-century Japanese diarist, one writes when some experience "has moved him to an emotion so passionate that he can no longer keep it shut up in his heart. Again and again something in his own life or in that around him will seem to the writer so important that he cannot bear to let it pass into oblivion." The creative emotion can be joyful as well as painful.

Recording Positive Emotions

If your diary points out that you seem to be caught in a negative frame of mind, you might ask yourself if you tend to dismiss your pleasurable experiences and concentrate on the painful ones. You might try making a list of the elements in your life you include in your diary and another list of the elements you forget or neglect to include. Or you might simply ask yourself in writing why you have a tendency toward negativity and allow the answer to come to you intuitively and spontaneously. You may find, like the woman who wrote, "I have this urge not to let myself come off in a positive way here," that the mechanism of guilt makes you feel unworthy of appearing happy to yourself.

Without eliminating other kinds of diary work you can experiment with including positive feelings in the diary. The easiest way to do this is to wait until the next time you feel happy and then to go to the diary with these feelings. Once you have experienced the pleasure of writing out positive feelings you will return to do it again and again. The following sensual description was one woman's first attempt to write out of positive emotions after years of writing only negative entries:

> As we walked to the fruit stand at twilight, I was
> overcome with ecstasy. Each house had a new charm and
> a story to tell. Colors seemed to have been applied with
> a brush. At the stand each orange demanded a caress. I
> wanted to rub each smooth mushroom against my
> breast. The green and yellows of the squash, the dark
> blue of the sky, the streak of crimson along the horizon
> made me drunk with color and air and space.

Recording her elation made it seem more real and consequently a more important part of her life.

There is magic in this process. By changing what you write, you begin to change how you perceive yourself and therefore who you are.

Witches who keep diaries believe that through some kind of magic they can influence the future by writing what they want to come to pass before it actually happens. The effects may seem magical, but the process is simple. You substantiate and give power to whatever you focus on in writing. As Virginia Woolf clearly observes in her diary:

> And now with some pleasure I find that it's seven, and must cook dinner. Haddock and sausage meat. I think it is true that one gains a certain hold on sausage and haddock by writing them down.

One gains hold of anything by writing it down. So if it's happiness and joy you wish to have a better grasp on, include these experiences in the diary.

Moreover, if you record moments of happiness in the diary you will find rewards as you reread. Your earlier self may be able to remind a later self how to be happy. The point is not to avoid the very important expression of painful feelings in your diary. Instead you need to *balance* them with other kinds of perceptions to achieve equilibrium and inner health, the prerequisites of happiness.

Finding Joy in the Here and Now: Active Receptivity

Actually you don't have to wait until a happy mood hits you to experience joy in the diary. You can use certain diary devices to discover it within you nearly anytime or anywhere. You can learn how to perceive in new and exquisitely gratifying ways. For example, writing detailed descriptions seems to enhance any experience. You may discover that describing your environment is sufficient to change the face of your world.

One diarist told me how she found herself waiting for someone in a bleak, cement parking lot. Rather than wait in boredom and irritation she seized her pen and some scrap paper and proceeded to describe the parking lot and herself sitting in it in as much detail as possible. Heightening her awareness by writing this description suddenly transformed her boredom into immeasurable interest, and she says that she still finds satisfaction in rereading this particular journal entry.

The diarist was doing a *here-and-now* exercise that reawakens all the senses and allows you to feel the wonder, intensity, and immediacy of your life. It is a description of the immediate present, an expanded awareness of the moment, and a reawakening of your senses.

Most of us have become desensitized; we have shut down many of our receptive circuits to our environment and to other people. It is as if eyes, ears, nose, mouth, and fingers had been coated or insulated, separating us from our physical surroundings. It may be the result of media and technological bombardment, a difficult childhood in which we built a set of defenses against a painful environment, or a variety of psychological shocks in adulthood. In the process of protecting ourselves, many of us have contracted like a sea anemone when disturbed by a rough touch. It is this contraction that makes people feel isolated and causes difficulty in becoming intimate with others.

The purpose of the here-and-now exercise is to open up your senses like the sea anemone spreading wide its feathery, sentient feelers. Perceive your environment in as many ways as possible, here and now, at this moment, letting the sensations flow into you. Then describe what you experience in the diary. I call this process *active receptivity*.

Here and now, at this moment: What do I hear? What physical sensations do I have in my body? Am I hungry? What is the temperature of the room? What do I see? What else do I see? What do I notice? What do I smell? What is the light like?

Marion Milner gives an example of how attuning her senses in this way opened a door between her and the world:

> Those flickering leaf-shadows playing over the heap of cut grass. . . . The shadows are blue or green, I don't know which, but I feel them in my bones. . . . beyond, there's a splash of sunlight leaping out against the darkness of forest, the gold in it flows richly in my eyes, flows through my brain in still pools of light. That pine, my eye is led up and down the straightness of its

trunk. . . . The air is full of sounds, sighs of wind in the trees, sighs which fade back into the overhanging silence. A bee passes, a golden ripple in the quiet air. A chicken at my feet fussily crunches a blade of grass. . . .

Milner later reflects on this exercise:

> I sat motionless, draining sensation to its depths, wave after wave of delight flowing through every cell in my body. . . . I no longer strove to be doing something, I was deeply content with what was. . . . hearing and sight and sense of space were all fused into one whole. . . . I had never suspected that the key to my private reality might lie in so apparently simple a skill as the ability to let the senses roam unfettered by purposes.

Even in periods of pain and confusion you can discover exquisite moments by opening the senses through consciously using active receptivity. Eyes and ears have a wisdom of their own that can offer an antidote to worry or boredom. During one winter of loneliness while I was separated from the man I loved, I wrote the following entry. I didn't think of it as a here-and-now exercise but it is almost that:

> Now I sit at the wooden kitchen table, next to the bird feeder. There must be more than a dozen birds less than three feet from me, outside the window. They take turns flying up the shelf, landing with a little thud. They come in combinations of colors—sometimes two male cardinals, electric red against a white world. The plain titmouse, the bravest, will sometimes arrive alone at the pane and look me in the eye.
>   I sit here, not caring what time it is. The birds disturb the trees in a sudden fearful movement, and snow falls on them in an avalanche.
>   Why does that big bluejay have so much trouble eating a sunflower seed? He hammers it against a branch and still cannot open it.
>   I watch the smoke curl from my cigarette. I listen to Satie's music. He must have have been a bird, those

quick, nervous notes, the game of frightening oneself, the hopping flights.

I am thinking about white. The car is snowed under, the roads are obliterated, the sky has turned as white as the ground. White thoughts: the white of homemade yogurt sitting in a ceramic bowl, the porcelain white inside my coffee cup, the white of the cream I pour into it, the white on the breasts of the junco, the towhee and the titmouse, the white of my long cigarette burning away the time, the white of the soapsuds in the sink, white specks falling from the sky, the white sound of silence.

It was an exquisite spot of time, perhaps made more indelible by the pain that surrounded it. If I had not recorded it, I suspect that my memory would have convinced me that this period of my life was entirely negative. Recording the here and now allowed me to stay in touch with the texture of my experience and the immediacy of my life.

Marion Milner similarly learned, from recording the moments of her greatest happiness in her diary, that they depended upon an "internal gesture" of expanded awareness. She observed that:

> In certain moods the very simplest things, even the glint of electric light on the water in my bath, gave me the most intense delight, while in others I seemed to be blind, unresponding and shut off, so that music I had loved, a spring day or the company of my friends, gave me no contentment. . . . So now I began to discover that there were a multitude of ways of perceiving, ways that were controllable by what I can only describe as an internal gesture of the mind.

She was then able to use this "internal gesture" voluntarily to cue her awareness in order to feel the intensity and wonder of almost any situation.

Milner found, as other diarists have found, that once this ability to evoke active receptivity is recognized, it can be used consciously to experience greater pleasure in the process of living. It is an *active* receptivity because it involves an active choice to be receptive to the magic of the moment. This choice has little to do with "resolutions" or "trying" or a "teeth-gritting effort" to have delightful moments. I have found that I cannot force myself to feel aware or happy or interested or satisfied, no matter how hard I try. However, I can choose to *allow* myself to enter these states by relaxing and by consciously directing my attention in certain ways.

You cannot make yourself see or think things that are positive; but you can choose where to look and what to think about. You can choose where to direct your attention. In this sense you can determine the interior quality of your life.

Selecting Your Perceptions

Diary writing shows the extent to which an individual has control over and responsibility for how he or she perceives. For example, if ten diarists were asked to record their experience of being in the same room with a sleeping cat: one might record boredom and irritation; another might try to capture in words the exact color of the cat's fur; another might write a meditation on the fragility of life; someone else might describe what she sees out the window; another might recall the symbol of the cat in his dreams; someone else might describe her own feline personality; another his allergies; another her worries; another a fantasy that seeing the cat had evoked.

The possibilities are endless, and yet we constantly forget that we are responsible for the quality of our perceptions. As Nin wrote in *Diary VI:*

> Every moment you can choose what you wish to see, observe, or record. It is your choice. So you create the total aspect according to your vision. We have a right to select our vision of the world.

Nin chose to look for the delightful and creative aspects of every situation. It was something she taught herself in the process of writing the diary. In a series of letters sent to her friend, author James Herlihy, to cure the blues she gave examples of how she chose to look at even difficult situations:

> If my lover is irritating I will think what a beautiful alibi he gives me for going on a journey.
> If my lover talks too much I will look out of the window and listen to the rain and think how well they synchronize.

You paint your own picture in the diary; you choose the colors. You even go into life to gather material for your journal, and you select the kind of material you want. Writing in the diary makes you aware of how you see the world, and you begin to choose what sorts of perceptions you wish to have—in your life as well as in your diary.

Learning to choose both the subject matter and the approach to life is especially clear in the diary of Emily Carr, a painter who, at the age of sixty-one, went to live in a van in British Columbia with a pet monkey, a rat, and two puppies. She chose a very unusual life for herself and then she chose how she would perceive it. Here is a here-and-now spot of time from her diary:

> *Sept. 19, 1933*
> The rain is thundering on the van top. The creatures are all folded down in sleep. . . . There is a solidity about the black night in this little valley as if you could cut slices out of it and pile them up. Not a light anywhere. The stream gargles as if it had a perpetual sore throat. A car passes up on the Malahat highway with a swift flash of light on this and that up above us and is gone like an unreality.

The moment comes alive and fills with excitement in her description. She could have chosen to worry about her age, loneliness, leaks in the van, or any number of other concerns, but she chose instead to open herself to the moment and receive its magic.

The diaries of recluses such as Emily Carr show how even an externally barren life can, on a subjective level, be full and rich with heightened moments. The accumulation of such spontaneous and chosen spots of time together contribute to the overall happiness of a life, whether it has been public and prosperous or private and modest. In her diary Carr described the relationship between such small moments of delight and the larger context of life by comparing it to a memory from her childhood:

> "Hundreds and Thousands" are minute candies made in England—round sweetnesses, all colors and so small that separately they are not worth eating. But to eat them as we did in childhood was a different matter. Father would take the big fat bottle off the shelf in his office and say, "Hold out your hands." Father tipped and poured, and down bobbed our three hands and out came our three tongues and licked in the "Hundreds and Thousands," and lapped them up, lovely and sweet and crunchy.
>
> It was these tiny things that, collectively, taught me how to live. Too insignificant to have been considered individually, but like the "Hundreds and Thousands" lapped up and sticking to our moist tongues, the little scraps and nothingnesses of my life have made a definite pattern. Thank you, tiny "Hundreds and Thousands."

Finding Joy in the Context of Your Life

Lists of Joys. Keeping a diary allows you to accumulate "hundreds and thousands" of joyful moments and to experience them together in rereading as the natural sweetness of your life. Even if you have rarely or never described personal joys in the diary, you can immediately experience the happiness of your life by making various lists. You can list those things that regularly make you happy or list what would make you happy. And you can make retrospective lists of the happiest moments in your life. Or at the end of a day you can list the day's small pleasures. Happiness is largely a matter of where you place your attention, and these lists can be an important tool for teaching yourself how to give attention to the positive aspects of your life.

For seven years Marion Milner made regular lists in her diary of her wants, whether she got them, whether getting them made her happy, and what regularly brought her delight. At first she found herself concerned with things she had been taught to do in order to achieve happiness: maintaining appearances to her friends, working for everyone's approval, and in general "keeping up" with other people's expectations of her. Then she found that what made her happy seemed to be changing as she became attentive to it by writing it down. Gradually, simply as a side effect of keeping her lists of personal wants and joys, she began to find happiness in the details of her life as they unexpectedly appeared in her lists of the day's pleasures: "someone playing piano in the distance" or "sudden bursts of laughter together."

If you were to list in your diary the happiest moments in your life you might be surprised to find that it did not include your graduation or wedding day or the acquisition of things you thought you wanted. Rather it might include the spontaneous wonder and surprise at certain unexpected events in your life, an encounter with a stranger in a strange place, a moment in a play, a feeling of physical exhilaration. One man's list of happiest moments included:

> The first time I was able to stay up on a two-wheeler bike
> The day Rita gave birth to Michael
> The day on a transcontinental motorcycle trip when we passed Chicago and headed further west than I or anyone in my family had ever been
> The day with Dan Murphy when we capsized in icy rapids, lost our paddles, then our canoe, had to ford four ice-choked deep narrows. I discovered I could do almost anything I had to, and that

I really wanted very much to live.
The first time I slept with a woman
The first time I did a one-handed cartwheel
The day W. H. Auden said they were all bastards
     and that I should keep going despite that and
     because of that

One woman's list included:

Driving through Big Sur with C.
Kissing W. on the street in Greenwich Village
Taking the glass bottom boat ride in Catalina
Dancing, floating and swimming in my dreams
Seeing the Bunraku puppets
Certain lines in Durrell's *Justine*
Seeing Frank Lloyd Wright's Hollyhock House
When I felt Cathy's new-born cheek with my
     forefinger and could hardly tell what was her
     cheek and what was my finger.

Both diarists said that in making these lists they suddenly realized how much genuine happiness they had known in their lives. Both also felt a strong sense of their own identity and individuality as a result of making the lists. The man, who thought he had had an unhappy past, began to view his total life from a more positive perspective. His past seemed transformed simply by acknowledging and emphasizing the joys in it.

You can also make lists of those things that regularly make you happy. For example:

Making music
A sense of community with others
A warm, clear day
Working through problems with L.
Teaching well
J. F.'s sense of humor

As reminders of how much enjoyment there is in your life such lists of personal pleasures can lift you into a positive frame of mind. The effect can be almost instantaneous. It is simply a new way of looking, as one of Dostoyevsky's characters says in *The Possessed,* "Man is unhappy because he doesn't know he's happy. It's only that. That's all! If anyone finds out he'll become happy at once, that minute."

I have found making positive lists so rewarding that I frequently list the pleasures of the day in my diary before I retire. I notice that even difficult days are full of pleasures. Making my daily delights tangible by writing them down has changed the way I see myself and my life. Lists seem to increase my own capacity for happiness. Instead of judging myself for what I haven't done, I seem to appreciate myself more by focusing on the pleasure I do give myself. I become aware of the joy in the texture of my daily life.

Sustaining Inner Balance

Such positive lists and other forms of intentional self-affirming writing help diarists sustain inner psychological balance. One writer says that the diary also shows her when she needs to use such techniques to take active hold of her thinking, "If I write about heavy stuff for a few days the question pops in—'Where is your laughing self?' Don't forget the absurd. . . . I know when the music gets flat." From the mirror of the diary writers can see when old, negative mental habits are taking over, and they need to evoke humor, perspective, and creative thinking for themselves. Rather than giving power to the voice that blames, "What a jerk" when they make a mistake, they intentionally listen while writing for the more positive inner voices that say, "Now what can be learned from this?" or "That was a mistake and it's past" or "That was unfortunate, but what are the positive aspects of this situation?"

At first the ability to take hold of and guide your thinking and writing in positive ways may be like discovering a muscle you never knew was there. People who have always been controlled by their moods are surprised when they discover that they can voluntarily affect them through redirecting their attention. However, through exercise in the diary the ability becomes stronger and your capacity to sustain happiness greater.

One technique for achieving inner balance, which can have almost instantaneous results, depends upon what would be called "principle of opposites." It means that inherent in every thought is its opposite. For example, inherent in despair is hope, inherent in sorrow is joy. It's a difficult concept for the Western mind to accept. However, you can discover the principle of opposites within yourself by searching within any negative mood for its opposite.

One diarist used this principle of opposites to help transform her negative beliefs about herself into positive beliefs. Feeling very depressed she made a list of her underlying assumptions:

> I believe I will never have a good relationship with
>   a man
> I believe I'm a loser
> I believe that I will be poor and wretched, and old
> I believe that I can't change these things

Once she had committed these negative thoughts to paper they seemed to lose their grip on her. In fact, her mind began to search for the underside of these beliefs and she came up with:

> I believe that I choose whether I will have a good
>   relationship
> I believe that I am loved
> I believe that I am worthy of success
> I believe that I will be secure and mature
> I believe that I control my destiny

Her depression contained its own antidote. Simply by allowing the opposite of her self-abasing thoughts to surface she was able to reaffirm her self-worth.

Marion Milner used the principle of opposites to cure herself of oversimplified thinking, wherein things are all "good" or all "bad," as if she were a soap opera character rather than an adult in a complex world. Milner kept an "opposites" notebook in which she noticed this oversimplified thinking in her attitude toward people:

> I was always wanting people to be either all lovable or all hateful. When I was getting on well with someone, everything they said was right and nothing was too good for them. Then, if some chance altered the emotional situation between us, they would become hateful to me, I would see all their weak points, and fail to remember that they had ever had any good ones at all. And it was only by recognizing my thought as thought that I could remember to look deliberately for the reverse side and remember to express it, so that I could widen my attention enough to view the irreconcilable opposites both together.

By searching for the reverse side of her negative thoughts she was able to sustain the inner equilibrium that is a prerequisite of happiness.

Because diarists have a record of the self through time, they begin to recognize their extreme ups and downs as only partial dimensions of themselves. One diarist reflects:

> I used to think I was my emotions at any moment. If I were depressed, it seemed I would always be depressed. My moods swung from Everest to the Grand Canyon in manic-depressive cycles. I have found that keeping the diary has given me a needed sense of perspective. When I get depressed now, there is a part of me that stays buoyed, and that buoyed part I sense as my center, as my continuous ongoing self through time.

This diarist now identifies her happiness with the fully conscious, buoyed self at the center of her being, instead of with just her extremely elevated moods. Happiness has become a total view of life that includes the rough places as well as the smooth. It lies in the diarist's ability and confidence that she can guide and balance her own perceptions, reactions, and moods, no matter what happens.

Choosing Self-Nourishment

Any of the diary devices can be used to direct your attention in positive ways. You can find pleasure in writing portraits of those you love or those who delight you, or you can experience the satisfaction of expressing your loving feelings toward them in an unsent letter. Refining such diary entries can become a way to communicate your affection for another in the form of a written gift.

You can also use guided imagery in the diary to please and nourish yourself. Or free-intuitive writing may offer gifts of delight from the subconscious. Milner discovered images in her free-intuitive writing that brought her joy: "a woman's breasts—a bird's breast, all soft and smooth feathers—the little white underneath parts of a dormouse."

You can also write dialogues that will put you in touch with the positive aspects of your own being. One diarist, for example, used dialogue to make active contact with the feeling of joy within her. Whenever she felt joyful she experienced a gnawing fear that the feeling would not last. She had learned to fly in her spirit but not how to sustain her flight, and she was never sure that she could remember how to achieve that elevation of joy again. With an attitude of experimentation she decided to learn about her own feeling of joy by having a dialogue with it in her diary:

> **Me**
> I'm afraid of losing you, Joy. And when you leave, it's like being abandoned by a lover. I feel worse in your absence than before you had visited.
> **Joy**
> I am inexhaustible. I can stay with you always, even in pain. I'm not a lover who leaves. I'm more like the sun, a great ball of light. Sometimes I'm hidden, but then I'm simply in a closet in your mind. I'm always here for you to reach.
> **Me**
> Why do I begin to be afraid now?

Joy
Because of old patterns. Because of guilt. Because you always want to put me into an object or a person or a goal.

Me
Exactly, so what can I do?

Joy
Relax, stay in the now.

Me
What about the guilt?

Joy
There you have to be active. Laugh it away or fight it off.

Me
But it will return. There will always be problems.

Joy
Yes, and there will always be solutions. Happiness is an active process.

Me
You know, you are gorgeous, Joy. You glow, you sparkle, when you smile light shoots from your mouth. I love you.

Joy
And I won't leave you. I won't ever leave you.

And yet, Joy did seem to leave the diarist. Many months passed and she found herself depressed again after all, and unable to feel joyful. But she recalled once having dialogued with Joy, and she knew she could do so again. Joy became her friend and companion in the diary, as in this example:

Me
Where is Joy?

Joy
I'm here, waiting.

Me
I want you.

Joy
You're not ready.

168 THE NEW DIARY

Me
I want you.
Joy
Look for me in the sky. Hear me in all the sounds of life
around you. Feel me in the future. Feel me in your
body. Move to me. Look for me and you will find me.

Within the diary the search is the goal, and the desire for
happiness is the major requisite for discovering it and rediscovering it, again and again. Joy is to be found in the process
of living, in an active receptivity to the moment, in the entire
fabric of your life as you record it in the diary.

George Sand wrote in her diary near the end of her
tumultuous life: "In striving for truth and happiness, we
should not allow ourselves to regard these two goals of human
effort as illusions. When we struggle for truth we find a part of
it. When we dream of happiness it is already ours." Or as Joy
told the diarist who was able to make it her companion:
"Look for me and you will find me."

8 | Dream Work

Diaries are a bridge between dreams and the waking life, a space of your own creation where the subconscious and the conscious mind meet and inform each other. Through the diary the dreaming self can deliver its messages to the waking self. And through the diary you can walk awake into your dreams—to observe, learn, and bring back images, insights, and creative ideas that will enrich your life.

Nearly all schools of psychotherapy emphasize the importance of understanding and working with dreams for mental health and self-knowledge. Dreams may indicate your destiny by introducing you to unrecognized aspects of yourself or to a figure who embodies the person you are becoming. They can provide whatever is presently missing in waking life—love, sex, companionship, adventure, travel, or creative freedom. They can serve as a release from anxiety, pain, or strong emotion that would interfere with daily life.

On a practical level a dream can offer guidance by reminding you of an appointment or a phone call you should make. Dreams can also suggest solutions to personal, business, and scientific dilemmas. Artists have always used inspiration from dreams for creative products—paintings, stories, poems, films, and musical compositions. Dreams can endow ordinary experience with the aura of ritual or mystery and give you a personal mythology that enriches life. And perhaps most importantly, dreams voice the unvarnished truth of your emotions and intuitions and set a standard of personal honesty for who you really are.

In many contemporary, nonindustrialized societies dreams are thought of as guides for daily life, a sacred level of perception that illuminates, and is part of, reality. For example, the Senoi Indians of Malaysia demonstrate this interrelationship of the dream with waking life. In their culture dreams are considered in decision making, shared, discussed, and lived out. Every morning at breakfast Senoi children report their dreams of the previous night. They receive from their elders congratulations on heroic or creative dream behavior, advice on how to improve behavior or attitudes in future dreams, and recommendations for social actions or for the creation of songs, dances, inventions, costumes, or projects based on the events in their dreams.

Psychologists, most recently Patricia Garfield in her popular book *Creative Dreaming,* theorize that the Senoi's remarkably cooperative and creative culture—which appears to be free of war, psychosis, and neurosis—owes its emotional maturity to the active integration of dream material into daily life. Our culture does not encourage such an integration of dreams into waking life, so it is up to the individual to make a personal synthesis. In writing a diary you immediately transform the dream into a creative product, as the Senoi do, and advise yourself on its practical application.

Working with dreams in a journal is a perfect opportunity to practice the art of sorting and understanding these images from your unconscious. However, dream work does not result in a verifiably correct interpretation of a dream, since there is no such thing. Instead dream work gives you access to important creative, curative, and renewing aspects of the self that might otherwise go unrecognized.

Integrating Night Dreams into Daily Life

Generally, dreams in and of themselves are neither useful nor interesting for very long. It is the interrelationship between your dreams and your life that gives meaning to both. And it is this interrelationship that a natural, chronological diary makes apparent. In the New Diary dreams are kept as part of the spontaneous, ongoing record of personal evolution. Dreams, memories, reflections, and the flow of your life all acquire meaning from their interconnections on the page.

There is a certain advantage to isolating dreams into a separate section, as in the Dream Log of Progoff's INTENSIVE JOURNAL, or into a separate book, as Jungian analysts often recommend. It allows the writer upon rereading to see recurrent dream imagery and themes and experience the inner continuity of the dream life. But rereading a separate dream log cannot show you what you were doing at the time the dreams occurred nor what your conscious feelings and concerns were. The dream and the life are dammed up into separate pools rather than flowing together as a continuous river of the self.

The benefit of isolating dream themes is achieved in the New Diary by titling dreams as you record them alongside waking thoughts, and then listing the dream titles. The added benefit is that the night dream and the day life remain complementary sides of an integrated being. You can tap the emotional energy and intuitive wisdom of a dream when it first delivers its message. In retrospect you can see even more patterns and interconnections, and you can also observe to what extent you successfully listened to and answered your dreams in your waking life.

Recalling Your Dreams

Of course, recalling and recording your dreams is the first step for doing dream work in the diary. All that is really necessary to recall your dreams is the desire. Everyone dreams and everyone can remember his dreams. You can even invoke dreams, nourish them, and regulate their quantity. For example, to stimulate dreaming, before you go to sleep tell yourself: "I want to remember my dreams," or address the dream directly, "Dreaming Self, send me a dream," or use whatever phrase feels comfortable to you. If you invoke dreams for three nights in a row, generally you will recall a dream by the fourth night. I repeat my phrase three times just to make sure my dreaming self hears me. Once dream recall begins you can invoke specific kinds of dreams by asking your dreaming self before you fall asleep: "Send me a flying dream" or "Help with this problem, please."

You should record the dreams you recall immediately, without interpretation. If your diary is small and flexible enough, you can keep it under your pillow or on your bed table along with a pen, and record a dream before rising or if you awaken during the night. Tenth- and eleventh-century Japanese diaries were called Pillow Books and used to capture dreams this way.

If the diary you use is too large for immediately recording dreams, you can keep a pad and pen beside your bed and transcribe the dreams into the diary when you have time. A cassette tape recorder also works well to capture dreams and parts of dreams that otherwise might elude you. Remember that if you go back to sleep telling yourself you will record the dream later, or if you rise and go about your day without at least jotting down notes, you are likely to lose the dream or many of its important parts.

The very fact that you begin to pay attention to your dreams and to collect them in your diary seems to stimulate your dreaming self to give you interesting, pertinent dreams. Like any other part of the self, if treated as an equal the dreaming self can become very cooperative. And, like any other part of the self, the more you give to your dreaming self of receptivity, interest, appreciation, and stimulation, the more it seems to offer you. You can choose food for your dreams through your life in the films you see, the books you read, and the activities that stimulate your imagination. Creativity, including the creative act of diary writing, seems to nourish the part of the self that is the dreamer.

Some people allow the diary to assist them in dream invocation by writing unsent letters to their dreaming selves. One diarist I know writes statements like: "A good dream, please. A dream to bring me joy!" Or, "I'm drowning in this flood of dreams. I want only one, and make it clear, please." After a few days her dreaming self seems to get the message, and she records the dream in the diary. If the dream did not correspond to the request in her unsent letter she writes another: "That wasn't very good. Too many confused images. Just a soup. I want a clear, gentle dream," or "That was just what I asked for. How about another on the same theme?"

The technique of using the diary to invoke dreams seems to work for her. Her entire diary proceeds as an extended, unstructured, written correspondence between her waking self and her dreaming self. Her waking self talks to her dreaming self through unsent letters and diary dream work, and her dreaming self responds in its dream language. The diarist explains the process in the following reflective passage:

> The diary and my dreams in it record the secret part of my life. In doing that my diary makes me whole—to myself. It is my ever-changing blueprint of the piece of work that I become. Only together—with dream and diary—do I make it possible to produce a product: my life. And the combination of my diary and my dreams does not present all I am; it records my becoming. Then I live that out, one day at a time, and *I* know where and what I am in that way.

During some periods the diary may be almost all dreams, and during others there may be no dreams at all. There are times when you are primarily learning from life and times when you are primarily learning from dreams. From experience with the diary you will recognize the inner wisdom in such fluctuations and will come to appreciate them. Although you can regulate the quantity of your dreams, my feeling is that one shouldn't tamper with the natural flow of dreams unless there is good reason to do so. The only time to interfere with the natural cycles of dreams and dreamlessness is when you feel too uncomfortable in one of the extremes. If you are thirsting in a desert of dreamlessness or drowning in a flood of dreams, you may wish to use the power of dream invocation to open or close the dam.

Recognizing Special Dreams

Since dreams are like radio transmissions that are always being emitted, you can tune in to them through the diary at will, when you have time. You needn't become obsessed with recalling and recording every single dream. It's one thing if you're a dream researcher but another if you're a diarist who wants to live simultaneously on many levels of experience. However, it's always a good idea to record any particularly startling dreams or any that impel you to remember them. There are also certain kinds of dreams that researchers believe may have special significance in the development of a more aware and integrated self.

The following list of special kinds of dreams is synthesized primarily from *Dreams and the Growth of the Personality* by Ernest Rossi, a contemporary American dream theorist. A dream falling into any of these categories deserves work in the diary:

1.   A dream that contains an odd, strange, unique, or intensely idiosyncratic image, such as a forty-foot green giant in Grand Central Station. Unique images are the "growing edge" of your personality.

2.   A dream that contains words, messages, poems, songs, advice, a soliloquy, dialogue, or other form of verbal or printed statement. Dream language represents important material for self-reflection.

Always record dream words in the diary. Speeches
made to yourself within a dream are of utmost
importance; they usually say something
about efforts to cope with an internal process of change.

3. A dream that contains multiple states of being. When
    you are yourself and also outside yourself watching in a
    dream, or when it is the present and also another point
    in time, or when you sense yourself in yourself and also
    in others, or when you have two selves in a dream,
    psychological change is in progress. You are gaining
    perspective.

4. A dream that contains self-reflection: An
    examination of your thoughts, feelings, or behavior
    while you dream. Narrative comments about the dream
    as you are dreaming indicate personality growth.

5. A dream that contains images of spontaneous
    transformations. If you suddenly turn into something
    else or an object in your dream suddenly transforms
    itself, the change may represent a process of inner
    becoming.

6. A dream that contains transcendent imagery.
    Circles, dancing, flying, floating, birth, flying saucers,
    mystical or religious imagery in dreams may be offering
    access to the highest part of yourself.

7. A dream that contains positive figures. A guru, a kind
    teacher, a lovely child in a dream may represent a new,
    positive self that is emerging.

8. A dream that is self-aware. Directing the dream
    as you dream it or having a dream within a dream
    is an indication of psychological talent. It suggests
    that you have developed a sophisticated dream life
    and that you can use it for self-directed change.

Such special dreams and almost all nightmares indicate
opportunity for fruitful dream work in the diary. Theoretically, any dream or even dream fragment is *prima material*,
rich ore from which the gold of insight can be extracted. But
you will probably record many more dreams than you will
work with in the course of keeping a diary. The accumulated

dreams gather meaning from the series to which they belong, and it's not necessary or even desirable to work with all of them.

You will know which ones to work with because they provoke you, either by leaving you with a strong emotion that colors the day or by tantalizing your curiosity. Some dreams even contain messages that tell you to work with them. For example, one diarist reported a complicated action dream involving a crippled boy who was throwing kerosene onto buildings and starting fires. The dream had a sort of epilogue that the diarist recorded:

> Much later (that is, after the action of the foregoing dream) I am talking to an acquaintance who says, "I want to dramatize your dream somehow. I never understood before the depth of your anger."

The diarist took the hint in the epilogue and worked with the dream by dramatizing it in various dialogues. Through these dialogues he found that the young pyromaniac of the dream was indeed his own unrecognized anger.

Dream Work Using the Diary Devices

Dreams are the oil that keeps daily life running smoothly, and the diary devices are a good way to get that precious oil into your life. Since dreams don't come from another realm but from the self, the devices for understanding your dreams are no different from the devices used to explore any other part of life—your feelings, your thoughts, or your experiences. If you have become familiar with the diary devices described in Chapters 4 and 5, you will find it easy to apply them to dream work in the diary.

Description. Descriptions, including short portraits of dream characters, are used to record the dream in the diary. Try to recall as many details as you can about the characters, setting, conversations, and your point of view in the dream. Don't edit or attempt to analyze the dream—simply get down as much as you can remember. Record your feelings within the dream as well as details of the dream "story." If you are copying the dream later from your bedside note pad, try not to alter anything. You may wish to write complete sentences instead of sentence fragments, and you may recall aspects of the dream with more accuracy, but try to refrain from interpreting the dream or making conscious judgments about it. Simply report the dream objectively. Too early an interpretation or elaboration may actually be a resistance to the dream's full message.

Even if you never work further with the dream there is great value in describing it. A diary that includes dreams contains a great deal of undisguised personal truth.

People seem to develop their best and most dynamic writing style in recording dreams. They easily use the first person, present tense, and the active voice. Notice the immediacy of the writing in this typical dream description:

> I am in a supermarket. The faces around me are dead or full of impotent anger and fear. Nervous women scream at their children. Husbands and wives select their groceries with controlled mutual disgust.
>
> I walk out of the electric doors and into a New York subway. Across from me sit three young American girls, returning from a trip to Europe. They are blissful, radiant. "I felt so free," says one of them, "I was fantastically happy. Every moment was exciting."
>
> Suddenly the subway comes to a halt. Panic. Alarms. The tunnels are crowded with people. We must escape. Run, run for the exit!
>
> I escape through one of the free passageways into a ghetto area.

As the writer describes the dream she reexperiences it. Her attention is concentrated on being true to her perceptions and feelings within the dream. It does not occur to her to disguise or impress. Dream descriptions create a personal standard for a direct and natural prose style.

Catharsis. In many cases the description of a dream in the diary is also simultaneously a cathartic process. Writing it down often releases for a second time the terror of a nightmare, the ecstasy of an erotic dream, the sorrow of loss, or the joy of a transcendent or spiritual dream. Diarists often report that they feel logy, sluggish, or shaky until they record an emotional dream. Some report that the dream causes a gnawing anxiety until they have unburdened themselves of its original emotion. Occasionally the emotion experienced in recording a dream differs from the emotion felt in the dream, because the insight the dream offers or its vision of an evolving self touches off a new level of awareness.

Catharsis or inner transformation may occur unexpectedly while one describes the dream in the diary. For example, one young man who felt great joy in a dream was moved to tears when he recorded it:

> I enter a large, spacious apartment with homemade staircases running up to sleeping lofts covered by heavy curtains. Everyone seems very trusting here, as if there is nothing really to steal. Now more and more people are coming in from other rooms, going about their lives, not taking great notice of me, but not unfriendly, either. Guitar music filters down from above, sad and beautiful. I look up to see a young black man perched in a rafter, playing to himself. Yet his music seems a gift to everyone; his way of saying that he is there, and that he feels.
>
> Everyone flops down for a rest together. I presume to join them, and no one objects. Our bodies all touch and I feel warm and secure, though I know no one. A young girl enters the room . . . I look closely at her face and it's fine, sensitive and clear through the eyes. She searches with her body for a comfortable place, and she leans against me. It's almost more than I can hope for. . . . She relaxes against my leg, and it's the warmest most wonderful feeling imaginable. I get an erection. It's as if my appreciation and attraction took on flesh.

> When it's time to leave and we are all getting up,
> she says to no one in particular, "But I think there are a
> lot of other things I've yet to experience." And she
> looks at me with a frank, unexaggerated warmth in her
> eyes. "Excuse me for that," I say to her, referring to my
> erection. "Don't ever apologize for that," she whispers
> to me as she brushes against my face.
> I feel so happy I could burst.
> As I type this page, I suddenly find myself crying.

The diarist underwent an inner transformation in this dream of inner harmony. It gave him a vision of all the parts of himself dwelling in peace and cooperation together. It allowed him to feel a spontaneous, tender sexuality that he was seeking. The catharsis he experienced in recording the dream released the frustration and rigidity that had kept him from achieving such feelings of spontaneity and harmony in his life. No analysis of the dream or dream work would have been quite so valuable as this natural emotional response.

If he had been a Senoi Indian child, his parents would have encouraged him to continue his sexual response through to orgasm in future dreams. They might have pointed out that the sensitive young girl was actually an emerging part of himself, and that the sexuality in the dream embodied fusion with that self. If he decided to work with the dream for greater intellectual understanding he might have written dialogues with the apartment, the black musician, the young girl and other members of the household. But no dream work could have been more valuable than the original catharsis.

Reflection. After recording a dream and allowing yourself to feel its imagery, you may immediately begin to understand its relevance to your life and concerns. In many cases simply reflecting upon a dream is sufficient to tap some of its wisdom. For example, one diarist recorded:

> Bob arrives at the door with a small bulldog. It's snarling
> and snapping and I'm afraid of it. He keeps exclaiming

how cute it is, getting my agreement. I say it's cute even though I think it's horrible.

Immediately following this the diarist reflected:

The dream is as if he is presenting some part of himself or our relationship to me that is ugly, and he wants acceptance for it. I see the unacceptable and dangerous aspects for what they are, yet lie to myself and say they are alright.

This reflective passage gave the writer the immediate insight that she had been pretending to herself about aspects of her relationship to this man. The use of other devices might open up deeper levels of significance in the dream. And further reflection after additional dream work would help the diarist absorb and integrate any other insights. It is also frequently the case that you will find previously unseen meanings in a dream if you reflect upon it days, weeks, even years after recording it.

Free-Intuitive Writing. Free association is the classical psychoanalytic method of discovering the underlying meaning of a dream. You can free associate through free-intuitive writing whether or not you know anything about Freudian dream interpretation. No one can really tell you what your dreams mean but you. A cup in a dream may be a classical female sexual symbol, but for you it might be a symbol of identity, nourishment, or something else entirely. Dream imagery is highly individualistic and personal. Only you can provide the context for the dream's meaning.

Free associating on a dream image is actually the opposite of interpreting it. You put aside the rational mind entirely. Here is an example of spontaneous free association on a dream image from one woman's diary:

Dream: I dreamt that I found Michael as a mummy in a casket in a drawer. He had had himself put to sleep for 50¢. I felt overcome with guilt. Then I could see that he was breathing faintly and slowly.

Free association: How does it feel to be that
mummy? Like a foetus. Ugly, resting, placid, frozen, monster, peace, no feeling, preserved
      mummy, warm mommy, breasts big, child
      still, ancient, cold, back to life monster
bandages unwrap
      I am the monster cocoon—the monster hiding
away baby

After the free-intuitive writing the diarist reflected on it:

The mummy seems to have contradictory
connotations, one of a monster hiding away
and two of a baby in its cocoon. It's a frozen
place without feeling, yet there is a baby
protected in it.

The free-intuitive writing represented the dreamer's state
of being at that moment in her life, when she had withdrawn
from a painful relationship and felt both unattractive and
unresponsive. But the free association also told her that she
was healing herself during that time. She was preparing to give
birth to a new self. The diarist probably could not have
reached the depth of meaning inherent in the dream image
through trying to analyze it intellectually. But by allowing the
dream to speak its own language of fragmented imagery and
feeling she was able to receive its message.

Guided Imagery. Guided imagery has several important
uses in dream work. Through guided imagery you can continue
a dream that was interrupted or remains unfinished in your
mind, and which seems to beg for completion. You simply
relax, close your eyes, breathe deeply and regularly, and imaginatively enter the dream again. Allow yourself to see the
dream images as you saw them when asleep, and then simply
watch the dream proceed and hear whatever the dream characters have to say. Some people will have vivid visual perceptions, others will not. It doesn't matter as long as you record

the waking dream spontaneously, without consciously judging or censoring it.

Of course, if you are using this device to continue a terrible nightmare, you will probably want to take a more active part in guiding its outcome. Guided imagery allows you to take control, to transform nightmares into opportunities for inner heroism, positive adventure, and creative ingenuity. For example, if you had awakened from being chased by a three-headed dream monster, rather than imagining the monster chasing, capturing, and torturing you, you could reimagine the dream as a *second chance.* In the guided imagery of a waking dream you could visualize yourself being chased, then turning and confronting the monster. You could single-handedly conquer and subdue him. Or, as the Senoi instruct their children to do while dreaming, you could call in friends and allies to help you defeat him and finally demand that he give you a gift. Or you could transform the monster into a friendly beast who would become your companion and protector.

These are especially valuable techniques to teach children who are plagued by nightmares. Through rewriting nightmares in their diaries children can learn to conquer their inner fears. But the benefits for anyone of imaginatively rewriting nightmares are immediate and far-reaching. A frightening nightmare can cast a pall over your emotions so that you feel insecure and troubled during the day. But reworking the dream as a second chance can help you feel better immediately and add to your memory a positive rather than a negative experience. In addition, imaginatively recasting your role in a nightmare in a positive light can create a strong self-image at a deep level. If you can stand up to the ghouls in your nightmares, you can stand up to the fears in your life.

One man I worked with had not remembered any of his dreams since childhood. At that time he had a recurrent nightmare that he was lost at sea and someone in a speedboat was trying to run him down. Through guided imagery the diarist visualized himself diving underwater, grabbing the side of the boat, pulling the driver out with a meat hook, scrambling into the speedboat himself, and taking off in full control. As a result of writing this violent little drama he was thrilled. He had conquered a fear he had not been able to face for thirty years. And the confidence he gained seemed to carry over into his life. He began to recall current dreams and reported that he felt more self-assured in his business dealings and social life.

Using guided imagery in the diary can also function as a form of *dream rehearsal* to prepare you to take a more active, positive role in future dreams. Improving your dream behavior in writing while awake may well be preparation for the same process while dreaming. Through guided imagery you may be able to teach yourself, as the Senoi teach their children, how to alter the outcome of a dream during the dream. First you develop a sense of what dream control feels like while awake in guided imagery, and then you make an effort to do the same thing in sleeping dreams. You become less the helpless victim and more the director of your own dream content.

On the other hand, you cannot manipulate the subconscious to grow or change in ways for which it is unprepared. Simply rewriting all your dreams with a positive outcome will not necessarily result in psychological change. The subconscious will respond to gradual and progressive guidance but not to forceful manipulation. For example, a student of mine recorded the following dream about her sister:

> My sister came to the door and wanted me to give her my coat. I closed the door on her. Then I felt sorry, opened the door again, but she was gone.

The dream made the diarist very sad the next day. Even though it was only a dream, she felt guilty about closing the door on her sister. She rewrote the dream using guided imagery:

> My sister came to the door and wanted me to give her my coat. I hugged her and asked her to come in. She sat

down on my couch and I gave her a cup of tea. I told her
I didn't want to give her my coat, but I had bought her a
present. It was a warm red coat. She put it on and
thanked me.

After writing this the diarist reflected, "I didn't like my
behavior in the first dream, but I don't feel entirely comfortable
with the outcome of the guided imagery either. I find it hard to
give to my sister. Somehow I don't want to give to her at all."
The guided imagery didn't work for the diarist. It didn't ring
true. It could not "cure" her of selfishness toward her sister, but
the "failure" of the guided imagery did begin a process of
self-recognition. Even when the results seem incomplete, dream
work in the diary brings a measure of self-awareness.

Dreams can also be guided and understood by transforming them into poems. Many poets find inspiration in their
dreams. In recording the dream in the journal the diarist is
struck by the symbolic sense of the dream or the elegance of
its images, so that he or she wants to give it further form in
poetry. Often writing the poem clarifies the dream's meaning.
Sometimes one poem may be formed by combining accumulated images that have appeared in many different dreams.

Occasionally several lines or an entire poem will come to
one in a dream. Try to record such unique dreamt expressions
immediately, before making a conscious effort to describe the
setting of the poem. Dreamt verbal expressions can be very
elusive. Samuel Taylor Coleridge awakened from a dream with
the whole of a poem, the famous "Kubla Khan," in his mind.
But he was called away while recording it, and when he
returned he found he had lost all but a vague impression of the
rest of the dream poem.

Dream poems and songs, though not common, are special gifts from the infinite resources of the intuitive self. One
diarist dreamt a Japanese haiku poem during her first trip to
Japan. Her diary entry of the day before expresses some
anxiety and a desire for unity with the culture she was visiting
as an American tourist:

March 26, 1975
On the first night in Japan, I was intensely aware of
cultural differences. I looked through a glass door at
Japanese men and women dining in another room in
semi-darkness. . . . I was silent, at that moment a part of
Japan. But some of our tour group came up behind me
and began talking loudly, asking foolish questions about
what was out there.

Later, I tried, unsuccessfully, to get in touch with
Julie, our friend in Tokyo, who would show us "her"
Japan, and was tense at not having reached her yet.

The following night the diarist dreamt the haiku:

Sometimes, when you come
To these places we wake you,
Loan you loneliness

The dream poem was a gift from her subconscious. It gave
meaning to her anxieties about being cut off from the "real"
Japan and resolved them at the same time by allowing her to
enter Japanese culture through her own intuitive creativity.

Lists. Lists are an extremely valuable device in dream
work. You might find it very illuminating to make a list of the
main themes of the dreams you have had within a recent
period. The list of themes would show you patterns of your
subconscious concerns. Making such a list is especially easy to
do if, when you record your dreams, you give them titles
taken from the dreams' key elements. For example, this is how
I record a dream:

| Slipping Seals |

I am teaching again, but I have seals as students behind
the desks and they keep slipping off their seats.

I draw a box around the title of the dream so that it stands out
on the page and will be easy to spot when I go back to make
my list of dream themes. If I record a longer dream, I simply
take one or two of the most startling or unique images in the
dream to title it:

| Flying for the Sake of Art |

I am attached to a helicopter by a rope and fly round
and round it in a huge arc, suspended high over the
ocean by my momentum. This is part of an art project I
have been helping Lori with.

Later Lori is making out checks and pays me
$1.25 for my participation. I had thought the pay would
be better, but I don't seem to mind because the flying
was so much fun.

Other ways to distinguish dreams from the ongoing diary
might include recording them in a different colored ink or
encircling the entire dream.

Titling the dreams makes it easy to go back at the end of
a week or two and compile a list such as this one:

Leo Has Kittens
Dream of a Newfound Mother
Slipping Seals
Kitten-Baby Dream
Mouse on a Cement Truck

Such lists allow the diarist to see the interrelationships among
the dreams in a way that would be impossible even from
reading through all the dream entries. The list above, for
example, shows interrelated themes of birth and mothering
and animal imagery, which I had not recognized before making
the list. In finding a new "mother" inside myself I was simultaneously giving birth to a new conception of myself, one that
permitted me all the emotions, needs, and natural instincts I
associate with little animals. I would not have recognized or
accepted this inner development without having made the list.

If you list your accumulated dream titles on the last few
pages of your diary, along with the date of your dreams, you
will have compiled an index to your dreams for future reference. Then when you have a dream about a particular image,
such as a deserted church, you can look through your dream
index for other dreams of churches and refer back to those

entries and the surrounding context to see what cumulative individual meaning that dream image has for you.

This system has more advantages than a separate dream journal, for it allows you to see the continuity of dream themes and images without losing the immediate connections between your dreams and waking life.

Maps of Consciousness. Since dreams are primarily visual they may frequently be recorded better through drawing than writing. Transcendent dream images such as flying saucers or dancing stars can be sketched and preserved for future reference and joy, and nightmare images can be transformed as you work with them graphically. Dream monsters can become funny creatures, or a tidal wave, a beautiful scroll design. Maps of consciousness, along with guided imagery, are particularly effective devices for children who suffer from nightmares. Like a miniature Frankenstein doll, a monster seems to lose its terror when the child can draw it smaller and less powerful than herself. Even if she could not find control over inner demons while dreaming, she can find it by drawing them.

Maps of consciousness are also useful in diary dream work because the spatial relationships between elements in a dream are sometimes important. If all the elements of a dream image are seen as parts of yourself, it is significant what elements are above or below the figure you identify with, as is the distance between elements. Stick figures with dialogue balloons (like comic strip characters) suffice to express the visual relationships in a dream.

Several years ago I sketched a dream in which my friends and I were trying to stay afloat on a raft in a rough sea. We were near my house, where brightly lit windows shone against the night sky. A beautiful woman leaned out a window and said, "I'm going to sleep now. I have to get up in the morning to paint my picture" (see page 188).

After sketching this map of consciousness I wrote a reflective entry:

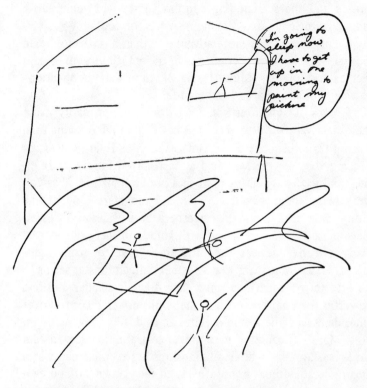

The house I drew looks rather like a face, and the woman is in the right "eye." Maybe that corresponds to my "right brain," the intuitive, creative, image-making part of myself. But in the dream I identified with the figure trying to stay on the raft, and in the drawing that figure is closer to me. I feel like that scared figure, plummeted around wildly by my emotions, almost gasping for air. The woman in the window is far "above me," what I aspire to, illumination, self-discipline, creativity. But I am she if I wish, because I went to sleep, dreamt this dream, and woke up and sketched it.

In this case the dream actually contained a coded message that I should draw a picture of it, the lines, "I have to get up in the morning to paint my picture." In sketching it I was able to see significance in the image language of the dream that would not have been evident without a map of dream consciousness.

Altered Point of View. In dream work as in other phases of diary work it is often desirable to gain perspective either by allowing time to pass or by using altered point of view, which will allow you to see the subject quickly from a new angle. When you are emotionally involved in a dream you may tend to miss its coded message. One way to gain immediate perspective is to record the dream in the third person. Rather than writing "In this dream I gave birth to a cat," you write, "In this dream a woman gave birth to a cat." Or, rather than writing, "I was caught in a storm," you begin, "A man was caught in a storm." The objective point of view, which you achieve by taking it out of the first person, can help you see the dream more clearly. Using an altered point of view encourages you to recognize hidden meanings that an outsider who had distance from the emotional drama might be able to offer.

You can also record your dream from the perspective of any of the characters in it or from the point of view of any of the images. Gestalt psychology, which concentrates on the relationship of various parts of the self to the whole, holds that all the characters and images in a dream are aspects of the dreamer's personality. "You can use *everything* in a dream," according to Frederick Perls, the founder of Gestalt therapy, in *Gestalt Therapy Verbatim.* "If you are pursued by an ogre in a dream, and you *become* the ogre, the nightmare disappears. You re-own the energy that is invested in the demon. Then the power of the ogre is no longer outside, alienated, but inside where you can use it." If you can give a dream lizard or murderer or tidal wave a voice through altered point of view or dialogue it will tell you what you need to know in your daily life.

Dreams themselves offer evidence that you are or can be any of the characters. Men occasionally have dreams in which they are inside the point of view of a woman character, and women also report dreams in which they relate to the world through the point of view of a man. And both men and women may dream from the point of view of an animal. Time, space, and identity are completely fluid in the dream. The release dreams can offer from a habitual perspective can be liberating, allowing you to experience altered point of view.

Generally, though, you are within your own point of view in a dream with your characteristic responses and emotions. I recorded this dream through my habitual perspective:

Dream of a Newfound Mother

I am leaving London and my newfound beautiful mother. She stands in front of her cottage, slender, youthful, and gentle. I am driving off in a sports car that has a long, rubbery handbrake. A Japanese and/or Arab young man is in the passenger seat.

My mother asks where we are going. I say I don't know, everywhere, around the world. The young man laughs.

As we drive away from the cottage, I already miss my newfound mother. The young man says, as we maneuver down a winding road, "If I had found a mother like that I would take the time to live with her and learn about her life."

I see her in the distance, with a female companion, watching us depart.

The fact that the mother was watching me at the end of this dream gave me the clue that it might be valuable to see it from her point of view. I rewrote the dream as if she had dreamt it:

My daughter came to visit me for a day. Now she is off again. She is so busy seeking adventures that she neglects the opportunity to know me better. But I am always here, waiting for her. She will return.

I could also have written the dream from the point of view of the young man in the sports car, my newfound mother's female companion, or from the point of view of that very sexual rubbery handbrake. But, like my persona in the dream, I was not yet ready to come home to myself so completely.

The natural resistances that allow a diarist to proceed only at her own pace toward self-recognition were at work. It was enough for me to feel, through entering the point of view of my newfound mother, that she was really a part of me that I had been neglecting. From my point of view in the dream I felt guilty, though set on my course of adventure with the "male" side of myself. But from the point of view of the newfound mother I was given a sense of hope and expectation that I would eventually find unity with the qualities of inner peace and feminine strength she embodied.

The fact that I had entered into her point of view through dream work was actually one way to get to know her, as the adventurous young man in my dream had advised. When later I reviewed my index of dreams for other idealized mother figures, I saw that the beautiful woman of this dream had been appearing to me for years—in different settings but always centered in her own peaceful home, beckoning me gently. The woman who was saying goodnight in the map of consciousness, for example, was one of her prototypes. Had I been aware of the device of altered point of view at that time, it would have been a valuable way to identify with her more closely.

Reviewing previous dream images of the same figure made me realize that she had always been with me and always would be, if only I would turn to her. I decided to make her one of the primary audiences in my diary. I felt her presence as I wrote, and I began to ask her advice in dialogues. In this mysterious way figures of inner wisdom rise from the subconscious and begin to take an active part in the diary. In this case altered point of view was only the beginning of other kinds of diary work. By letting me transcend the dullness of my habitual perspective it allowed me to expand my sense of identity.

Dialogue. Gestalt psychologist Frederick Perls's most important contribution to the understanding of dreams was his use of dialogues that permit each part of a dream, each of the characters or images, to speak to the dreamer. Through altered point of view you can enter the perspective of any dream figure and experience that figure as part of you. Similarly, in the dialogue you enter the point of view of any part of the dream and you are also able to ask questions of the dream figure.

Writing dialogues with dream characters or images is a good way to open the messages enveloped in your dreams. For example, one diarist recorded the following dream, which she did not understand:

> I am part of a group of prehuman creatures. We stand erect most of the time, but we are lizardlike, dark-skinned and scaly. Our fingers and toes are long and pointed, our bodies thin and snaky. We have migrated to a place, the delta. When we see the mud we rush for it. It is our destination. We spread out on the mud, staking out territory. We are claiming it as ours and will protect it from our enemies.

She followed the description of the dream with a dialogue, hoping to gain some insight into its images:

Me
Creatures, who are you?
Creatures
We are the beginning. We are your primal instincts.
Me
Why am I aware of you at this time?
Creatures
Because you need to know that you are instinctually self-protective. Underneath you are like all animals—self-defensive.
Me
You give me the creeps.

Creatures
Let us develop and we will stand erect. Let us develop
and we won't appear so ugly.
Me
You aren't vicious in your behavior.
Creatures
No, but we will defend what we feel is ours. We are
returning to our source, and you, too, are returning to
your inner resources.

Dialoguing with the creatures allowed the writer to hear something she needed to know at that point in her life—that she
had the inner resources to take care of herself, to survive by
her own instincts.

It is especially helpful to write diary dialogues with any
frightening figures or images in dreams. The result is generally
a story of Beauty and the Beast. What seems terrifying in the
dream turns out to be a powerful friend in disguise, once you
can get him to tell his story. For example, I recorded this
frightening dream in my diary:

Fist through the Door

I am shutting the front door of my house, which is held
locked only by the chain. Suddenly a huge fist crashes
through the opening and hits me hard, right between my
eyes. I awaken from the shock with an intense pain in
the center of my forehead.

The impact of the dream was so great that it demanded dream
work. I might have continued the dream through guided imagery but my intuition suggested a dialogue:

Me
Fist, what are you?
The Fist
I am power, your own personal power. You won't admit
me, so I'm banging down the door to get to you.
Me
But you hurt me.

The Fist
To wake you up. I hit you right between the eyes, right
where your third eye is—that's where your power is.

Without extending the dialogue further I recognized that
this dream fit into a cycle of dreams I had been recording in
my diary since its inception. By referring to my dream index I
could relate the dream to those I had had of looking in a
mirror, seeing a third eye in the middle of my forehead, and
being so embarrassed by it that I wouldn't leave the house. I
had also had dreams of furry little creatures who wanted my
love but who repelled me, because they had only one eye. I
had these dreams long before I knew that the "third eye" has a
meaning of inner vision in Eastern philosophy and art.

But now, by relating this dream of the fist in my
forehead to those in the past about my third eye, I could see it
suggested that I was still fearful of the strangeness of my
powers of inner vision, my intuition. The dream also showed
me that I could no longer simply disregard my "third eye" by
locking myself up in my house. The door between me and the
world was now being forced open. The dream that seemed to
be a nightmare actually contained a message about my psychological and spiritual growth.

Sometimes you might wish to allow all the dream's
images and characters to have their say in an open dream-
forum. In this entry the diarist first used description to record
the dream and then gave all the elements in the dream a
chance to speak:

Caught Naked

I am riding on the front of a cart, and like a child, I
propel it with my legs. I have dropped a sweater off at
the cleaners and now I have a sheet wrapped around my
nakedness. The rest of my clothes are in the back of the
cart.

I stop on a residential street, in someone's
driveway, in front of the garage. I begin to put on my

clothes. A chubby little girl sees me and says, "What are you doing?" "Haven't you ever been caught naked?" I ask. She laughs.

Her father enters the back door to their house. The right side of his face is burnt scar tissue.

Burnt scar tissue on father's face—"I am the past, the pain from which you may release yourself."

Chubby little girl—"I am like you, but not yet free. You can teach me."

The cart—"I am your hesitancy. Your lack of confidence. You move, but I keep you close to the ground."

My nakedness—"I am the process of freedom you are engaged in. You are beginning to accept yourself as you really are." *

The sweater at the cleaners—"I am your old image of yourself which you have left behind."

The driveway—"I am the place where you stop. You become afraid and retreat into the past again."

This dream work reflected a psychological transition at that point in the diarist's life. When she allowed all its parts to speak, the cumulative message of the dream seemed to be saying that she was on the right path. Her feelings of vulnerability or "nakedness" symbolized a growing freedom, which her painful memories of the past and "old clothes" or habits were keeping her from totally enjoying. The dream offered the diarist the comfort of self-understanding and kept her company on her journey toward inner liberation.

Using the dialogue device to work with this dream had quite a different effect than interpreting it would have had. If the diarist had made a Freudian interpretation of the nakedness in the dream, she might have assumed it was a symbol of sexual fear. But the dialogue put the writer inside the movement and energy of the dream and gave her a fresh perspective. It imposed nothing on the dream; instead it allowed the dream to unfold its own meaning.

As in all work with diary devices, sometimes one device will satisfy a need that another cannot, and sometimes one device will give access to the significance of a dream while another will not. You may have to try many until you find one that works. But the object is not to come to a "final understanding" of a dream, because that understanding is always changing and growing with you. A dream preserves its power by preserving its mystery. If you can enter the mystery of the dream on its own terms, you can share its power. But if you try to reduce it to a code that tells you what the images are supposed to mean, you are likely to distance yourself from the dream's power by intellectualization.

Dreams are messages from your inner wisdom giving cryptic answers for your life. But dreams do not give final answers. A single dream may work on many levels simultaneously and offer very different insights in different contexts. The diary devices are simply a way of crossing the bridge into the subconscious, of asking the right questions and listening while your dreams deliver messages in their own mysterious way.

9 | Eroticism

Inside the diary as in life, sex is part of the discovery of self. Outside in the society, sex has been isolated and sensationalized. Pornography and commercialism distance sex from the individual just as repression buries it. Both sensationalism and repression take eroticism out of the context of an individual life. But the inclusive method of the diary offers an alternative—the opportunity to become intimate with sexuality as an integral part of your total personality.

We have been so bombarded by cultural messages of what sexuality should be—from the media, advertising, pornography, religious education, family attitudes, and the pressures of fashion—that few people really know themselves sexually. We are only beginning to recognize the extent to which sexuality evolves and changes, along with the rest of the personality, throughout a lifetime. Each of us needs to discover what pleases or displeases us, what frightens or intrigues us, what we want to give and what we want to receive in a sexual relationship, and this self-knowledge is only in part a physical exploration. It is also a matter of reflection, imaginative experimentation, and careful observation of feelings and responses. For becoming familiar with sensuality and sexuality the diary provides a safe and private place.

Perhaps because of the tradition of secrecy and silence on both subjects, diaries and sexuality have become linked in the popular imagination. Personal diaries have received notoriety in court cases as evidence of marital infidelity, and a number of fictional pornographic diaries have been published. But in general there is much less sexual "confession" or revelation in diaries than the public might expect. People are often afraid—in their journals as well as in themselves—to reflect upon their sexuality. Ira Progoff's INTENSIVE JOURNAL, for example, contains no specific section for exploring sexuality. Though you could explore sensuality in the section called "Dialogue with the Body," to do so would limit eroticism to a purely physical experience rather than an integral part of your life energy, mixed with and heightened by emotions and complex psychological patterns.

Many diarists tell me they would like to explore sensuality in their books but are fearful their spouses or other family members might read them. Diarists who have these fears might consider locking their diaries securely in a cash box or writing about their sexuality on loose sheets of paper that they could later burn. The benefits of exploring the sensual self in writing are great, even though admitting such reflections to yourself on paper may initially seem frightening.

Some writers of natural diaries practice deliberate vagueness, or a personal form of obscurantism, when they write about sexuality. They may use fictional names or initials for the people involved in a sexual encounter or write erotic sections in code or shorthand. Frequently diarists record actual sexual experiences using altered point of view—"she" or "he" instead of "I"—as if the sexual encounter had happened to a fictional character. Some diarists even have a separate persona for their sexual fantasies. One woman I know has projected her sexuality onto a fictional character named "Forbidden Fuschia." Another has named her character "Trouble." A reader of these diaries would probably be unable to distinguish between what is fantasy or embellishment and what is actual experience. Diarists sometimes blame themselves for not being able to write about their sexuality in a straightforward manner, but the compromises they make with themselves, the little tricks and disguises they develop at least allow them to write about it.

Even when diarists decide they want to write about sexuality in a totally open, original way they may encounter difficulties. They have to create their own language for eroticism, since most terms used to named sexual parts or positions are depersonalizing, either because they are too clinical or because they are slang. Finding a personal erotic language is especially a problem for women, since until very recently women played almost no role in creating slang vocabulary. Sexual slang has generally evolved from a male perspective, colored with anger or fear of women's bodies. For many diarists it may be necessary to go through stages of awkward, imitative, or artificial writing before discovering a natural voice for eroticism.

In a women's writing class I taught at UCLA, I asked the students to try erotic writing in their private journals and to share what they wished of it. To my surprise, the same students who had written powerfully and authentically about their personal experiences suddenly assumed a common pornographic voice that seemed male rather than female when they tried to write about their sexuality. The solution for establishing an intimate tone and for asserting their eroticism was found through writing their individual sexual histories in their journals. Through this process they began to learn their unique sexual identities.

Then as they learned to write freely and personally about sexuality they experienced a creative liberation in other areas of life. One diarist cured herself of a serious writing block that had prevented her from completing any of the numerous short stories she had begun. She discovered in herself a fully developed and sophisticated fantasy life that, when written out in the diary, seemed to free her to use creatively the energy that had previously gone into repressing her fantasies.

Another diarist said that giving herself permission to write about her sexuality helped her with a particular sexual problem. She found that she blocked her creative energy and her sexual energy in the same way. When she was writing, when the ideas were rushing through her and she felt the high excitement of inspiration, she would stop and get something to eat, or masturbate the energy away, or make a phone call. She similarly curtailed her own sexual intensity before it could naturally peak and ebb. She found that learning to sustain the intensity of her erotic writing helped her accept intensity in a sexual relationship. My research has given me the opportunity to read many private diaries, and I have often seen such interrelationships between eroticism and other aspects of the writer's personality.

Sensuality evolves along with, is influenced by, and influences all other parts of the self. Learning about your sexuality can eventually help you balance and integrate it with other aspects of your life. And the more you know about your own sexuality, the more likely you are to find sexual satisfaction. Most erotic material in diaries seems to fall into five categories: sexual memories, complaints, celebrated experiences, erotic dreams and fantasies, and behavioral rehearsals for sexual encounters.

Memories

Since sexuality is a continuum that begins with infancy, one way to free yourself in the present is to understand and accept your past sexuality. Over the years as you keep a journal, you may find yourself spontaneously recalling, recording, and reflecting upon sexual memories. Traumatic or guilty memories can be released and worked through in the privacy of the diary. Repressed memories, which may be influencing present feelings and responses, can surface and be worked through as you are ready to understand and accept each one.

In addition to permitting this spontaneous evocation of memories, you may find it useful to write the stepping-stones of your sexuality, a list of the major events of your personal sexual history. Like all lists that give an overview of some aspect of your life, this one changes each time you write it, depending upon your current state of mind and stage of personal growth. Because you are likely to bring to light formerly hidden personal patterns as you make such an outline of your sexual development, it is valuable to record any insights that come to you in the process and then reflect on them. You may wish to explore certain items on the list in more depth, and you can either do so immediately or come back to it later, when you have the time and inclination.

To list the stepping-stones of your sexual history, begin by sorting through your memory, asking yourself generally about your childhood sexual fantasies, experiences with masturbation, what happened to you sexually during adolescence, how your sexuality evolved from there, what significant changes your fantasy life or desires underwent, and what you would like to achieve in the future to fulfill your individual sexuality. These general areas and the list of questions that follows may lead you to recall and work through your sexual memories.

> Can you recall any childhood sexual dreams or
> fantasies? What were they? (Try not to limit
> your imagination by social taboos and condition-
> ing.) Did you fantasize or dream about cartoon
> characters? Machines? Strange people? Odd
> situations?
> Try to recall your feelings about masturbation when
> you were a child. Describe your feelings as you
> discovered your own body. Did you use a pillow,
> a toy animal, water, a certain position?
> If you did not masturbate as a child, why do you think
> you did not? Were you ever caught and punished
> for touching yourself?

Did you stop masturbating at a certain age? Can you
   recall why?

What did your parents tell you about sex? How did you
   learn about it?

Did you have romantic fantasies about love and sex? A
   knight on a white horse? Movie or TV stars? Your
   wedding?

Did you have any sexually traumatic experiences?

Can you remember sexual feelings toward a parent?

How did you feel about getting your period? Having a
   wet dream? How was this event treated by your
   parents?

How do you feel about your body? Your sexual
   organs?

Recall the first time you had intercourse. What were
   your feelings?

If you are still a virgin, explore your fears and desires.

Do you have any recurrent sexual dreams?

What was your best sexual experience?

What sexual positions give you the most pleasure?

Have you ever "faked" an orgasm? Do certain things
   "turn you off"? Explore your feelings.

How do you feel about having children?

Recall the birth of your first child and your other
   children.

If you have had an abortion, describe the incident
   and your feelings.

Fantasize and describe your ideal sexual situation.

Describe your sexual frustrations.

People tend compulsively to repeat past sexual patterns
or fears until they finally understand their origins. But the
pain of past sexual confusion, mistakes, and negative experiences can be released and cleansed through cathartic writing.
You can also begin to develop ease with your own sexual
language through describing past experiences, and you can free

sexual and creative energy through honestly exploring your early fantasies and feelings.

Complaints

Many diarists first confront their sexuality by writing their complaints in cathartic entries. Sexual frustration and disappointment can make you feel helpless, powerless, and angry. But the ability to describe an aggravating sexual experience is an important step toward recognizing and taking responsibility for your sexual preferences and needs.

Such cathartic descriptions have helped some diarists begin to deal with the need to improve a sexual relationship. For example, one woman wrote the following entry about her eroticism and her marriage. Emotional catharsis interweaves with, and counterpoints, objective reflection:

> *October 26, 1975*
> My body feels as if it has broken into pieces and I am
> beginning to fear that I will fast grow too old to gather it
> back together again. I have lost the throbbing sexuality
> that I used to wear like perfume. This house is sterile;
> sensuality has dried up. I blame my husband (to myself),
> but underneath I know that I fear that it is me. If I want
> sensuality, I should be able to generate it for myself.
> (Wrong. Wrong. Something is wrong with that!)
> Last evening we sat together on our bed reading.
> He pored through his borrowed copy of *Playboy*,
> periodically exclaiming: "My gawd, those are so BIG,
> they're repulsive! Don't you think? Here, look!" I
> scanned the photos and passively agreed, but then felt
> angry. I reminded him that he says the same thing every
> time he has a copy of that magazine. Annoyed, he
> denied that. Why is it that the last time I can remember
> that he (we) made love with any passion—months
> ago—was after an evening he'd spent engrossed in
> *Playboy*. . . .

The headache that had been lingering all day settled in and gripped me like a giant hand squeezing my head and making it smaller. The strands of hair on top of my head stung as if they were being pulled out one by one. I undid the hairpins and let my hair down. He turned on the TV and returned to the bed where he began his mechanical fingering of my thigh and vagina while he debated philosophies out loud with the image on the TV screen. I didn't want more mechanical sex—no kissing, no playing, no caressing, no loving—just c'mon, c'mon, I come; pound, pound, you come. Slam, bam, thank you ma'am. (And how could I ever complain out loud when I am assured of an orgasm with almost every encounter, an orgasm of machine oil.) The giant hand on my head gripped harder and blurred my vision. I told him I was hurting. The *Playboy* lay on the floor where it had been tossed, its pages fallen open.

Instead of midnight sex, we drowsily watched Michael Sarrazin in the late movie and I longed for Michael Sarrazin, young, thick-lipped, piercing blue eyes. I felt bad and guilty that I wasn't longing for my husband. Is it that I only want him when I think I'm going to lose him? And I worry: If I no longer feel like I have lips or breasts or cunt—a body—how will I ever have a passion again? And I am confused. My sexuality has always been defined by my partners. What does that mean now? I have danced delightfully in pits of decadence behind closed doors; I have wandered through the golden, smoky haze of delicious, detached orgasmic nights and days; I have swum naked across the sky, loved forbidden fruit . . . yet, with this man, to whom I'm married, with whom I live, I am shy and silent and embarrassed and undemanding. I blush at the thought of things that, in other times, were easy habits. . . .

I'm afraid soon it will be too late. No, that's not what I fear as much as I'm afraid I will someday walk into a room, stroll down a street, look into a window and suddenly be face-to-face with that being who will drive me to a white heat with just the look of him and I will have to choose *between* fidelity and passion. I don't want that, all that again, not split again and lies and sneaking. I want to be whole, intact, faithful to myself, and to him.

There is a part of me that is peasant, that is whore, that beats with thick, red blood, that is lusciously "evil," that laughs from the gut, that walks above the ground buoyed by that heady aroma. To have one side of myself, it seems necessary to deny the other facets . . . and always to mourn what is missing or broken away. Why can't I ever be whole?

This is authentic, searching erotic writing. It undermines the cultural cliché of woman as the object of man's passion rather than the guide of her own. The difficult admission of dissatisfaction is mixed with reflection, the need to know how much of this dissatisfaction must I take responsibility for? What are my alternatives? Should I be able to generate my own sexuality? Do I just want my husband when I think I may lose him? Will I ever feel passion again? Can I ever be whole—wife and passionate woman together? The writer recognizes that her fantasies of Michael Sarrazin are equivalent to her husband's Playboy bunnies, and that an extramarital affair would not bring the happiness she seeks. As yet she has no answers to the difficult questions she poses.

As an experienced diarist she is willing to place the questions in the diary and wait for the answers. She trusts the process of the diary, knowing that she has done all she can for the moment in being completely honest with herself. She feels she is not ready to discuss these questions with her husband nor to allow him to read of her frustration. Her intent is to discover answers within herself that she will eventually be able to share with him.

Another diarist makes the same important journey to understanding her sexuality outside of marriage. Again the initial entries are in the form of cathartic complaints, which lead to reflection:

At lunch today we made love.
   At a certain point J. decided to come.
   I felt it. I saw him switch.
   It didn't matter where I was.
   He had spent five minutes or so stimulating me
and me stimulating me as well as him—I was on my way.
   And click—it's all over.
   I said—right then—"Why did you do that? You just
decided to come."
   "I felt like it."
   "Why?"
   "Why do you have to bring it up right now?"
   The voice in my head squeezes my chest—pressure
in my head. Don't talk to him now. Don't break the
spell. Don't break his mood—he's relaxed—just came—if
you say this now he'll get mad. He'll probably leave you.
   Why is it still, after all I've learned, so difficult to
say what I feel about sex? Why must I pad the walls,
stuff cotton down my throat about sex?

This entry is a cathartic expression of emotional as well as
sexual frustration. It does not separate sex from the individual's emotions and personal growth. Writing it offers no immediate solution, but it helps the diarist acknowledge as valid her
perceptions and feelings. This is a first step toward eventually
recognizing and finding the sort of sexual relationship she
desires.
   A short time later the same diarist wrote:

I realized the other day that it has been years, perhaps
longer, since I've had sex with someone who I felt really
loved and cared about me. Touched my face and eyes
and breasts for me, because they loved me. In realizing
that I don't have that, I am moving to my own center,
my own needs and awareness of me.

Writing about feelings leads to a deeper respect for them,
which eventually brings about changes in your relationships
and in the sexual partners you seek. A good way to discover

what you want is to concretize what you don't want through writing cathartic complaints.

Celebrating Experiences

Some people find that celebrating a pleasant erotic experience by describing it in specific detail in the diary helps them develop a personal language for their sexuality. They also find pleasure in savoring these descriptions as they write them, and later in rereading them. Like recording other personal joys, including sexual pleasures in the diary reinforces and develops a long-range sense of happiness.

This entry of celebration reflects the individuality of the writer and the uniqueness for her of each night of love:

> We just held each other last night, floating in sensuality. When he touched me, it had a quality of immediacy, comfort, and affection. It seems to me that I have never been touched this way before, in the past men have always touched me with their egos.
>
> We respond to each other's touch with small sounds. We are gentle like children, pure in our sensuality like cats.
>
> I felt vulnerable. I wanted the night to continue forever, the night to last as all nights. The fear of loss mingled with joy of affection and made the experience all the more immediate, all the more precious.

In capturing her memory of the night the diarist feels she can preserve its fleeting preciousness.

From recording important sexual and sensual moments along with other important moments of grief, joy, insight, and hope, diarists begin to recognize the tides and moods of their unique eroticism. They also come to see how sexual perceptions are related to, and influenced by, many other factors in their lives. The diary has the power to integrate sexuality into the total emotional and intellectual harmony of a life.

Erotic Dreams and Fantasies

An erotic dream can be treated in the diary like any other dream—recorded and, if the diarist wishes, worked with to discover its relevance to waking life. The Senoi Indians encourage erotic dreams even if "inappropriate" or incestuous because they recognize erotic dreams as creative fantasies about parts of the dreamer's personality, rather than as signals for behavior. Taking a cue from the Senoi, psychologist Patricia Garfield in her book *Creative Dreaming* suggests that if we allow open sexual expression in dreams, "we may actually be freeing creative thinking on all levels of consciousness." Abraham Maslow, the well-known humanistic psychologist, has also found that sexual dreams are characteristic of women who are self-assured, poised, independent, and generally capable. And another study reported that particularly creative university students tend to have more active and nonconventional erotic dreams than less creative students seem to have. The conclusions show what I have found in countless diaries: Giving permission to imaginary sexuality seems to release creativity in other areas.

Within the diary erotic fantasies are not significantly different from dreams. Erotic fantasies are actually waking dreams, a form of guided imagery. Just as you would work with a dream, a sexual fantasy or obsession can be recorded in the diary and then decoded as if all the parts of the fantasy were parts of yourself. After all, the creator of the fantasy actually generates all its parts.

For example, one middle-aged, married man used the diary to work through an erotic fantasy he did not want to live out. He had a recurrent Lolita fantasy of picking up one of the very young girls whom he often saw hitchhiking on the highway and taking her to a motel with him. He wrote out the fantasy in great detail and afterward felt no need to act it out. Savoring the fantasy as fantasy was the experience he really wanted, and the diary allowed him to have it as such.

Once he had recognized and accepted his fantasy as a creation of his imagination, he decided to write a dialogue treating the images and characters in the fantasy as if they were elements in a dream. He allowed the highway, the motel, and the girl to speak:

The Highway
I am the open road, the life of infinite possibilities. You feel your life closing down on you. I offer escape.
The Motel
I'm impermanency. I'm irresponsibility. I'm the opposite of marriage and obligations.
The Girl
I'm the part of you, you have never admitted. I want to find fusion with you. I am youth and innocence. I'm gentleness and goodness. You want these qualities in yourself.
Me
How can I get you?
The Girl
Begin to allow the little girl in you to come out. You can discover the child in yourself, in your delight in the new and the unusual. Stop judging everything from that old-man point of view. You don't have to prove your manhood in every situation, you can be soft like me sometimes.

In this instance the sexual fantasy was an embodiment of internal emotional needs, rather than a cue for future behavior. The parts of the fantasy were parts of one person calling out for integration.

By recording and working with erotic fantasies in the diary—along with dreams, reflections, events, relationships, feelings, and the other aspects of a life—you come to see how they are all interrelated. Sexual fantasies cannot be understood apart from the larger context of a life; they are influenced by activities you are engaged in, what you are reading, thinking, feeling, or studying. Your sensuality is colored by many other internal choices, attitudes, and interests.

Behavioral Rehearsals

If you are timid about communicating your sexual preferences to a partner, unclear about your feelings in a sexual relationship, or displeased with your fantasy life, diary work may help influence or solve the problem. The diary is a perfect place to practice articulating sexual desires. For example, one man wrote an imaginary dialogue with his wife, trying to find a language that would communicate his sexual preferences without making them sound like demands or complaints. One woman wrote an unsent letter to her lover to see if she could express her desires. She began reflectively:

> The real problem is that I don't know how to express my desires so that they can be fulfilled. And I'm afraid of hurting his ego.
>
> Let me imagine that he were different, that he really wanted to know, and that I could explain how I'd like him to make love to me.
>
> Well, slowly, for one thing and with the assurance that I won't be left hanging, even if it takes a long time. Yes that's it—with enough time to build up slowly and gently. I'd like you to stimulate me gently and enter when I tell you I'm ready.
>
> There, that wasn't so bad. He wouldn't object if I told him that.

In the process of writing the diarist recognized that a large part of her fear of her lover's reaction was her own fear of actively admitting her sexual desires to herself. Rehearsing in the diary relaxed her anxiety about speaking to her lover and gave her the words she needed.

Another woman, who felt a lack of intimacy with her lover and was unclear about her own feelings, decided to write in her diary about one of their encounters. She wrote first from her own point of view and then from his, using altered point of view:

Me
My hands are cold because I am nervous. He observes that. He takes my hand and places it at his groin. I fear my hand will feel unpleasant. I am full of self-doubts. Does he find me attractive?
Him
(I take on his physical bearing)
    I am in bed, finishing a cigarette. I take your hand, which is cold, and slip it under the covers. Immediately I feel aroused. Your attention is with me. I desire you.

In writing this entry the diarist observed something revealing about her choice of pronouns. As "Me" she thinks of her lover as "he," distancing and objectifying him. But when "he" speaks, he addresses her directly as "you," which is certainly more intimate. She recognized that the lack of intimacy she felt was, in all likelihood, created by her own fears. Once she began to take responsibility for her own fear of intimacy rather than projecting it onto her lover, she felt more accepted and more comfortable.

Besides rehearsing to communicate preferences or to gain insight into the dynamics of a sexual complaint, you can actually alter undesirable patterns of sexual behavior or habits of mind through imaginatively rehearsing alternative behavior in the diary. For example, a woman who has always been sexually passive and unable to say clearly "yes" or "no" to sexual overtures could use guided imagery to visualize herself taking a more active, decisive role on a date. By allowing herself in the written fantasy to be actively seductive or firmly uninterested, she could begin a process of self-programming to accept her sexual drives and choose when and where to act on them.

Similarly, people with repetitive fantasies could work with them as if they were dreams, altering the point of view to see how they are actually the source of all the parts of the fantasy. The fantasizer is both the masochist and the sadist in a sadomasochistic fantasy, both the rapist and the raped in a rape fantasy.

A woman with frequent rape fantasies could begin to take responsibility for her own active sexual drive by assuming the point of view and the voice of the rapist in either a dialogue or guided imagery. Such practice in an imaginative, written form could gradually help her take conscious responsibility for her sexual desires. It's unlikely that she would become a rapist. More likely, by identifying with both extremes of activity and passivity in her fantasy she would eventually reach a balance and come to know the full range of her sexual potential.

Taking Possession of Your Sexuality

Diarists who record eroticism along with emotional, intellectual, and spiritual aspects of the self don't need to repress sexuality because diary work gives them a means of understanding it. By staying intimate with their own sexuality they can take responsibility for when, where, or whether they will act it out. They begin to understand that they are not sexually dependent on others so much as on themselves. Ultimately they are able to develop an independent self that is secure enough to know its own pleasures and mature enough to keep them within nondestructive bounds.

By taking possession of their own sexuality they learn that it can be a source of imagination, humor, pleasure, creative energy, and physical aliveness that no one can deny them or take away. One diarist who had worked hard to know, recognize, and create the kind of sexual relationship she wanted began to have anxieties that it could not last, because her relationship was changing in other ways. She wrote a dialogue to explore these feelings and take possession of her sexuality:

Me
You bring me tremendous pleasure. You are a great mystery and joy in my life. Yet I fear your power over me.
Sexuality
I am a place of mystery in life. You can never
completely tame me, because when you do, you lose me.
I have to maintain some of my wildness and irrationality
to exist.
Me
You threaten me.
Sexuality
You threaten me.
Me
How?
Sexuality
Your tension. Only when you relax can I feel free.
Me
Give me some advice for my anxiety.
Sexuality
I'm inexhaustible. You don't know all about me yet.
You and I are going to continue to change. But you can
be sure, I'm not going to leave you.
Me
Even when I'm old?
Sexuality
Yes, even then.
Me
I think it would be a good thing for us to talk here
together from time to time.
Sexuality
Me too. I like you.
Me
You talk like a person.
Sexuality
I'm just the energy of attraction and you can feel it
toward yourself, toward a painting, toward an animal,
toward people you would never make love with.
Me
I don't know what to say.

Sexuality
You don't have to say anything. Just feel my presence in your life and as part of who you are. Then you won't be afraid of losing me.

As Sexuality suggests to the diarist in this interchange, people who find sexuality centered in themselves and defined by themselves can look forward to fully sensuous lives, enriched by the recognition of the varieties of pleasure available at all ages. As you begin to understand the amazing intricacy of feelings involved with your own sexuality, distinctions between sexual and sensual, body and mind eventually dissolve. The diary gives you a means of appreciating the moods and cycles of your sexuality, its unique evolutions, myriad forms and influences. Expressing eroticism in the diary is part of an overall search for self-acceptance, psychic integration, and creative freedom.

10 | Overcoming Writing Blocks

In a diary you can experiment, play, loaf, relax, confess, and be alone and enjoy yourself. It is a safe place, immune from the need to impress an audience. Yet even within the diary self-consciousness sometimes blocks the flow of the writing. Particularly in the beginning stages of keeping a diary people often experience fears about writing and internal voices of self-disdain or self-censorship. Even those who keep diaries for years have difficulty at times articulating their feelings. They may find themselves avoiding writing for weeks or even months. Or, when they do go to the diary to write, the pen won't seem to move, they stop in the middle of a paragraph and their thoughts run away, or they suddenly become very tired, too tired to write.

Generally such blocks, or inabilities to write, are caused by one of two basic fears, which might be called the Internal Censor and the Internal Critic. The Internal Censor represents fears about the "OKness" or acceptability of the content of your thoughts and feelings. The Internal Critic represents fears about the quality or style of your writing. Both are powerful inhibitors, so it is important to understand what they are and how to deal with them if and when they arise. If you can get to know them in yourself, focus them, talk to them, and get them to assist you, you will have taken an essential step in freeing your creativity.

The Internal Censor and How to Outwit It

The essayist and novelist Virginia Woolf first gave the Internal Censor a name when she observed in her diary how in modern times writers seem to be affected by "invisible censors." Because these censors are buried deep within, it is difficult at times even to know that they are inhibiting you. Censors reveal themselves when you find yourself hesitating to write something, omitting certain elements of your thoughts, or blocking and unable to write altogether.

Woolf visualized her Internal Censor in a woman's form, and wrote a portrait of her in an essay called "Professions for Women":

> She was intensely sympathetic. She was immensely charming. She was utterly unselfish. She excelled in the difficult arts of family life. If there was chicken, she took the leg; if there was a draft, she sat in it. In short she was so constituted that she never had a mind or a wish of her own, but preferred to sympathize with the minds and wishes of others. Above all, I need not say it—she was pure. . . . And when I came to write, her wings fell on my page: I heard the rustling of her skirts in the room. . . . She slipped behind me and whispered. . . . Be sympathetic; be tender; flatter; deceive; use all the arts and wiles of your sex. Never let any one guess you have a mind of your own. Above all—be pure. And she made as if to guide my pen. I now record the one act for which I take some credit to myself. . . . I turned upon her and caught her by the throat. I did my best to kill her. My excuse, if I were to be had up in a court of law, would be that I acted in self-defense. Had I not killed her, she would have killed me.

As Woolf implies, the Internal Censor is a form of guilt particularly opposed to writing about sex, bodily functions, or feelings that "don't seem nice." It forbids expressing anger or committing to paper any thoughts that will stir up trouble or make you take action in your life. The Censor is like the superego in psychoanalysis, the embodiment of societal values. It is the authoritarian voice in our heads that says things like: "Why, you can't say *that*. Why, that's nasty! What kind of person are you to think such things?"

The Internal Censor is also like the judgmental "Parent" in Transactional Analysis, who says "You're not O.K." The logical extension is "You're not O.K., so anything you write can't be O.K." The Internal Censor dreads facing feelings or taking responsibility for them. It fears any feeling it judges to be "unfeminine," "unmasculine," or "childish."

Fortunately, it is not too difficult to get around the block that the Internal Censor tries to pose—if you simply remember not to make judgments on yourself while writing. And since self-judgments seem to come from the intellectualizing part of the self, those devices that permit a nonrational expression of feelings and attitudes are particularly helpful for circumventing blocks. Free-intuitive writing, maps of consciousness, and guided imagery allow you to write a symbolic language that will slip right by your Censor.

Write about the Block. Writing about the symptoms of the block itself is a good way to outwit the Censor. The Censor has no power against such a head-on offensive. If the pen won't move, write about that fact. If you feel afraid, write about your fear.

One diarist named Richard Watts noticed that sleepiness was often a symptom that he was avoiding something inside. Rather than giving in to the inertia, he wrote about his tiredness.

> When I sit down at the typewriter, I become very tired, I have no desire to do anything but sleep, I stare up at my eyelashes. My bones ache. I sit down at the machine, I'm languid. The noisome smells of inactivity vibrate through my body and I want to sleep. I am frightened. I

withdraw my thoughts, ideals, feelings into the shell of
my body. . . .

In my mind's eye I see: myself sitting on a large
muscular stone shaping itself into an egg; milk spouting
from my large full breast, the empty sack of the
donkey's head pulled down securely over my own. This
vision is there now, right in front of me, floating in the
transparent waters over the machine. I feel as if I am
looking at myself through a microscope.

The entry moves from a reflection upon the nature of the
writer's resistances to images that give form to still-preconscious
feelings. He used the block as an access to the deep emotions that
his Internal Censor was suppressing. Writing about the block led
to guided imagery, which, as the entry continued, opened the
door to his emotions.

Dialogue with the Block. Another way to confront the
Internal Censor is to get a block to speak to you in a dialogue.
Once a block has been made to expose itself, it seems to lose
much of its power. For example, one night I felt out of touch
with myself and unable to write. So I wrote about the block
itself and then got it to speak to me:

It's so hard to sit down to write, so hard to articulate
myself. I'm all choked up with pain. I'm not even sure of
that. I'm only sure that I'm going to write, fast, until I
can write no more. I'm so out of touch with myself. . . .
I'm blocking. I can't. I shall allow the blocking voice
to speak.
Voice
You're going to make trouble. When you realize what it
is, you may have to act. And you're afraid to act.
T.
But this is awful. I can't go on in this confusion. I know
I'm a coward when it comes to action, but I have to
change that.
Voice
You're so much of a coward you can't even write it.

T.
But it's worse when I don't know my truth.

The entry that followed this preliminary dialogue eventually covered seven pages and led me to an awareness I had been repressing—that my arrangement with the woman I was sharing my house with was unsatisfactory, that there were no signs of change, and that I would have to ask her to move out. I cared about her very much, so it had been a difficult awareness to come to. However, the courage it took to confront the block and get past it inspired the courage needed to take action in my life.

Write Your Fear. You might release a block created by the Internal Censor by asking yourself when your pen stops, "What am I afraid to say? What is it that I'm afraid would be too shocking or unconventional or upsetting or nasty to articulate?" Write the question in the diary and then answer yourself. *Write exactly what you are afraid to say.* By exposing the fear this way, you use the writing block as an opportunity for an important insight. Your fear contains a secret, and the secret is usually a gift to yourself. If the blocked thought remains repressed it will only cause trouble for you and others. Once you have expressed it in the diary you can work toward transforming it (if that's what is needed), or take action, or simply stay with your self-knowledge for the time being.

Make a Deal with the Block. There may be some things that the Internal Censor feels are so terrible that they can be written only if the diarist promises to throw the paper away afterward. In such cases the writer asks the question, "What am I afraid to write?" and puts the answer on a piece of scrap paper rather than in the diary. One diarist began, "I promise to throw this away if I can just get it out." Once on paper and out of your head the thoughts may not seem so terrible, and you may wish to preserve the scrap of paper in your diary after all.

The Internal Critic and How to Tame It

Whereas the Internal Censor tries to inhibit certain kinds of expression related to the content of your writing, the Internal Critic creates self-consciousness about the quality. The Critic constantly judges your writing style. He can be felt in anxieties such as, "What if *they* read this someday?" or self-deprecation such as, "I can't write great literature. I don't write well at all," or comparisons such as, "X writes so beautifully. My writing is awful."

The Internal Critic presents a standard of writing elevated far above the writer's ability. He is generally a perfectionist and an aesthete with a well-developed taste for great literature. But the Internal Critic is self-defeating because his impossibly high standards of excellence are likely to inhibit the experimentation and experience necessary for the writer to develop. From his perspective any attempt at writing is an exercise that will be judged and "graded." He cannot distinguish between a personal diary in which you write for self-discovery and a test booklet you write to impress the teacher.

The Internal Critic must be kept in his place in the diary because he does not understand its process of nonlinear, intuitive evolution. He can tell you what is wrong with your writing and will even try to do so before you have been able to write two sentences, but he cannot write creatively himself. He can comment on your writing severely and sometimes brilliantly, but he is much better at stopping the flow of writing than encouraging it.

While the Critic is a valuable resource in the mind of someone who aspires to write well and a useful commentator as you reread, rewrite, or edit your diary, he has no place in the original expression of ideas. He has no place in a first draft. And since diary is all first draft, he has little function in the diary unless you eventually decide to edit it.

Still, you can't just banish him from yourself, you cannot kill him off because, like any genuine part of the self, he will just come back to life again. Instead, you need to tame the Internal Critic and educate him to become a balanced, integrated part of your personality.

The Italian director Federico Fellini depicted this process of integrating the Critic to free creativity in his film *8½*. Fellini personified the Internal Critic as a taciturn writer-critic who disparages the filmmaker's every inspiration with intelligent and rational arguments. In exasperation the filmmaker, Guido, has the writer-critic hanged. Yet in the next scene the Critic reappears, alive and well. Fellini finally resolves the conflict between the critical and the creative aspects of the self at the end of the film by having Guido's child-self lead all of his other selves, including the writer-critic, in a circular dance.

In the creative process—whether it be Fellini's intuitive process of filmmaking or diary writing—the spontaneous, creative child-self must lead the way while the rational, critical adult-selves follow and do their parts.

Like all creative and educational pursuits, diary writing requires that you relax, give yourself permission to experiment, take chances, and go on. You have to quiet down the Internal Critic because he can interfere with your natural evolution and keep you stunted. The Critic in you needs to trust your writing-self to grow intuitively on its own, in its own way, sometimes making errors as part of that growth. As in Fellini's film, you need to give your creative inner child the lead.

Dialogue with the Critic. One of the best devices for bringing the Internal Critic into line is the dialogue. As with the Internal Censor, the first step is to hear its voice in your mind and to identify it in some way. For example, one diarist allowed the Internal Critic to interrupt her and have his say right in the middle of a sentence:

> The diary will be a chronicle of my efforts (your pitiful efforts). If only I could put a face on that person and exorcise him . . . instead of struggling against the

blackness, the impact, the "in-print" authority of his voice.

The diarist records the Internal Critic's deprecating remarks ("your pitiful efforts") and then identifies him as the "in-print authority." "Putting a face on him," perhaps through writing a portrait or using guided imagery, in addition to getting him to dialogue, would help the writer come to know her Critic better. Eventually she can educate him to become an ally, and not a block.

The Internal Critic can be pacified by allowing him to express his bitter attacks on your writing, by letting him get it all out. He may begin as a nasty bully, but if you reassert your right to experiment as you please and answer him firmly, he loses his power.

For example, you might be writing an entry in your diary when you hear an inner voice that says:

> That is sentimental crap, drivel! I'd be embarrassed to let anyone see that. That's not literature. It's the outpourings of a sick mind.

Write out everything this voice has to say and then be sure to answer it:

> Listen, Critic, it may be true that this is too sentimental, though someone else might say "written with feeling." I think it's too early to tell. I'd love to hear what you have to say at another time. I know how intelligent you are and what good advice you will have for me later. But you're butting in at the wrong time. Let me get the ideas and feelings out and onto paper. ,

Continue the dialogue until the Critic gives you permission to proceed:

> **Critic**
> Oh, alright, go ahead with your garbage. You'll regret it later.

Me
At this point I'm not writing for anyone's eyes but my own. I will be interested in your opinion if and when I ever decide to do anything else with this writing. So why don't you let me just wing it without interference, till I finish this?
Critic
Go ahead. I have to admit, you generally write better when you let it happen spontaneously.

The Internal Critic comes under control when the diarist relegates him to his proper time and place—after his feelings are expressed on paper. This Internal Critic has already learned that even he likes the product of spontaneous writing better than hesitant, intellectualized prose. A reeducated Critic will give the diarist permission and even encouragement to write with an open heart and a free hand.

Circumvent the Block with Altered Point of View and Altered Audience. Another way to deal with the Internal Critic is to circumvent the block he presents. Rather than confront it directly in a dialogue, you can sail around a block by altering your point of view. Using another pronoun—"she" or "he" rather than "I"—can allow you to record an experience or feeling that is difficult to admit to in the first person. The fictional disguise of writing about "she" rather than "I" seems to fool both Internal Critics and Internal Censors.

Altering your sense of audience also helps circumvent a writing block. The Internal Critic and the Internal Censor are both inhibiting audiences. You can ignore them by concentrating on a more supportive listener. "Audience" in any piece of writing is the person or presence you are consciously or unconsciously thinking to as you write. In a work prepared for publication the audience is generally "them," the "public," or "posterity." But in a diary a preoccupation with "them" in the future signals an avoidance of intimacy with yourself in the present. If you find yourself thinking about "them" as you

224 THE NEW DIARY

write, you can redirect your attention toward a more receptive, encouraging audience.

For example, when I first became aware that I had unconsciously been writing my first diary to my former boyfriend, I consciously chose to change my audience to write to myself as a woman. Similarly, if you find yourself writing in the diary for "them" or with a disapproving parent or mate in mind, you can choose to write instead to a best friend, a child, a future self—any uncritical, receptive audience that will support and encourage your spontaneous writing and discourage your Internal Critic.

One of the unique characteristics of the diary is that the audience can be fluid; you can change whom you are writing to at any time. And the audience you choose at any time can reveal important psychological truths about yourself and your state of mind. Different audiences, like different people you know, allow you to express different sides of your personality.

In some ways finding the right audience or audiences in your diary is like finding the right people to share your life with. After you have been keeping the diary for a while it may be helpful to ask yourself, "Whom do I write to here?" If the audiences you identify encourage you to be the person you feel most comfortable being, if they allow you to grow, to be sincere and spontaneous, to discover new aspects of yourself, and to develop in the ways you wish, they are probably the right audiences. But if certain audiences limit your potential, make you feel unsure of yourself, make you feel boring or repetitive, cause you anxiety, interfere with your development, or keep you from being sincere and spontaneous, you need to concentrate on evoking a wiser, more receptive audience as you write.

Constructive Blocking

Not all writing blocks are negative. A block can be a messenger in the road who will not let you proceed until you receive his very important message. Once you get the message you can go on. Frequently a block is the harbinger of the very thing you need to face and deal with. Sometimes a block occurs if you are trying to write about something else and avoiding pressing inner issues, if you are writing insincerely or through a mask, or if you are being self-destructive. One diarist found that the imagined commentary of a friend of hers entered the diary as a block whenever she became too self-critical. In life this friend wouldn't allow her to punish herself, and he played a similarly constructive role in her diary by interrupting her in self-deprecating passages:

> I should have worn makeup and set my hair every time I saw him.
> Bullshit.
> Who is that? Is that Ron? Get out of here.
> I should have been sweet all the time and never gotten angry.
> Ron, you're embarrassing me by looking at this.

Of course, Ron was looking at the writing only in the diarist's imagination. But becoming aware of his predictable reaction allowed her to see how self-critical she was being. In this case the writing block was a signal to the diarist to go deeper into her feelings instead of remaining on the surface.

Preventive Strategies

So far I have been suggesting devices and tricks for dealing with writing blocks after they arise. There are also techniques to keep in mind that don't give writing blocks a chance to develop.

Writing in Fourth Gear. The best antidote to writing blocks may be simply to write so fast that they don't have time to catch up with you. If you can write down all your feelings speeding along in fourth gear, neither the Internal Censor nor the Internal Critic will be able to stop you. Richard Watts, for example, writes at a breakneck speed and with a sort of robust defiance of both the Critic and the Censor:

> It is not important what I write, it is only important that
> I do write. It is not important whether I sound like
> Henry Miller, Thomas Wolfe or Hemingway. In the
> end . . . I will always return to what I am.
>   Therefore this book is about me. I spit. I bite my
> nails. I walk about with a clownish rictus. I am deformed
> in spirit and without hope. (So what!)

"So what!" the diarist says to the carping critical presence in
his mind, and then goes on with the business of free expression.
At the first sign of hesitancy or of inhibition he immediately
speeds up rather than slowing down.

Free-Intuitive Writing. Working on the same principle of
writing so fast and freely that writing blocks don't have a
chance, some diarists begin all entries with a spree of free-
intuitive writing. Prescribed earlier for bursting through a
writing block when it has occurred, free-intuitive writing is
also a good preventive strategy. Once you have loosened up
with free-intuitive writing it's much easier to write quickly and
openly with any other diary device you may choose.

Lists. Sometimes a writing block is simply the result of
feeling overwhelmed. You have so many thoughts and feelings
that they all rush to be released at the same time and cause an
internal traffic jam. In such cases a list will get all the important topics out and onto the page. Once they are on the page
before you, you can tackle them one by one or concentrate on
the item that gives you the most discomfort, for that is
probably the source of the block.

Relaxation. Another way to prevent writing blocks is to
relax your body. Letting go of tension in the body seems to
help eliminate tension in the mind. If you can learn to relax
and attune yourself to your inner voice, you won't have to
worry about using any other devices or tricks to free you.
Marion Milner used various relaxation techniques in conjunction with diary writing as part of her personal search for
happiness. She noticed how she could stop the intellectual
clamor in her head by lying flat on her back and imagining her

body's being massaged or by making a mental gesture of withdrawing all the energy from her limbs.

In *A Life of One's Own* Milner describes the rewards of learning to relax: "Experiencing the present with the whole of my body instead of with the pin-point of my intellect led to all sorts of new knowledge and new contentment. I began to guess what it meant to live from the heart instead of the head."

Methods for relaxation can include running or other strenuous exercise, yoga, deep breathing, taking a shower, sauna, or bath. I also find some techniques of mental relaxation helpful. For example, similar to Milner I imagine pushing tension out of my body. Either lying or sitting, I start at the top of my head and imagine slowly pushing the tension down and out of my body through my toes, as if they were faucets. Sometimes I massage my feet to get it all out.

Or you might use guided imagery to visualize a beautiful, peaceful spot where you are in harmony with your environment and yourself, and where your body feels light, free, and joyful. Some diarists also use some form of meditation in conjunction with their writing, concentrating on their breathing, on an internal sound, on a white light, or simply on their silence. The ten minutes or so spent relaxing using any of these techniques are never a waste of time, for the effort spent fighting tension is much more time- and energy-consuming.

Still another way to avoid writing blocks is to borrow creative energy from someone else: by listening deeply to music, looking at works of art, or reading poetic writing. Anaïs Nin frequently read the stream-of-consciousness novelists Marcel Proust or Marguerite Young, because the free flow of their prose released her to flow in her own writing. Reading Nin's writing does the same for me.

You can learn a great deal about the interconnection between mind and body by experimenting with various relaxation techniques before you write and even while you write in the diary. For example, if you become sensitized to your own handwriting in various moods, it can tell you when you are tense. When your handwriting reveals tension take several deep breaths and stop writing long enough to relax your body.

Being relaxed helps you write in tune with yourself whatever your mood. Marion Milner compared it to singing in tune. As a child she had been teased for not being able to sing. Only as an adult did she notice that when she was humming to herself without thinking about it, her voice was on key. She discovered that if she relaxed and listened to the melody coming from her voice, she stayed in tune. But if she thought about the fact that she was singing, her voice wandered off key. The same is true of writing. If you relax and listen to your inner voice, the writing will flow. But if you think about the fact that you are writing, you may begin to block.

From keeping a diary you will learn how concentration depends on relaxation. Concentration is not a matter of effort but of trusting yourself. In diary writing concentration means that you try to write well out of respect for yourself rather than out of fear of judgment. Fear of judgment blocks writing or results in dull, unimaginative, stilted prose. If you relax and listen to your inner voice and record what you hear, writing blocks don't have a chance. You will write through the limitations that Internal Censors and Critics try to pose and discover that in the diary, anything is possible, everything is admissible, all things may be tried, said, remembered, and imagined.

11 | The Diary as Time Machine

People who keep diaries inevitably become aware of time as one of life's ineffable mysteries. Some of them even become time travelers, unhooked from the limitations of time and place that confine most people. The diary becomes a time machine that takes them into the past—where they can learn who they are by understanding where they have come from. And it takes them into the future—where they can clarify their goals and discover their destination.

The diary is the genre of the present moment. And on the continuum of time between past and future, the present moment is the point of power from which you can influence the meaning and direction of your life. The present moment contains all you have experienced, felt, and thought in your lifetime—and even what your parents and grandparents have experienced, felt, and thought in theirs. It also contains the seeds of all you are to become. The present moment is the portal to past and future, and the diary is the vehicle that enables you to travel into both dimensions.

Inner health, psychic balance, depends upon a sense of personal continuity through time. Some emotional "law of completion" seems to require that any part of a life not fully or genuinely experienced at the time needs to be felt through at some later time. As a result, adults who led very sheltered youths may break up their marriages to live out their missed years of social and sexual experimentation. Or an individual who seemed unaffected in her youth when a parent died may suddenly feel overwhelmed with the illness of a friend in the present.

Rather than allowing the past to invade the present as blind behavior, it can be more beneficial to complete yourself through time travel in the diary. Self-completion is a reaching backward in time through memory as well as a reaching forward in time through focused desire. Through written recollections you can gain self-knowledge, release delayed or repressed emotions, find hidden misconceptions that have influenced your self-image, forgive and forget past offenses, and imaginatively explore the roads taken and not taken to discover present fulfillment as well as future options.

Recalling the Past

In general you record memories spontaneously as they arise. In this way the diary replaces the arbitrary chronology of time with an emotional calendar of your own making. You may recapture moments from the near or distant past for the simple joy of reliving and savoring them. Particularly haunting or emotionally charged memories will often spark further creative writing, such as a story, a song, or a play. You may also wish to recollect certain incidents and feelings to gain insight into a present dilemma.

One diarist in her early fifties began to suffer diminishing eyesight. Besides seeking the proper medical care and writing dialogues with her eyes, she began to recall all the early incidents and feelings related to her eyes and the influence of her farsightedness on her childhood. In working through the history of her eyes in the diary she began to understand the psychosomatic elements of her failing sight, while the ophthalmologists were looking for physiological causes. Her memories were the laboratory in which she sought personal clues for a cure to her present ailment.

Some people have memory gaps, periods of time, some-times several years, that seem to be missing. Such missing periods of time leave holes in your sense of personal con-tinuity. If you have such gaps or if you have forgotten much of your childhood, you may wish to develop your powers of memory. The technique for recalling involves imaginatively placing yourself within whatever fragment or wisp of a remem-brance you have and allowing your senses to gather additional information.

For example, you might take your first childhood memory and expand it through description by imaginatively placing yourself back into that period of time. Try to feel, see, taste, smell, and hear as you did then, and record these sensations as concretely and specifically as possible. Recall details such as the house you lived in, whether you slept in a crib or a twin bed, where you ate, where you played. Try to recall exactly where the first memory took place. Try to feel the size of your body: If an adult took your hand, how large did the adult's hand feel? You may suspect that you are guessing and inventing details, but it is not the literal truth you are searching for. The object is to expand imaginatively your sense of who you are and who you were.

After you have described your first memory to your satisfaction you may wish to reflect upon it in your diary. Carl Jung held that one's earliest memory is the key to the meaning of an entire life. The first memory contains the psychic pat-terns that will repeat themselves again and again as the mature personality evolves. You may wish to reflect whether this has been true for you. The same methods of imaginative descrip-tion and reflection can be applied to any subsequent memories you wish to recapture. The results may lead to further creative work: a poem, a painting, or reflection for an autobiography.

You might also use childhood photos as an aid in spark-ing recollection. For example, you might have a photo of yourself at a birthday party about which you remember noth-ing. By analyzing the photo carefully, as Dr. Robert Akeret suggests in his book *Photoanalysis*, you can gain a sense of who you were at that moment. Are you touching anyone in the photo or do you seem aloof? Are you hiding behind someone else or are you the center of attention? Can you imagine what you were feeling? The body language in the photo can tell you a story about your past.

Then you can imaginatively set in motion the scene in the photo. You might visualize going into your old room to get something, perhaps a favorite toy you had at the time. What did your room look like? Notice your height in relationship to doorways and objects in the house. Recall or imaginatively fill in the scene until you have expanded the memory as far as you can and recorded it in the diary.

In the case of traumatic or painful periods of time, you may have to work hard against your natural resistance to remember. Reflective questions, as in this diary excerpt, can help push you forward:

> I am in that room, that room I don't want to remember, but that I will never forget. It was white, and there were, let me count them, one, two, three . . . five arched windows that looked down upon a courtyard. But the room itself. Shall I pace it in my mind as I paced it so frequently then? I don't want to remember it, the queen-sized mattress on the floor, a telephone. The room was particularly bare then.
>
> It is that day I must remember. How was it different from the other days? Had I left the house that day? I left the house infrequently then. . . . There was something cold in me at this time. Frozen like that room was frozen white, frozen in time, frozen space. The mystery is that I was frozen but I cried. I cried cold tears. They fell on my hands in Baltic floods.
>
> Why do I write this? I write to remember. I write to discover. Because somewhere there is a missing link. What is the secret I am hiding from myself?

The entry continues for many pages, until finally the diarist reaches a catharsis and discovers a hidden secret of personal responsibility she had been afraid to face for years. There is a great deal of resistance in this example, which can be felt even in the rhythm of the writing. But whenever she begins to block, the diarist asks herself a question. Even though she avoids answering her questions directly, they do push her to remember.

Releasing and Recycling the Past in the Present

Writing about the past can provide an important catharsis for delayed or deferred emotional responses, unburdening the writer of pain or guilt, freeing him or her from old misconceptions, and relieving years of accumulated stress. In the diary the past can be recycled—refelt and transformed. Sometimes the original reaction to an incident was the only one that could be admitted at the time, particularly if the event was painful or threatening. But as a person's life changes, as he or she acquires maturity, an incident from the past can be made to reveal the true feelings that were never fully experienced or were hidden beneath the surface reaction.

One woman finally found the leisure and personal security in her retirement years to work through recollections of a difficult childhood she had had to put firmly behind her: "I awake now, fifty years later," she writes in the diary, "to pain I thought I had forgotten, to bitterness I thought I had not tasted, to recognition of realities and values I could not then accept but had to live with." By recovering her childhood memories she is recovering herself; and in working them through she is completing the business of her life. Since she intends to give her diary to her grown children, her efforts will have the additional value of helping her children understand themselves by understanding their mother and her struggles.

Sometimes the purging of past emotions is absolutely essential to a process of self-acceptance in the present. For example, one woman was able to admit her genuine anger and regret several years after having had plastic surgery to enlarge

her breasts. She wrote a description of the event in her diary,
trying to be as honest and revealing as possible:

> He took my height and weight and said that I could
> handle a "hefty" size bosom. I was in a state of not
> thinking; if that is what he felt was right, he must be
> right—he must have the power—the power of aesthetics,
> the gift of knowledge, the magic of being able to change
> flesh, the god-like effect on flesh, the superior
> transcendent ability to do better than god did. To be,
> more than any other kind of surgeon, a transformer, not
> a healer of physical pathology, but a shaman-surgeon, a
> surgeon of the mind, cutting years of insecurity and
> inferiority out of a person, not just changing a nose or a
> chin, lifting a breast or filling one out, but cutting out or
> altering what seemed to be a permanent disfiguration of
> the being. What power. So I just went with it, stunned. I
> never even said goodbye to my breasts.
>
> I remember a poem I wrote about six years ago.
> My breasts are small and white
> I hold them in my hands.
> Today I long for truth,
> A truth as real and white
> As my breasts.
> I intend to explore this incident fully.

A significant association emerges as her memory of the surgeon leads to an earlier memory of a poem she had once
written about her breasts. In the intervening years the power
with which she had endowed the surgeon had almost eradi-
cated the acceptance she had once felt for her natural self, and
she has a powerful need to recapture these earlier feelings in
the present. She recognizes the importance to her sense of self
of recalling again and again the event of her plastic surgery,
until she has worked it through. It is precisely this circling
back to the past in the present, each time gaining greater
understanding, that creates the spiral of inner development in
the diary.

In the case of neurotic problems, people seem to bring into their lives situations that echo unresolved parts of their past. Diarists can work with these repetitive situations to discover an awareness that will finally release them from self-perpetuated traps. For example, one diarist who had, in her childhood, experienced a pattern of trust, broken trust, and withdrawal from her father found herself repeating this pattern in adulthood with the men she dated. At the onset of a new relationship with a man who happened to remind her strongly of her father, she decided to observe her pattern carefully in the diary.

She recorded the development of her new relationship in great detail. At the same time she recorded any childhood memories about her father that rose to the surface, evoked by incidents in the new relationship. She described her feelings of trust and joy during the blossoming of the new relationship, and she recorded the spontaneous childhood memories she began to have about playing games with her father and learning from him. As she anticipated with dread her boyfriend's departure on a business trip, she began to recall the exact moment when her father had left home and filed for a divorce from her mother.

These associations of past with present enabled her to recognize why she was feeling her boyfriend's departure as a broken trust. Perhaps most importantly it allowed her to experience, on the pages of the diary, the original sorrow she had not permitted herself to feel as a child. Her exploration of past memory was painful, but in releasing the emotion she had held onto for twenty years she was finally able to learn from the memory what she had been too young or too vulnerable to understand at the time—that her father's departure was not a broken trust with her, but that she had mistakenly interpreted it as such. Releasing the past in this way was a first step toward helping her stop compulsively reliving it.

If you wish release from neurotic patterns of self-pity or guilt about the past, try reflecting upon spontaneous memories

236 THE NEW DIARY

for illumination, insight, and understanding. Self-pity and guilt are symptoms of needing to push further, go deeper, remember more, and be more honest with yourself. The joy that finally comes with illumination and release from the past will always erase self-pity and replace it with a sense of responsibility and personal strength.

To get to the truth of your feelings you must discover *who you were, what you chose, what you decided.* It is more important to ask yourself, "Who was I when that happened? How did I choose to react? How did I choose to feel?" than to ask, "Who was my mother (or father or teacher or stranger) that she/he did this to me?" You can never really know another's intent or motivation. But with a little effort and persistence you can remember what you decided and what you felt, and it is this discovery which is essential for self-understanding.

In the process of releasing and recycling the past you can often correct childhood misconceptions and discover new insights that you were blind to in earlier years. The little girl who decided she was unworthy of love because her father left home and divorced her mother can now, from her adult perspective, revise that assumption by exploring its origins. Mistaken assumptions from the past based on limited information, limited experience, and a child's narrow perspective can be reviewed and altered through descriptive and reflective writing of your memories in the diary.

Recognizing the Past in Present Emotions

When you have an inappropriate or extreme response to a current situation, it is often helpful to describe the situation in the diary and then ask yourself reflectively, "What in my past might be responsible for my feelings in this current situation? Was there a time in my past that I reacted this way? Is that why I feel (angry, in love, overwhelmed, etc.) now?" Spontaneous, reflective responses to such questions can be personally liberating.

Here is a hypothetical example. Your neighbor brings over a letter addressed to you, but which was mistakenly put in his mailbox and opened accidentally by him. He is apologetic and assures you he didn't read the letter, which contains nothing of a personal nature anyway. But you are furious inside, and you cannot understand why, for you have always liked your neighbor.

Such moments when your feelings baffle you are always good times to sit down and work in the diary. You ask yourself, "Why do I feel so furious about this incident? Does it recall something from my past?" You might remember, for instance, that your older brother used to open your mail when you lived at home. Then you write an entry, perhaps using altered point of view for that period of time, perhaps as a dialogue, about your genuine anger at your brother for having violated your privacy. In this way the justified anger is released and directed at its true source and is no longer unfairly projected onto your neighbor.

As you keep the diary over an extended period of time, you may come to recognize characteristic, intense responses that accompany recurrent situations in your life. You may come to know one or several child-selves (you at various ages) who bring strong emotions into the present. The child you were is still the child within, and to understand yourself in the present you need to give attention to your inner child of the past.

Since the child within is very willing to travel to the present and affect—sometimes even dictate—our lives, it is important to use the diary to travel into the past to get to know him or her better. One diarist began by allowing her childish emotions to spill out in a cathartic form of free-intuitive writing:

Nobody loves me. Everybody ignores me. I want to be loved. Nobody loves me. I just want to cry.

She reflected as her adult self, "How old is this voice?" and it answered, "Seven." So the diarist decided to have a dialogue through time with this unhappy seven-year-old self:

> **Adult Me**
> My situation is not one in which your feelings are appropriate.
> **Seven-Year-Old Me**
> Nobody loves me. I just want to cry.
> **Adult Me**
> Now cut it out. I love you, but I'm not going to give in to your feelings.
> **Seven-Year-Old Me**
> Nobody loves me.
> **Adult Me**
> Look, you are back there in a time bubble, but I am also you. I am the woman you have become. And I am loved. My friends love me. I love myself. I'm no longer a helpless child.
>   There, you seem to have stopped crying. Here, dry your tears. I'll always be here now, and I love you very much.

By disciplining the inner child when it is being unreasonable, telling it to "cut it out," and by giving it the love, understanding, and nourishment it may have needed and not received, you can become your own loving parent.

Transforming the Past

Another way to heal old wounds is to apply the salve of humor or irony in the present. One diarist described the adolescent discomforts of a summer as a National Science Foundation scholar in a way that transformed uncomfortable memories into an amusing story. As an adolescent she had felt powerless, but in the present she had the power of her adult perspective to purge the hurt of the past:

> *March 31, 1976*
> Seventeen years ago, I remember, I remember, I was one

of the top science students in the nation—no, wait. I
must remember. The top forty were awarded
scholarships by the National Science Foundation to
attend a summer session for the study of advanced
chemistry and mathematics. As a high school junior that
year I had placed forty-first, the first alternate. One of
the forty was unable to attend and I became number
forty. I was the only individual who knew exactly where
she ranked within the group.

I handled the classwork; I learned complex laws of
probability; I photographed a maple leaf using X-rays,
etc. I was not a stunning #1 in the class, I was not
fantastically desirable to the boys, the few words that
dropped from my mouth were not pearls of wisdom. I
didn't know why or what I was doing there. The
thirty-nine others seemed to know. They had no
confusion; they were, every one of them, unrelentingly
brilliant. I was a seething bag of emotions sitting in the
midst of thirty-nine magnificently programmed
automatons. . . .

I was terribly, terribly alone.

After classes and studying in the evening, after all
the others were in their rooms, I would go down to the
recreation hall bringing the few books of piano music I
had with me and sit at the old upright piano playing
and playing till I became lost in the act and could dream
myself out and away: talented, beautiful, admired,
loved. . . . I became glued to one piece: W. C. Handy's
"St. Louis Blues." . . . I lived the day to play that song
at night on the old, out-of-tune piano.

Near the end of the session . . . we were to have a
Talent Night. I gathered up my courage and decided to
hell with them, I wasn't going to be excluded. I sat
sweating while so many of them played flawlessly on
their cellos and violins: inspired concertos, lively rondos,
etc., etc. God, how unbearable. They were absolutely
perfect people. They knew everything, could do
everything: math, chemistry, music, breathing, walking,
talking. My time came and I walked up and sat down at

the beautiful, polished, unsoiled grand piano. I had never touched a grand piano before. I had never played any kind of piano for anyone before. I began in a flurry and stumbled my way through one of my lesser interpretations of "St. Louis Blues" . . . The only response I recall was from a short little guy with greasy hair who approached me later with a sneer on his face asking: "Did you ever take lessons?"

I bit my lip and replied, "Yes, a few when I was very young."

"It sounded like it," he snarled back.

I was devastated.

That song had gotten me through lots of nights and he was declaring it wasn't good enough!

If, somehow, someway, this page of words should ever be read by anybody, but especially him, and he recognizes himself, I have a message for him: In your ear, you greasy, little bastard! May all your hair fall out! And all your sneering teeth! But one. And that one should ache you for the rest of your life!

Through a combination of humor and descriptive powers the writer has released and avenged her pain.

Another way to transform the pain of the past is through understanding and forgiveness. If you can empathize with the fear of confusion or ignorance that led another to hurt you, you may be able to let go of personal resentment or anger.

Exploring the Road Not Taken

In Progoff's INTENSIVE JOURNAL there is a section called "Intersections: Roads Taken and Not Taken." Progoff suggests to people working in this section that by returning their minds to an important intersection in their lives, when they consciously or inadvertently made decisions that determined their future direction, they may reacquaint themselves with potentialities, interests, or talents that are still waiting to find fulfillment. In natural diaries many people have also found it valuable to explore imaginatively the choices or paths they did not pursue. A diarist who decided not to go to medical school and became a businessman instead found that the road he had not taken continued to call out to him from the past. Using guided imagery he pursued the career he might have had in medicine, visualizing himself studying nights, deciding on a specialty, and doing his residency.

His rejected career may have been an early intimation of capacities or talents that needed more time to develop. In rediscovering his road not taken the businessman awakened his lay interest in medical research and a buried social conscience, which might lead him to do some form of therapeutic counseling in the future. Abilities, projects, and relationships that could not be pursued for whatever reason in earlier years may become feasible with the passage of time.

The purpose of exploring roads not taken is not to compare them with your present life, nor to feel "if only I had...." No one can know what actually would have happened on another path. But by returning to important intersections you may discover future options. The road not taken may still lead to a point in your future.

Charting the Future

Recalling the past and working with it in the diary can be entertaining, therapeutic, liberating, and informative. But it is a misuse of memory to dwell in the past to the exclusion or neglect of the present and the future. Traditionally diarists have written about the immediate past. And perhaps because people who have a personal record of the past can become fascinated with it, diarists have sometimes been accused of being "stuck" in the past. However, one of the benefits of keeping the New Diary is that it provides devices that allow the diarist to reach forward in time and to visualize the future as well.

Just as memories of the past exist in the present, so do seeds of the future. You already know certain facts about the future—for example, that you will age and eventually die. You have other predictable information about the future that you may not allow to reach consciousness. You may also have expectations and assumptions, perhaps some of them false or negative, that will play a part in determining what comes to pass.

In the diary you can lay all your information, your assumptions, your desires, and your hopes before you, and in so doing construct a vision of the future. You can work on correcting negative assumptions that are likely to cause future problems. And you can learn to use your power to influence the future constructively and creatively.

Nearly all the diary devices with which you are already familiar could be used to focus goals and direct you on a positive path. Through the rest of this chapter you'll see how four devices—lists, guided imagery, dialogue, and altered point of view—are expecially valuable instruments for charting the future.

Lists. The simplest and most direct way to focus the future is through list making. Just as you can make stepping-stones of your past life, you can make stepping-stones of your future life as you would like it to be. Stepping-stones of the future may vary each time you make them, as will stepping-stones of the past. Even so they indicate direction and create a sense of continuity in your life. A list of future stepping-stones might look like this:

> My divorce was finalized
> I moved to New York
> I started taking painting classes again
> I found a focus for my art
> I sold some pieces
> I moved into a beautiful loft
> I found spiritual peace

This list of future stepping-stones is also a list of wishes, but they are all possible. Why couldn't all these things happen if the diarist wanted them enough?

Another list you can make to understand your own power in determining the future is a list of assumptions or expectations. Everyone has powerful assumptions about the future even though they may often be unconscious. And everyone will recognize the influence that these unconscious assumptions or expectations have had on their lives.

Listing your assumptions makes them conscious and brings them under your control. You might make a list of all the things you assume will never change about yourself. And you might ask yourself, are these assumptions realistic or do they reflect negative, self-punishing thinking? You might list what you assume will change about you in the next year, five years, ten years. Again, are these positive or negative assumptions? Negative assumptions such as:

I will fall ill
I will be abandoned
I'll always be depressed
I'll end up like my poor father/mother

need to be altered because, unless you change them they are likely to come true. People tend unconsciously to bring about what they believe or assume about themselves.

Unrealistic negative assumptions can be reversed on an "opposites" list:

I believe I can maintain my good health
I take responsibility for making myself be
   abandoned
I can make myself happy
I'm not my father/mother

You can work further with other diary devices, such as a dialogue with inner wisdom, to help bring about psychological changes in the present that will influence your future.

Of course, the most obvious uses of lists for guiding the future are making lists of things you want to accomplish within a few days or weeks, lists of short- or long-range goals, and lists of steps required to accomplish a particular goal. Even people who don't keep diaries make such lists, but I have found an added advantage to keeping them in the diary. I can return to a list of long-range goals made years ago to see how my objectives have remained the same and how they have changed.

When I did this recently I saw that most of the elements on the older list concurred with my present list of goals. And I was delighted to note that I have already achieved several elements on the older list. This gives me a sense of continuity and accomplishment. I also find that I have had to change the order of my priorities to adjust to the actual opportunities before me. If my life is long and I perceive it as a whole, the order in which I accomplish my goals is not of great importance. I may be able to fulfill only one aspect of myself at a time. But in the diary I can be whole and one whenever I make an inclusive list that represents the fulfillment of all aspects of my personality.

Some diarists make lists to help them with decisions. This is a common method of visualizing and guiding the future. They list the predictable consequences of each alternative or the pros and cons of each choice to make sure they have thought through their options. They include such speculations as "What is the worst thing that could happen?" and "What is the best thing that could happen?" They add their feelings and intuitions about each alternative. Finally they ask themselves, "Am I sure these are my only options?" When they have all this information before them they know they have done all they reasonably could to prepare before choosing a direction. The lists will not make the decision, however. A decision is always a leap into the unknown.

But the diarist has an advantage over the person who writes such decision-making lists and then discards them—the opportunity to learn about one's own decision-making process from rereading the list later, with the knowledge of subsequent events. The diarist can see whether an oversight was avoidable, what blindness he or she had, whether the worst fears or the greatest hopes were well founded, and whether intuition, feelings, or logic was indeed the best guide. The diarist has a record of the reasons that prompted the choices that were made at certain junctures in life. Every decision-making list is an opportunity to learn more about your process of decision making as well as a device for imagining, guiding, and choosing the ingredients of your future.

Guided Imagery: Daydreams. Guided imagery in the form of daydreams is another valuable instrument for charting the future. Daydreams are a language of hopes and wishes. Yet they can give you clues that will direct you on a positive, realistic path. Like night dreams, daydreams provide a bridge to your inner consciousness, giving you insights into thoughts you might not consciously admit. By recording and working with your daydreams in your diary (just as you would night dreams) you increase your ability to recognize and value fantasy as an access to important aspects of yourself, and not to treat fantasy as realistic expectation.

Daydreams can be particularly valuable to record if you are having difficulty determining or focusing your goals. For example, one diarist who felt too blocked and inhibited to make a list of goals wrote out an "impossible" daydream instead. She asked herself, "What would I like to happen that couldn't possibly happen, but that I would like to happen if it could?" and she wrote:

> I met a fabulously wealthy man who took me on a trip around the world. When we got back he set me up in my own antique business. I imported and sold fine furniture and became an expert on interior design. I had very chic parties that everyone wanted to attend and I went out nearly every night.

This is pure fantasy, but the diarist knew that as she wrote it. Like any form of guided imagery it had value simply in the pleasure it provided for the moment. It had even greater value, however, because the diarist was able to extract from it a list of realistic goals:

1.   I want to get a job with a travel agency.
2.   I want to take a course in interior design.
3.   I want to have a party and see more of my friends.

Each of these items represents a goal the diarist can bring about through her own volition. The daydream contained information in a symbolic code, the very concrete goals for her future, which the diarist had been unable to list in a more direct way.

Daydreams, however, are not always sweetness and light. Recording them may bring you in touch with the pettiness or anger in yourself. But recording even vengeful or opportunistic fantasies has cathartic value. And it seems that admitting to everything you are or seem to be is an essential aspect of self-acceptance and inner development.

Dialogues with the Future. In daydreams you can imagine the future unrealistically because you recognize the dreams as symbolic language. But it is also valuable to give a voice to your realistic future projections to discover your view of the future as you would like it to be and as it can be. You can do this by concentrating on aspects of the future that *you* can bring about, those seeds that already exist in you as potential. In dialoguing with your own voice of positive potential you automatically affirm faith in yourself and in your capacity to make life meaningful.

Using the diary as time machine you can speak with your potential future self and find in it a listener, a helper, and a healer. For example, a woman who had recently divorced was very depressed and could not see a way out of the depression until she wrote a dialogue with her own positive future. First she released her feelings in a cathartic entry about the present, and then the woman she was to become, became her guide:

Negative Present
I'm depressed, insecure. I believe that no one will ever love me, that I'll never have a good job, that I'm going crazy. I'm becoming an alcoholic and I can't even admit it to myself.

Positive Future
I worked through these problems in therapy and I joined AA. I got very firm with myself. Giving up the booze wasn't as hard as I thought it would be. I grew closer to all my friends, the new ones and the old ones.

    The pain of the divorce seems very far away now. I asked to be promoted in the office. Mr. Drekler refused and I quit. I went to an employment agency and found a much better position.

In the process of writing this dialogue the diarist gave herself a set of goals to accomplish and a vision that they could be accomplished.

A dialogue with the future can also give consolation in the present by allowing the writer a broader perspective on a particular problem. The following entry was written by a widow who was very attached to her children. Her oldest son had decided to leave home and travel indefinitely. She wrote this dialogue with the future, not as an impossible fantasy but as a realistic option:

Present
My son is leaving. I feel that I'll never see him again. My feelings are inappropriate, of course. I'm not supposed to cling. He doesn't even think of me. He can't wait to leave, while I iron his clothes.

Future (as I wish it to be)
I got used to Jonathan being gone. It was easier than I thought. In later years we got to be good friends, a mature relationship of adults. It's brought me great joy.

One aspect of this dialogue verges on fantasy, since the writer cannot be sure that her son will ever return. However, it is not an unlikely possibility. And through the dialogue she was also able to foresee an independent inner peace.

Some diarists carry on extended dialogues and develop a strong, ongoing relationship with the wiser, older, future self who will eventually read the diary. This older self frequently offers advice and guidance when the diarist is caught in present dilemmas. You can, in the present, evoke the self you wish to become and in so doing establish a loving relationship with yourself through time.

Such dialogues with your own positive future or future self are uplifting. By learning to give the future a voice in the diary you can develop new habits of mind that may eventually influence your thinking, even when you are not writing in the diary. For example, if you find yourself dwelling on painful memories when you arise or during the day, you can begin to recognize them as the past and replace them with your voice of a positive future, developed in the diary.

Altered Point of View: Remembering the Future. For many people the best device for visualizing the future seems to be altered point of view. Rather than straining to foresee the future you simply put yourself into the point of view of the future and remember the "past." For example, you might use the date of a future time as the date of the entry and write an overview of your life up until that date. One diarist at the age of thirty-three tried to visualize her life three years hence by recording a future date in her journal:

> *July 20, 1980*
> My thirty-sixth birthday last week. I finished my law degree with honors. Have been so busy that I haven't had time to write here for an entire year.
>   I'm joining the Public Defender's office. Me—a trial lawyer. I can hardly believe it!
>   The worst is over. I visited my daughter in Maine this summer. She's old enough to talk about what happened now. I think I was able to help her understand my

decision. Oh, and my article on recidivism among
middle-class women was published. So it's all worked out.

From reading this diary entry you get a strong sense that the
woman who wrote it will be able to accomplish her goals, even
though they only existed as hopeful future projections at the
time. Making goals concrete is more than half of obtaining
them.

Shifting your point of view into the future is also a
useful device for exploring alternative courses of action. One
young woman, who had a promising career as a ballet dancer,
wanted to decide whether or not to marry her boyfriend. On
July 6, 1975, she wrote at the beginning of her entry:

July 6, 1991
I'm now forty years old, still in good shape and thinking
about getting a facelift, but I'm afraid of an artificial
look. How do I evaluate the past sixteen years with
Jerry? It's been hard but worth it. Sometimes I've hated
him, other times loved him intensely. It's never been
boring, though often frustrating.

I never became really famous. I never set the world
on fire, but I've done what I wanted, what interested
me. All and all it's been good. It's the next ten years that
worry me, forty to fifty. Will I pay now for having
played it safe before? This is the time I had hoped to be
most productive, to have my own dance troupe and be
directing and choreographing. Now I know that won't
happen. Unless I can do something earth-shaking at this
point, I will be disappointed in myself. I have no desire
to grow into a pleasant matron. Glamour no longer
attracts me.

Then she wrote: "And, if I didn't marry at all . . ." and the
same date:

July 6, 1991
Well, I've done what I set out to do. I have my own
dance troupe which is world famous. We just finished
the European and Soviet tour.

Why I had to go it alone, without a man, I'm not
sure. Women envy me and I resent their ignorant envy. A
side of me has never been fulfilled, the girl-woman who
needs to be loved and for whom the real proof would
have been a lifetime of intimacy and devotion.

On the balance, I'm grateful for the specialized
gratification I've had—freedom, the masculine pleasure
of seeing my mind create form as dance and affect
others at a deep level.

I'm sick right now over negotiations for the next
season. Will I never be calm about this stage of it? I seem
to work off my own stress. Even in production I can't
say I *enjoy* it—not like one enjoys being held.

But my babies, my creations, seem worth it when
it all comes together. There's the pleasure of marriage
and birth with each new ballet.

After she had written both these entries the diarist analyzed
the present conflict they expressed. She wrote a reflective
comment:

I think what's interesting to observe here is that I set
marriage and career as mutually exclusive options, as in
a 1930s "woman's film." I see a place for some career
within marriage, but strangely, no place for marriage
within the career I really want. The work replaces both
marriage and children. I suppose because I assume that
any man—Jerry included—would be too threatened to
live with a woman director-choreographer, and that I
wouldn't want him to play the role of "wife" to me.

As a result of writing this future projection the diarist began to
recognize her assumptions about career and marriage and saw
the need to discuss her ambitions openly with her boyfriend.

Another use for altered point of view could be alternate
projections of the future, given the continuance or discontinu-
ance of present habits. One diarist reflected, "How will I feel
in ten years if I begin to jog regularly?" and wrote out a
portrait of himself full of energy, stronger and healthier than

he was in the present. Then he asked himself, "How will I feel in ten years if I continue working night and day without any exercise?" He wrote a portrait of himself pretty much unchanged—tired, tense, but more overweight and more stooped. His future projections strongly reinforced his growing desire for change. Like Scrooge in "A Christmas Carol" diarists can, through altered point of view, foresee their future and make changes before it's too late.

Once you have visualized the future through lists, guided imagery, dialogues, altered point of view, and other devices you may wish to hurry up and enter the next phase of your life. You can give yourself a push by beginning a "new chapter" of your life in your diary. Summarize the last chapter by writing an overview—in the past tense—of the latest period of your life, which you wish to move out of. For example, "I *was* obsessing about my children during this time." When you have completed your summary of the past period, consider that part of your life closed. Release yourself from it.

Some people ritualistically burn their diaries as a means of releasing themselves from the past. Though it seems to work, this is an extreme measure and diarists often regret it later. It may be just as effective to draw a line across the page under the last entry and then to skip a few pages before beginning a new chapter. Or you may wish to begin a new book right away without needing to fill the old one, and put that finished period of your life away with other old volumes of the diary—out of sight, out of mind.

As you begin a new chapter or book of your life you can give yourself permission to make changes you have been forestalling, and you can identify your present point of evolution. After doing the preliminary work of focusing yourself in time by reviewing the past and visualizing the future, always return to the present moment. That is your point of power. And if you stay true to the present moment, you will always grow and change, for the present is always moving.

Using the diary as time machine lets you travel back and forth on the rails of memory and imagination to see yourself at any age. You may use it as a lever to speed yourself up into a positive future or slow yourself down to contemplate your cumulative experience and extract wisdom from your past. You may use it to establish a relationship with yourself—an expanded form of self-love whereby you can nurture, discipline, appreciate, or heal the younger self you were and receive nurturing, guidance, understanding, and inspiration from the wiser self you will become. In this way you acquire a deep sense of your own continuity through time, because in the diary all time is one.

12 | Diary Magic

A personal magic begins to enter the diary through time. Diarists seem to develop special sensibilities—a perception of meaningful subjective patterns, fateful coincidences, and prophetic dreams—as they learn to follow their feelings and intuitions. These intuitive capacities may not be available to scientific proof because they are by nature unrelated to linear thinking. Yet many diarists report strong, intuitive perceptions, personally significant coincidences, foreknowledge, and predictive dreams, all arising out of the diary-keeping process.

Synchronicity

As they observe their personal patterns through time many diarists become aware of *synchronicity,* or meaningful coincidence in their lives. Synchronicity, according to Carl Jung, "takes the coincidence of events in space and time as meaning something more than mere chance." A synchronistic experience is a concurrence of events that has special significance in the psyche of an individual. Like insight into one's dreams, an appreciation of synchronicity can give depth of meaning to life, especially when recorded in one's diary.

For example, on the afternoon of September 18, 1975, I was typing a screen adaptation I had written of Anaïs Nin's "Houseboat" story and considering whether to add the character of Sabina to the screenplay. Although Sabina is a character who appears in much of Nin's other fiction, she does not specifically appear in "Houseboat."

Unable to make up my mind I went for a walk on the beach with my neighbor's little girls. We met for the first time a third child, about their age. This child's name was Sabina, and she was walking with her father, a film producer.

Soon after I returned to my house I had a visitor, an actress I had met once before at a party. She did not know of my interest in Nin's writing, but I saw that she was carrying a copy of Nin's first novel, *House of Incest.* In the course of our conversation she suddenly opened the book and pointed to a passage that began, "Sabina was no longer. . . ." I had never mentioned Sabina to her.

This coincidence of thinking about Sabina, meeting a child named Sabina, and having a passage from a book about Sabina pointed out to me—all within a few hours—had personal significance even beyond what I have mentioned here. I recorded the coincidence in my diary. Eventually all its elements came to have importance in my life, as if the coincidence were a condensed version of dominant themes that would develop in time.

Those few hours had what Carl Jung has called a "numinous" quality; they were charged with inner meaning. I have since come to think of synchronicity as the art of human experience, because it suddenly pulls what has special significance out of everyday life, combining and condensing it in such a way that it forces your attention.

Sometimes synchronistic events indicate human fate: the coincidence that brings two people together who eventually marry, or the coincidence that leads someone in the direction of a life's work. In such cases coincidences seem to be letters of God dropped in the street. The diarist alone has a means of keeping these letters for future reference.

Coincidences don't always turn out to have the significance you originally attached to them. Jung himself recognized that synchronicity can be a trickster, setting you up to expect something that never materializes. Further, unless a synchronistic event is experienced with another person (which seems to happen frequently when people fall in love), it generally has no meaning for others. If someone were to approach me and say, "The most amazing thing happened! I was thinking about cooking fish for dinner, I was wearing my new Pisces necklace, and I opened my *Newsweek* and there was a feature article on underwater life, full of pictures of fish," I would probably think, "So what?" I might even be irritated at her making such a big deal out of a mere coincidence. Nevertheless, the incident of the repeated image of the fish might have deep significance for that person's intellectual, spiritual, or emotional life.

It may often be better to share the significance of synchronistic experiences with the diary and not try to impress such experiences upon others for whom they may have no meaning. It is more helpful to use the diary to test for yourself the personal validity of synchronistic events over an extended period of time than to test their validity for others. Synchronicity relates to a personal fate; its significance is individual rather than collective.

Foreknowledge: Predictive Dreams

Diaries offer proof, perhaps the best possible proof, that some people have knowledge of the future. Diaries are full of examples in which the writer had a dream or a flash of intuition that foretold a future occurrence. Throughout history diarists have recorded famous military battles, important events that influenced the course of a career, important first meetings with another person, a premonition of someone's death, and many other phenomena—all before they occurred.

In "The Diary as Time Machine" I suggested ways to evoke foreknowledge through altered point of view and dialogues with the future, but many diarists experience foreknowledge as an involuntary message from the subconscious. It comes through a dream or a sudden visual flash when the conscious mind is preoccupied with something else, through guided imagery when the images gain predictive significance with the passing of time, and through free-intuitive writing when the subconscious is allowed to speak.

Diarists most often observe foreknowledge in their dreams, where conscious laws of time and space do not apply. They may dream about a new person, place, or event before they encounter the same in waking life. They tend to notice this phenomenon more frequently than those who don't keep diaries for an obvious reason. If they record their dreams upon arising, and if they record the day's events in the evening, they see correspondences between dream and reality. If the dream and the actual event are days or weeks apart, the diary still contains a record of the predictive dream to which the diarist can refer.

Most predictive dreams seem to foretell occurrences or images that materialize in the following day or two. But some dreams seem to predict the future well in advance—months, even years before the materialization in reality. Such far-reaching dreams often have a particularly vivid quality, as if crying out to be remembered until life catches up with them.

The ability to dream the future is neither unique nor uncommon among diarists. A good many of the diarists whom I have worked and corresponded with were eager to tell me what they had discovered about their ability to foresee the future in dreams. In my case, most of my predictive dreams are of specific images of places, but I have had emotional dreams that worked predictively in quite a different and a very helpful way. Occasionally I live out my reaction to an emotional situation the night before it occurs. Then when I confront the actual situation, I glide through it calmly, having released my emotional reaction already in my sleep, and having recorded it already in my diary.

Some diarists have predictive dreams nearly every night. One of them, a young woman named Shirley Marcoux, found a way to illustrate the dream/life correspondences she saw in her diary by setting the entries side by side. Here are only a few of her many examples:

> (Dream) I dreamt I met a Mexican-Indian man dressed in a white "T" shirt and jeans. He was in trouble with the law and needed a place to stay. I brought him to my friends' (Cheryl and Dave's) house to hide. (April 2, 1976)
> (Reality) The following night, Cheryl had the same dream. She described the man identically to the man in my dream—same situation. (April 4, 1976)

> (Dream) Two men walked into the office to rob me. I ran into my boss's office and pulled a small gun out of his top desk drawer. The men were were afraid and left. (Nov. 4, 1975)
> (Reality) Boss called in from L.A. office and asked for information on a piece of paper in his top desk drawer. I went into his office, opened the drawer, and there was the small gun that was in my dream. (Nov. 5, 1975)

> (Dream) I was walking through a canyon and came across some woodpiles. Then I saw a locked gate. (April 28, 1976)
> (Reality) At a healing celebration, I woke up early and hiked through the land. I came across a canyon that was used as a junk yard. Lots of wood had been thrown there. I walked on and came to an iron gate that was locked. (May 1, 1976)

> (Dream) I was talking to a girl with blonde hair by the name of Cathy. (June 24, 1976)
> (Reality) Camping in Big Sur I met a young girl with blonde hair named Cathy. We had a long conversation and I learned a lot from her. (June 25, 1976)

Shirley embraces the many correspondences between her dreams and her life joyfully, accepting them as mysteries to be celebrated rather than understood. Other diarists, however, have been frightened by their talent for dreaming the future, probably because foreknowledge is not accepted as a normal capacity in this culture. Several diarists have told me they have chosen to "forget" the future, and they stopped having predictive dreams. Just as people can put certain aspects of the past out of their minds, they can similarly choose to eliminate foreknowledge from their consciousness for as long as they wish. (That may be what most people do all the time, which leads them to believe that such intuitive capacities don't exist.)

However, a diarist who has developed the talent of predictive dreaming and finds in it nothing to fear perceives ordinary life experience to be charged with inner meaning. Nights begin to feed days with magic and illumination, and days begin to feed nights with appreciation and confirmation. The most mundane experience can become an inner adventure when it is also a reflection of your dreams.

Again, the personal wonder that predictive dreaming has for the individual can never really be shared with anyone. As with synchronistic experiences, the significance makes no sense to another person, unless he or she has shared the inner experience. There may even be a loss of personal power when you try to share transcendent experiences indiscriminately. They are inner experiences and, as such, the best place to express them is in a diary where they begin to build a pattern of inner meaning for you.

Being in tune with the interrelationship between dream and life doesn't mean that you will become "dreamy" or "cut off" from others. You can be aware of inner mysteries and still remain active and focused in the world, just as meditators can repeat a mantra that keeps them in touch with a timeless self while efficiently performing their daily tasks. The human mind is dialectical, which means it has the capacity to maintain dual perceptions, not just alternately but simultaneously.

Anaïs Nin's diaries demonstrate how one can live in the timeless realm of the imagination and never lose touch with reality, never sever the cable of connection to others. She writes in *Diary II*:

> I never get cut off from pity, sympathy, participation, in spite of the fact that I am living out my own dream, my interior vision, my fantasies without any interruptions. I dream, I kiss, I have orgasms, I get exalted, I leave the world, I float, I cook, I sew, have nightmares, write in my head, compose, decompose, improvise, invent. I listen to all. I hear all that is said. I feel Spain, I am aware, I am everywhere, I am open to wounds, open to love, I am rooted to my devotions. I am never separate, never cut off, never blind, deaf, absent

The numinous awareness of the dream running parallel with the day need not diminish the intensity of reality. Rather it makes reality more essential, more meaningful, and more magical.

Past and Future Lives

Diary magic can involve some intriguing "time games." You can imaginatively travel back to the tenth century or forward to the twenty-first century simply by entering the appropriate date, for example, April 21, 2021, and writing as if you were there. The following entry, which uses altered point of view, is one diarist's attempt at such time travel. She allowed her intuition to write a date of the eighteenth century and from that flowed the rest of the passage:

Jan. 4, 1794
I am in London. I see the barges being pushed down the river. The afternoon is dingy. The sky, the water and the stone arched bridges give me a grey chill.

I'm wearing my bonnet, carrying a parasol. A man in a tall black hat walks up and takes my arm.

I am worried about something. He is a friend, an advisor.

Someone I love—a husband, a lover—is away at sea or in another country. My friend in the top hat has news for me.

"Marguerite," he says, "You have to be brave."

I feel I am going to faint. He holds my arm.

"I want to go to him," I say, sure of my mind.

He is on a plantation on an island. Does he want me to come? Why doesn't he send for me?

"Marguerite, you have to forget."

A marriage is being arranged. Someone of his own station.

I am a governess. What can I do? I am in despair. My grief will drive me mad.

I think about the cruel peace of the river, the cold bleak water. I wish that I could rest there.

Writing the date 1794 seems to have put the diarist back into that time period, into what seemed to be a previous life.

Regardless of whether "past lives" discovered this way are genuine or a projection of the writer's emotions or anxieties in this life, the process offers an opportunity for self-insight. I quote the example not as proof of anything but as a way of illustrating that the opportunity for time travel within the diary is limitless. Just as you can become your own psychologist, your own nourishing mother or father or friend in the diary, so can you become your own psychic.

Time travel can be thought of as a creative game or used for its therapeutic value. For example, one woman had a recurrent voice inside that called out to her, "I want to go home!" She could never understand what this meant because she couldn't associate the "home" with either the house she grew up in or with her present apartment. So, using intuition and altered point of view she allowed a past date to enter her mind, and she recorded the date in her diary: "Dec. 26, 1864." Then she simply allowed the following guided imagery to come to her as she wrote:

Dec. 26, 1864

A carriage. London streets. I am a child. A boy of seven

or so. I am waiting for my mother. Two men take me by either arm. Put me into the carriage. Drive. I am confused. I don't know if this is supposed to happen.

"Where is my mother?" I ask.

"We're taking you to a better place," they say.

"What place?"

"A land of treats and sugar-candy." I become very excited. I imagine this land. We drive for hours.

Finally we arrive at a country cottage.

"Is this it?" I ask.

"No, we'll go there in the daylight," they say.

When I awake a woman brings me a cup of soup.

"When will we go to the magic land?" I ask.

"Here's your magic land!" One of them hands me a sucker. I look at his face. It's creased, unkind, and desperate. I want to go home.

I begin to shout, "I want to go home!"

"Shut up!" they tell me.

I continue to scream. One of them hits me.

"I want to go home," I whimper.

Again, whether or not this story of being kidnapped by high-waymen actually represents a past life is less significant than the mind's eagerness to give form to such fantasies. There seems to be a psychological release that accompanies such time-travel games. After writing out her vision of the kidnapping the woman was no longer plagued by the inner voice crying, "I want to go home."

The Power of Predictive Titles

Some people practice a custom of naming the volumes of their diaries. Anaïs Nin gave a title to each of the original volumes of her diary, but her editor objected to them so they are not included in the published volumes. One of them she titled "Les Mots Flottants," "The Floating Words." While she was writing in this volume she unexpectedly found a houseboat to live on and her writing began to take on a flowing, floating quality of extraordinary ease and spontaneity. Observing this she wrote in that volume:

> Day and night the river laps at the wood and rocks the houseboat gently. It gives me a feeling of departure.
> What a strange coincidence that I wrote on the title page of this diary: "Les Mots Flottants." The Floating Words. A prophecy.

I have always given my diary books titles before writing even the first word, and I have found that the title of the book seems to prophesy what I learn and experience during the period I write in it. The title gives a focus to my search and therefore I find what I am looking for.

At first my titles were very general, simply alternative ways of saying "diary," such as "The Mirror Book." Then I became very interested in time—diarists generally do. I knew that mystics conceptualize time as circular, as one, but I had never experienced it as such. I deeply wanted to have that experience, so I titled my next diary "The Time Book" and drew a large circle with a dot inside it on the front page. This seemed to focus my search, and during the year and a half that I kept that volume I learned everything I wanted to know about time, and perhaps more than I thought I wanted to know. I recorded the same things I usually put in my diaries, but I also recorded quotes from books on relativity and insights about time that occurred to me during my daily life. One day it all fell together for me with a line from Walt Whitman's *Song of Myself:*

> I do not talk of the beginning or the end
> There was never any more inception than there is now.

Having prepared for it in the diary, the single line of poetry provided the missing link that allowed me finally to experience time as one and circular.

Using predictive titles to give the diary a specific orientation has had mixed results for some diarists. One woman told me she wanted to explore the concept of self-love in her diary. She tried to cut out a mylar heart to paste in the front of the volume, but found herself with the shape of an apple instead. Rather than begin again to execute her original plan, she impulsively put the mylar apple inside a heart she drew on the page. Then, thinking of the Garden of Eden, she named the volume "The Bitter Fruit of Self-Knowledge."

On rereading this diary she realized that unfortunately she had gotten exactly what the title promised. She reflected as she concluded the volume:

> What a fool I was to name it "The Bitter Fruit of
> Self-Knowledge." That is exactly what I got. Why didn't
> I call it "The Joyful Fruit of Self-Knowledge"? I could
> have learned as much and enjoyed myself much more."

Titles of diary volumes are often self-fulfilling prophecies because they give the writer an expectation to fulfill, a future orientation to the search. With predictive titles you can write your own life, not only after it happens but also before it happens. However, anyone who wishes to experience the effect of predictive titles should remember the wise adage: Be careful what you wish for, you might just get it. Predictive titles are a form of diary magic, and magic is unreliable and sometimes tricky.

Through recording numinous experiences, such as synchronicity and prescient dreams, and playing time games, such as writing past or future lives or creating predictive titles, you can develop the "sixth sense" of intuition. However, before the capacity to interpret and evaluate your intuitions has fully matured, you may have strong intuitions that turn out to be misleading. Even people who are highly intuitive may filter out parts of an intuition by oversimplifying the complete message, making it all positive, or all negative, or making it mean what they would like it to mean. It requires years of attention, experience, patience, and caution to learn to interpret intuitions accurately. And in this process the diary is a valuable aid.

A dream, a coincidence, or an intuition preserved in the diary reveals its full, cumulative significance with time. Over the years you can reread your diary and see for yourself what aspects of an intuition you tended to filter out. Using the diary you can become sensitive to your intuitions, learn to interpret them more accurately, and develop what some important contemporary theorists consider to be a hopeful, newly evolving channel of knowledge and awareness.

13 | Rereading the Plot of Your Life

Scientists use journals to observe and record changes in any living organism they are studying over a period of time. A botanist, for example, may keep a journal on a particular variety of plant life, noting its growth on a certain day, its reaction to an altered amount of light another day, a change in its color the next. By rereading the journal and looking for patterns developing over a several-month period the researcher can learn many things about the nature of that particular plant.

In the same way the diarist comes to see patterns of experience and personality on rereading the journal. The patterns are completely individual and deepen the understanding of one's own nature.

In rereading the diary you observe links, webs, and themes of self; you see the plot of your life created by your subconscious slowly through time. Just as you can follow the silvery thread of a garden snail on the grass or human footprints in the sand, so on the pages of a spontaneous diary can you observe the characteristic trail of your own being. You gain self-knowledge and experience self-recognition that can be acquired in no other way. Half the benefit of writing a diary lies in completing the process through rereading.

266 THE NEW DIARY

Rereading can bring pleasure as well as self-knowledge. You may delight in preserved memories of yourself as you once were, recollections that would have been lost forever if they had not been recorded. You may savor an experience that, like a well-aged wine, at first could not reveal its full character. But the pleasures of rereading are possible only if you approach the diary with an attitude of self-acceptance.

Preparing to Reread—and Its Benefits

Since diaries contain the struggle for growth and emotional equilibrium rather than the final achievement, it is essential to reread with an acceptance of your human, incomplete, in-process nature. It may be worthwhile to prepare yourself to read with a nonjudgmental openness to what you will observe. Relaxing and trying to empty your mind of other matters is good preparation for rereading, to help you to be as receptive and objective as possible.

Diaries reveal the people behind their masks—without their personality makeup or carefully selected social clothes—and all are vulnerable, flawed, sometimes awkward, childish, or mean if they have been writing honestly. Therefore you need to assume the qualities of a good friend, therapist, or counselor in rereading. You must offer the person you appear to be in the diary sympathy, tolerance, insight, and patience, but not pity or harsh judgments.

You need to read with an eye for your expanding awareness and growth. You must be prepared to advise yourself and offer direction and sincere encouragement. And, so that you won't be sucked into inappropriate feelings from the past, you need to remember that you are not the person you were, but the person you are now—the person who is able to perceive and understand the situation from a more objective point of view.

Rereading is especially helpful whenever you feel the need to put your ongoing life in context. Whenever you feel stagnant or grounded, or when you feel you are ending one period of your life and beginning another, rereading helps focus your energies and clarify the present. You may also reread whenever you simply wish to appreciate the life story written in your book.

Diarists reread at various times as well as for various reasons. Often a diarist will read an entry immediately after writing it and achieve instant perspective and clarity on a problem that had seemed confusing and opaque. Then the writer may add a reflective paragraph of observation recording insights gained in reading the entry. But at other times the same diarist may write cathartically to purge feelings and not stop to reread the entry, wanting only to push forward. Particularly if it's late at night the writer may just want to go to sleep, having gained release, comfort, and relaxation from the process of writing.

Some diarists read back five or six entries before writing a new entry to get a grasp on the current cycle of their lives. From such a brief scanning they can often discern dream patterns and grasp their meanings, reinforce their perception of a particular current issue that they might otherwise try to ignore, and sometimes see that they have entirely neglected to confront a certain anxiety, though it has been in their minds for some time.

Rereading accumulated entries, the work of several months or of an entire volume is especially important because it gives you a sense of the inner movement and continuity of your life behind the words, the river of self discovering its own path. Some people traditionally reread the year's entries at the end of each year. Others ritualistically reread when they finish a volume. The ideal condition is when you can give yourself an undisturbed block of time so that you can read straight through a period of your life or to the end of a volume. The most serious limitation of Ira Progoff's INTENSIVE JOURNAL lies in its fragmentation of life into separate sections, which makes it nearly impossible to read with a sense of

continuity. In contrast a natural, chronological diary allows
you to read the story of your own life like a book.

The greatest benefit of rereading a diary is obtained
when you can follow it through chronologically to the present
moment, and then flow into the future with the clarity of the
past as your guide. It allows you to compare one period to
another and to see your passages of inner change and growth.
Rereading becomes a process for discovering the unique
meaning of your life. As Anaïs Nin writes in *Diary II,* "There
is not one big cosmic meaning for all, there is only the
meaning we each give to our life, an individual meaning, an
individual plot, like an individual novel, a book for each
person."

In researching this book I asked many people to reread
all their diaries from beginning to end to find examples for me.
The response was invariably enthusiastic and generous. Within
days I would receive Xeroxed diary pages along with a characteristic comment:

> Thank you for giving me the excuse to go back and
> reread all my diaries at one time. I had completely
> forgotten so much of it—events, lessons, and insights I
> had promised myself always to remember. Sometimes it
> was uncomfortable, because I saw destructive patterns
> I'm still playing out and mistakes I still make. But I also
> found wisdom and honesty I hadn't realized I was
> capable of. Feelings that didn't seem to make sense at
> the time and dreams I wasn't able to understand became
> clear. I thought I could see the hand of destiny in my
> life, tracing a path. I fooled myself about so many
> things; I often blinded myself from what seems obvious
> now, in retrospect. But I also saw my growth.

As the diarist observes, you may feel discomfort in
rereading your diary. It can be an extremely intense experience. You may reexperience the pain of the past as well as the
joys. You may feel confusion, despair, arrogance, envy,
beauty, resentment, and passion—the entire panoply of your

moods and emotions—within a concentrated period of time. In rereading you must inevitably acknowledge some of life's chaos and recognize the determination of chance.

You may also see traits you ordinarily hide from yourself and others and feel shock, pain, or embarrassment. A few diarists report reading and using old entries as evidence against themselves, as "proof" of their imperfections. But if you use the diary to judge and blame yourself it is likely that you put yourself in this uncomfortable position in other areas of your life as well. Learning to reread with acceptance of your incompleteness can be an important step toward ending such self-punishing habits of mind.

Some people forget when they reread that the diary represents *process*, not product. Unedited diary writing is never a finished product like a published work. The diarist who thinks he or she is a "terrible writer," a "bad person," or "insane" from rereading should try to remember that this seeming "insanity" may appear in the diary precisely because it is kept out of the external life, that "evil" thoughts may appear in the diary because it is a safe place to vent hostility. A diary that is a watershed for all the things the writer doesn't want to subject other people to, or a diary that seems negative or terribly fragmented may still be an extremely valuable tool for its writer. Moreover, a fragmented, incoherent diary or an emotional, painful one may be a necessary step toward a relaxed, coherent diary, which reflects a more relaxed and self-accepting writer.

Self-recognition can be the most difficult confrontation in life. But in recognizing the incomplete aspects of yourself, you have already begun the process of changing them. For example, the man who consistently makes decisions based on monetary profit and later blames himself for having ignored other, more important human values may become conscious of this pattern from rereading his diary, and therefore capable of changing it. The pattern emerges not because he had an intentional plan to reveal it, but inadvertently, because people tend to record what is still unresolved and troublesome in their lives.

Or the woman who avoids accepting personal responsibility for her decisions and her life is likely to see that trait appearing in the diary in a number of ways. It may show itself in entries in which she blames other people for her personal unhappiness. It could appear as a predominance of daydreams without any practical application. It might even influence the diarist's style of writing. She might consistently avoid using the personal pronoun "I" and write many of her sentences in a passive structure, making it seem that other people were responsible for her actions. (For example, "My mother had me drive her to the store," rather than "I drove my mother to the store"). Individual patterns and traits show up in rereading the diary, because in writing spontaneously the truth slips out.

Writing and rereading the diary helps you change old habits by first permitting you to record—inadvertently and without self-censorship—undesirable unconscious behavior. As you reread the diary these habits are brought to conscious awareness. Though you may continue to think and behave in the same ways, you will become increasingly self-aware as you continue to write. It is easier to see patterns of thought when you write them down than when they just go on in your mind. You may find yourself recording in the diary such observations as: "I'm criticizing myself unfairly again" or "Here I go . . . can't I stop this?"

At this stage you may experience an internal split between your desire for change and the persistence of old habits. You may feel nauseated or repelled by some of the patterns you observe repeatedly in the diary. But it is precisely that distaste and the impatience you feel with yourself that pushes you to change. You change partly because you become so fed up with reading about the same old patterns. You feel the change in your life, and it is reinforced when you reread new volumes of the diary that reflect new habits of mind, new issues of concern, and new patterns of behavior.

Awareness and change, then, are direct results of writing spontaneously and later rereading. As your intuition becomes the "memory" of the future, you learn from self-feedback and become immersed in the process of your evolution. You grasp the inner story of your life and develop the talent to determine its direction.

Reading Yourself from Rereading Your Diary

When you read through your diary you need do no more than feel the continuity of your spirit through time. But you may also wish to "read yourself" in more specific ways. People attempt to interpret themselves through the I Ching, astrology, palmistry, tarot cards, handwriting, body type, and through many forms of psychological typing. The diary offers an opportunity for self-understanding based on something concrete and specific—your own words—what you write and how you write it. For example, you may discover interesting insights from considering the following questions. They are divided into: (1) word indicators, (2) content of the writing, and (3) observable trends and patterns. All of these offer clues to how internal language influences thinking and behavior and may reveal what sorts of things you tell yourself about reality. However, these questions are no more than food for thought; you need not hold them in mind as you reread.

Word Indicators
1. Do you label people? That is, do you refer to your therapist as "the shrink" or to a certain woman as "the blonde" rather than dealing with them as individuals?
2. Is the use of the word "I" negligible? If "I" does not begin a good proportion of the sentences in your diary, you may be avoiding personal responsibility for your thoughts, feelings, and actions.
3. Are there any slips of the pen or significant misspellings that reveal the unconscious?
4. Do you frequently use the words "always," "never," "stupid," "should," "ought," or judgmental expressions

such as "how dare she!" "not again!" or "poor dear"? Such absolutes and judgments are often used by the part of the self that creates guilt and blaming. In Transactional Analysis it is the stern voice of the "Parent." Learning to identify this voice in the diary can help you identify the judgmental part of yourself.

5.   Do you frequently use the phrases "I wish," "I want," "I don't care," "I guess," "I don't know," or superlatives such as "best" or "worst"? In Transactional Analysis these are the verbal cues of the "Child." Learning to identify this child-self in the diary can be a great aid in helping you to know your own inner child.

One diarist finds an entry:

> I wish he would prove his love. If I were to get sick would he get serious, look at me, and finally say "I'm sorry" and tell me how much he loves me? I want to make him show his feelings.

Next to this passage she makes a note in rereading, "This is the child speaking." It is the child-self that feels her every desire must be satisfied and reacts emotionally if it is not met.

6.   Do you ask questions in the diary without insisting on absolute or simplified answers? For example:

> I find Deb materialistic, selfish. Are some of my feelings disappointment that she didn't become my dream of her? Do I see some of myself in her?

Such reflective questions are characteristic of the reflective "Adult." The adult-self is also characterized by tentative words such as "probable," "possible," and taking personal responsibility for your perceptions, as characterized by phrases such as "I think," "I see," and "It seems to me. . . ."

Content of the Writing

7.   Do you reveal your feelings fully or hide them even from yourself?

8. Do you keep secrets from the diary? Why? What kinds of material do you tend not to write about?
9. Do you concentrate on future wishes or past memories and neglect writing about the present?
10. Do you record dreams? If so, what relationship do you notice between the dreams and the rest of the diary?
11. Is your memory of the past more or less consistent with your record of it in the diary?
12. Are there significant differences in the content of the entries in this volume and that of earlier ones? How would you characterize the differences?
13. What changes, if any, do you wish to make in the next volume?

Trends and Patterns of Behavior

14. Do you seem to be stuck on a certain problem? That is, does your diary reveal any repetitive emotional reactions that you wish to change?
15. Do you see any destructive habits of thinking?
16. Is there a great discrepancy between what you write in the diary about a certain person and what you reveal to that person? If there is, you may wish to consider in the diary how you can make your relationship more open.
17. Does guilt or self-blame appear in the diary in particular contexts?
18. Can you connect any frequent references to physical ailments (headaches, stomachaches) with some recurrent emotional state?
19. Do you record pleasurable moments as well as complaints?
20. What personal strengths do you notice? What do you wish to reinforce?
21. What do you like about yourself from your rereading?

You will certainly have questions of your own to consider when you reread. You may wish to search through your personal document of the past for keys to current questions that have never occurred to you before.

But rereading should not be and need not be a purely intellectual process. There is no "correct" way to write the diary and no "right" answers to the questions you may ask yourself. Rather, rereading is a process for feeling an intimacy with yourself through time.

Summarizing a Volume and Focusing the Next

After you reread allow yourself to meditate quietly upon the content of your diary. There's no need to drill yourself with questions as if you were taking a quiz. Simply permit feelings and insights to rise to the surface of your mind as they will, and then record them. For example, "I used to have extreme emotions and few gentle feelings. Now I often have subtle feelings. I like the change."

If you leave a few pages at the end of a volume to make a final entry about what you observe in rereading, your diaries will have natural, meaningful conclusions. Moreover, from interpreting a volume you have just completed you will get a good sense of what direction you wish to take in the next.

For example, one diarist summarized a volume this way:

Reread this entire diary. The writing as a whole degenerates. Too many experiments without a coherent narrative to carry the flow of my life, to make sense of it. I find little vulnerability in this volume. I find distrust of the self. So many dialogues, so much dream work, indicates effort and also a manipulation of self, as if I had lost confidence in the process, in the flow of my own being.

There is great anger in this recent book, and frustration. Even the handwriting is ugly and troubled compared to a clarity and simplicity of form in the previous book.

From her dissatisfactions with the volume just completed, the diarist recognizes that in her next she will want to allow herself to be more vulnerable, less manipulative, and less intellectual. She will want to allow a flow and spontaneity to develop in her writing, and probably use fewer special diary techniques. She will also want to work through the anger she has observed in herself. The summary concludes one volume and prepares a focus for the next book and the next phase of the diarist's life.

Another diarist concluded a volume with a set of "Rules to Grow By" evolved from observations about himself, which he made from rereading his diary:

> **Rules to Grow By**
> First and foremost: Avoid feeling sorry for yourself.
> This manifests itself in many ways. Be on the lookout,
>   for it is best if recognized early. Some typical
>   manifestations are:
> Setting yourself up to be hurt.
> Comparing yourself to others.
> Living in the beauty of the past.
> Blaming others—very rarely does one person
>   intentionally hurt another.
> Not accepting full responsibility for yourself.
> Making others feel guilty for holding you back (it's
>   you who holds you back—you're just using "them"
>   as an excuse).
> Not wanting to hurt someone (the indirect hostilities
>   are much more painful, and time and growth won't
>   really hurt another).
> Thinking that growing is more painful than not
>   growing.
> Denying yourself joy and play in the name of growth.

From meditating on the volume he has reread the diarist is able to provide the self-guidance he needs. It is the Silver-Lining Voice that seems to have written the list. His rules have been developed from recognizing what has made him happy and unhappy in his own experience.

Another diarist summarizes her diary as follows:

At the moment of death one recalls her entire life in a flash. The end of a diary is a kind of death, and to prepare for it, I reread this volume. The beginning still recalls the persona as writer, but the middle is sincere, coherent, well written. I like myself there.

Somehow, when S. came to live with me, the writing became more scattered and I notice a gradual corruption of my values. I seemed to fall into a well, and in it I assumed I had been that unhappy through this entire diary. Only in rereading was I able to remember my path.

This summary illustrates a tremendously important benefit of rereading the diary. The writer was able to recognize, from seeing a segment of her life in a larger context, that she had not been as unhappy as she had assumed, nor for as long a period as she had thought. The diary reminded her when and how she had forgotten her path. In rereading she experienced a return to prior values; she saw a part of herself that she liked and that she can reassert in the next volume.

Especially after they have been working in the diary for several years diarists begin to like what they see in rereading. Virginia Woolf, after years of writing many volumes that displeased her, finally felt she had, through writing fast and freely, achieved a style she enjoyed. To confirm this she wrote in her summary of that volume:

> *Easter Sunday, April 20, 1919*
> I got out this diary and read, as one always does read one's own writing, with a kind of guilty intensity. I confess that the rough and random style of it, often so ungrammatical, and crying for a word altered, afflicted me somewhat. I am trying to tell whichever self it is that reads this hereafter that I can write very much better; and take no time over this; and forbid her to let the eye of man behold it. And now I may add my little compliment to the effect that it has a slapdash and vigour and sometimes hits an unexpected bull's eye. But what is more to the point is my belief that the habit of

writing this for my own eye only is good practice. It loosens the ligaments. Never mind the misses and stumbles. . . .

The main requisite, I think on rereading my old volumes, is not to play the part of censor, but to write as the mood comes or of anything whatever, since I was curious to find how I went for things put in haphazard, and found the significance to lie where I never saw it at the time.

The significance of what the writer has recorded haphazardly becomes clear later, when she rereads. It was precisely in not worrying about what went into the diary—by allowing it to be spontaneous and uncensored—that it took on meaning. Writing this summary Woolf confirms the effectiveness of her random, impulsive method and encourages herself to pursue it in future volumes.

Rereading from a Different Perspective: An Experience in "Emotional Relativity"

The summaries written of a volume may or may not be accurate. Sometimes the shock of discrepancy between your memory of a period of time and your record of it in the diary may be so great that it affects objectivity. Nevertheless, your summary has its own value as a record that can be compared with observations about the same volume written at another time. If you reread the same material at various points in your life and record your observations, you will experience how much your perspective in time determines what you see in the diary and what you learn from it.

The process of writing a diary and rereading it at different times develops an awareness of what I call "emotional relativity." You experience such a significant change in your perception of reality from each position in time that you come to realize nothing is absolute; everything is relative to the vision of the beholder at a particular moment. Emotions and anxieties that seemed overwhelmingly important at one time may seem trivial from a later perspective. What makes no sense at one point may take on deep significance at another. Whether you consider yourself a success or a failure, fulfilled or unfulfilled; whether your life seems meaningful or meaningless depends upon your mood, your attitude, your perspective.

Many diarists find that each time they reread the same volume they seem to read a different book. Sometimes you may think the writing is dreadful and the book should be destroyed. Sometimes you will think certain entries are quite effective. Sometimes you will think, "Things weren't as bad as I remember them." And at other times you will think about the same material, "I'm sure glad I'll never have to go through that again!" The book hasn't changed, the writer has. Your mood, needs, values, and perspective have changed. How you respond to rereading the diary tells you as much about yourself in the present, as what you have recorded tells you about yourself in the past.

A summary that Anne Frank wrote upon rereading her diary helps illustrate how one's perspective changes with time:

Sunday, 2 January 1944
Dear Kitty,

This morning when I had nothing to do, I turned over some of the pages of my diary and several times I came across letters dealing with the subject "Mummy" in such a hot-headed way that I was quite shocked, and asked myself: "Anne, is it really you who mentioned hate? Oh, Anne, how could you!" I remained sitting with the open page in my hand, and thought about it and how it came about that I should have been so brimful of rage and really so filled with such a thing as hate that I had to confide it all in you. I have been trying to understand the Anne of a year ago and to excuse her, because my conscience isn't clear as long as I leave you with these accusations, without being able to explain, in looking back, how it happened.

I suffer now—and suffered then—from moods which kept my head under water (so to speak) and only allowed me to see the things subjectively without enabling me to consider quietly the words of the other side, and to answer them as the words of one whom I, with my hot-headed temperament, had offended or made unhappy.

I hid myself within myself, I only considered myself and quietly wrote down all my joys, sorrows, and contempt in my diary. This diary is of great value to me, because it has become a book of memoirs in many places, but on a good many pages I could certainly put "past and done with!"

Anne's philosophic distance from her anger is no more "true" than her hot-headed hatred for Mummy. Each entry is true to its moment. The rereading gives perspective and self-awareness but cannot invalidate the sincerity relative to each point in time. Had Anne lived she might have reread at another time and felt that her anger had, after all, been justified.

As you become aware of the relativity of your emotions and attitudes you develop perspective—an important aspect of maturity. In addition, rereading your diary gives you the opportunity to compare yourself to yourself ("From rereading my diary I see that I am more fearful of taking chances than I used to be. Why?") rather than measuring yourself against others ("He was mentioned in *U.S. News and World Report,* therefore I am less successful than he is"; "She has two children and a four-bedroom house, and she is younger than I am"). When you cease judging yourself against external standards you begin to experience the meaning of your life's drama.

Balancing Yourself Through Balancing Your Writing

Personal growth through the process of diary keeping depends upon the close interrelationship between you and your writing. When you change yourself, your writing seems to change; and when you change the way you write, your perceptions seem to change. For example, if you notice in rereading that you often exaggerate, you could consciously stop exaggerating in your writing. You might work on avoiding the use of superlatives, for instance. Things are not generally the "best" or the "worst" but lie somewhere in between. Changing your writing in this way would force you to think in terms of more subtle gradations in evaluating your experience and sensitize you to the complexity of your feelings—the subtle as well as the dramatic. In this way changing the self and changing the writing become complementary activities that accelerate and reinforce each other.

I once heard the poet Robert Bly explain that balance in writing corresponds to Jung's concept of "balanced consciousness." According to Jung, the four functions of perception— that is, feeling, sensing, intuiting, and thinking—exist in everyone. But in most people some of these functions are dominant while others are undeveloped. To balance the personality, then, the weak functions need to be strengthened.

Coincidentally, Jung's four functions of perception correspond to the four basic modes of expression—catharsis (feeling), description (sensing), free-intuitive writing (intuiting), and reflection (thinking). As a result, you may be able to gain insight into your personality by observing which of the devices is prominent and which is least represented or nonexistent in your writing.

If how you record experience reflects how you perceive it, then practicing a mode of expression that seems to be absent from your writing may, in fact, expand how you experience your life. For example, some of my students have become increasingly aware of their physical environments by including more description in their diary writing. Others have developed greater intimacy with their feelings by consciously including them in the diary.

The following highly oversimplified formulation should not be taken as a proven system for balancing yourself through balancing your writing. Rather it is, like the questions suggested earlier in this chapter, simply food for thought on how personality might be coded in, and developed through, your writing.

Consciousness of Feelings. If you find rhythm, sincerity, accuracy of tone, a strong code of personal values, and a sense of sustained involvement with others in your writing, it may indicate an intimacy with your feelings. However, in rereading for feelings you need to distinguish between affected or overly dramatized writing and vulnerable, honest writing. If you sound like the reporter of your emotional experience rather than its source, it may indicate distance or a fear of your feelings.

If your writing seems to you weak in genuine feelings you might ask yourself when you write, "What did I feel? What do I feel now? How do I really feel about that person, place, or thing?" You might try to allow yourself to feel vulnerable as you write, permit cathartic writing, and work with your dreams in the diary.

Consciousness of the Senses. If you write concrete, descriptive prose, full of specific detail, it may indicate that you are very much in tune with your physical environment. Samuel Pepys's famous diary is sensually specific in this way, and he was a very sensual person. You can see, hear, taste, smell, and touch an experience from reading such writing.

If you are weak in this area of consciousness, your writing may seem abstract and generalized on rereading. To develop descriptive abilities you could focus more attention on your environment, write "here-and-now" exercises, listen more carefully to your body, and ask yourself while writing, "What physical detail would help me illustrate this experience or idea?"

Consciousness of Intuitions. The highly intuitive person may not use free-intuitive writing specifically, but freedom of form and a spirit of surprise and experimentation will be evident in the diary. An intuitive diarist might visit a friend and write a free, unstructured impression of the experience; something like the following:

> Energies of their own accord synchronize given time
> Dreams can grow rich or die
> > a fly touches the rim of my glass
> > a touch of his wing can break the balance.
> Tread gently, fly; sip the sweet wine that binds love to love.

Intuitive writing often has a magical, poetic quality and sometimes contains fanciful or poetic flights. It may also be obscure. The intuitive diarist frequently notices dream correspondences and synchronicity, and may tend to overidentify with other people's feelings.

If your writing seems matter-of-fact and lacking in lyricism, you could develop intuition through dream work, free-intuitive writing, and future projection through altered point of view.

Consciousness through Intellect. The diary of a strongly intellectual person frequently contains a significant amount of reflection. The writing may be very coherent so that you can follow a consistent train of thought throughout the entries. There may be an element of irony or humor or the presence of a strong Internal Critic. Or the writing may, if not balanced with description and intuition, tend toward abstractions and sweeping generalizations and seem overly intellectual.

If serious thought or significant insights seem to be missing from your diary, you could reread entries immediately after writing them and comment in a final paragraph on what you observe, include other reflective entries, and dialogue with a figure of inner wisdom.

By developing modes of expression you may previously have ignored you open up new areas of perception and personal strengths. The diary becomes a laboratory of the self where you can expand capacities that allow you to experience life more fully.

You need the objective and concerned spirit of a good scientist to reread and evaluate your own diary. Harsh self-judgments only impede growth. Just as there is no perfect diary, there is no perfect self. There is no goal. There is only the continuous process of self-completion. Anaïs Nin's description of this "goalless" orientation (in *Diary II*) provides a guiding principle for rereading the diary:

> There is no progress of the personality like a pyramid converging to a point of perfection. Fulfillment is the completion of a circle. All aspects of the self have to be lived out, like the twelve houses of the Zodiac. A personality is one who has unrolled the ribbon, unfolded the petals, exposed all the layers. It does not matter where one begins; with instinct or wisdom, with nature or spirit. The fulfillment means the experience of all parts of the self, all the elements, all the planes. It means each cell of the body comes alive, awakened. It is a process of nature, and not of the ideal. . . . All the errors are necessary, the stutterings, the blunders, the blindnesses. The end is to cover all the terrain, all the routes. No spaces to skip. Any skipping of a phase only retards the branchlike unfolding. Growth, expansion, plentitude of the potential self. To live only one aspect or one side of the personality is like using only one sense, and the others become atrophied. There is greatness only in fulfillment, in the fullness of awakening.

All the errors are necessary for they lead to the "fullness of awakening." Rereading your diary with self-empathy and self-acceptance prepares you for the next phase of personal expansion.

14 | Therapy and the Diary

The New Diary and psychotherapy have developed independently though along parallel paths throughout the twentieth
century. Quietly and creatively diary writers have absorbed
and applied psychological theories and methods, and recently
some psychologists have incorporated autobiographical journal
writing into their programs for personal growth.

Freud recognized the importance of the diary as a key to
the psyche in his preface to the *Diary of a Young Girl.*
Jungians have always asked their patients to keep dream logs.
And Morita therapy, now recognized by Japanese psychiatrists
as one of the most effective therapies for neurosis, uses journal
keeping as an essential part of the treatment.

Morita therapy, which was developed in 1920 by Professor Masatake Morita at the Kikei Hospital in Tokyo, usually
lasts forty to sixty days and consists of exposure to nature,
light manual labor, the therapeutic relationship between doctor and patient, and keeping a journal. The patient is
instructed to record past traumas as well as his behavior and
feelings of the day, and the therapist reads the entries and
makes comments. Morita therapy has proved to be particularly
effective for patients who tend to be intellectually oriented
and use their rational capacities to analyze their seeming
imperfections. The goal of the therapy is to decondition the

person's obsessive concentration on his shortcomings by encouraging him to focus attention on nature, on work, and on an acceptance of life as it is.

In the United States clinics that treat many outpatients have also used the diary as a means of helping people gain a more objective view of their mental processes. At the Mood Clinic of the Hospital of the University of Pennsylvania, Drs. Aaron Beck and Maria Kovacs use the diary as part of what is known as "cognitive therapy." Cognitive therapy attempts to identify and correct negative and unrealistic thought patterns found at the root of depression. Patients are asked to write down their thoughts when sad or depressed, and they are taught to identify and to challenge their self-criticisms. They are also asked to record achievements and gratifying activities and, in so doing, they come to discover that they may be accomplishing more and having more pleasurable experiences than they had previously realized.

Besides such programs in which journal keeping is central, there are many more instances in which the diary functions as a complement to other forms of therapy. Researchers Snadowsky and Belken in 1974 published the results of a study in which they had asked half of the participants at intensive growth weekends to keep diaries, while the other half did not. Those who kept journals were shown to have experienced greater measurable gains in self-concept from the intensive weekend.

Some therapists suggest that patients keep a journal of their thoughts, dreams, and behavior as a complement to the traditional therapeutic hour. They may recommend specific exercises depending on the patient's particular problem—such as listing how one is like and unlike her mother or reviewing collected dreams on a particular theme.

If you are engaged in some form of psychotherapy that does not incorporate journal keeping, you may wish to take the responsibility upon yourself to use the journal to accelerate your progress. For example, a topic that may have been glazed over during the therapeutic hour can be explored more fully on your own in the diary. Some diarists adapt particular techniques learned in therapy into their journals, such as dialogues between the "Adult" and the "Child" used in Transactional Analysis, or fantasy journeys into the subconscious used by some Jungians. Other diarists record certain of the therapists' comments so that they can go back and review the advice when they need it.

In many cases the diary provides a place to sift insights and feelings that occur after the therapeutic hour, integrating and reinforcing the healing process. For example, one diarist, recovering from a bad experience with drugs, writes after a session with her therapist:

> After seeing Louise today, I felt like crying. "Will I get
> well?" I asked her. And she leaned forward, saying
> earnestly how she had sensed from the first moment that
> I was strong and that she could feel the healing in me. I
> believe I feel the healing too. It is gradual. I think there
> is something in me which is instinctively wise.

With a personal record of the therapeutic process the diarist can accelerate her growth.

You can also prepare to make the most of the therapeutic hour by sifting through your thoughts and feelings in the diary before meeting with the counselor to get a sense of what needs attention. And you can use the diary for self-guidance when the therapist is unavailable. The formal time scheme of the therapeutic hour cannot always correspond with personal patterns of growth. There are occasions when an urge to explore an insight or feeling cannot wait for an appointment or when the energy will have dissipated by the time you meet with the therapist. In a diary the insight or feeling can be captured when it occurs, fostering a familiarity with your individual rhythms of growth and tides of emotion—an important aspect of self-knowledge.

The diary may also serve as a gauge to the openness of your therapeutic relationship. If you notice a significant disparity between the relative intimacy of what you share with your therapist and the total intimacy of what you share with your journal, you may wish to assess the reasons for this disparity and perhaps discuss the problem with your therapist.

Frequently the therapist becomes an important figure in a journal. The diarist may write unsent letters to the therapist or dialogue with the therapist on paper for solace and advice. There are many places in her diary where Anaïs Nin seems to be thinking to her analyst:

> I feel well, Dr. Bogner. I feel I can now earn my living. I look for pleasure in small events. For example, I now enjoy the foghorns in New York. Years ago I thought of the foghorns as signaling all my frustrated dreams of travel, they seemed like wistful sounds of ships leaving without me aboard. Now I think of them as joyous proofs that the ships are there, sailing back and forth, and that any day I will be on one of them. Isn't the miracle in the interpretation of events, in this transformation of nostalgia, regret, longing into hope and faith?

Nin associates the ability to transform painful ways of perceiving into positive ones with attitudes learned in therapy. And so she naturally evokes her analyst as a way to connect with these attitudes in herself.

The presence of the therapist in a diary as a healing figure or a figure of wisdom can be very reassuring. But if the diary becomes primarily an extended unsent letter written to the therapist, you may wish to examine your level of dependence on the therapist and perhaps work on reasserting your capacity for self-guidance.

The central relationship in the diary is with yourself. And it is precisely this active, positive relationship with self that therapy works to facilitate. However, there is sometimes a temptation to get lazy in therapy and allow the counselor to provide the support that must ultimately be supplied by you. Overdependence on a therapist can actually retard maturation and self-reliance. Developing a strong relationship with yourself in the diary by writing to and for yourself, as if the diary were another therapeutic session, can counterbalance this temptation.

In the diary you take on the roles of both patient and therapist. As the writer/patient you express your fears, pains, hopes, and needs; and your job is to be spontaneous, honest, and vulnerable. As the receptive listener/counselor you take on the role of active self-helper and self-healer; and your job is to be observant, compassionate, and constructive. Used in this way the journal-keeping process can help you accelerate your progress, carry you through any interruptions, create a natural bridge out of therapy, and facilitate continued progress after its termination.

Finally, as I have tried to demonstrate throughout this book, the New Diary is a marvelously effective, life-long tool for self-therapy and self-guidance. For a great many people who cannot afford therapy or who feel they have all the necessary resources within to act as their own counselors, the diary can substitute for psychotherapy.

To carve a mountain path all by yourself gives a greater sense of personal power than to follow a path that is shown. Similarly, a personal search carried on in the diary gives rise to a well-founded feeling of confidence in your capacity to meet predicaments successfully and not feel lost without external guidance.

15 | Expanding Creativity

Creativity and therapy become one and the same in the New Diary—an active communication with self. Each complements the other, and arises out of the other. Creativity, like self-awareness, depends upon being in touch with your intellectual and emotional processes, upon listening for, valuing, and cultivating what comes from within. As a diarist you are immersed in the habit of genuine self-communication, so that creativity becomes part of your daily life. Once your creative spirit has been freed and nurtured in the journal you are likely to discover an added benefit of the diary—as a source book for creative projects.

In this book I have discussed the New Diary as a tool for living creatively: for transforming a personal problem into a creative solution, for gaining insight and inspiration from your dreams, and for developing the skills of perception and self-expression. The principles of working in the diary—patience with your own process, faith in your intuition, and the search for correspondences and synthesis—are essential to all original, creative activity. You will find that these principles, once acquired, seem to expand naturally to other creative pursuits.

In fact, all of the diary devices are, at the same time, self-help techniques and tools for creative expression. In learning to use the devices you fully exercise your instrument as a writer. Just as a guitarist first learns a set of basic chords, which he can then augment, invert, combine, and play upon in an infinite variety of ways, so have you as a diarist learned the basics of creative expression, which you can now play upon imaginatively and freely, both inside the diary and out.

To begin with, the four natural modes of expression open up universal channels of creativity. Lyric poetry and songs spring from catharsis, the free expression of feeling. "All my poems," said Robert Lowell, "are written for catharsis." Narrative writing depends upon description, the ability to translate sensory perceptions into language. The delightful nonsense lyrics of Ogden Nash or Lewis Carroll and many other forms of humorous expression evolve from the quick, nonlogical associations of free-intuitive writing. And literary, film, music, and art criticism rely on the intellectual observation of reflection.

The special diary techniques also have limitless direct creative applications. An outline for anything from a speech to a novel is simply a list arranged in a considered order. Portraits are part of most fiction and much nonfiction. (A magazine article may simply be an extended portrait of an interesting character.) Maps of consciousness may lead to further exploration of the visual arts—drawing, painting, or photography.

And every creator and inventor goes into the uncharted realm of fantasy and reverie that I have referred to as guided imagery. (Fantasy, science fiction, poetry, children's stories, adventure tales, and romantic novels are actually polished examples of guided imagery.)

Altered point of view is the basic device of all fiction. Anaïs Nin was able to fill in the "missing parts" of her edited diary through the use of altered point of view in her continuous novels. In *The Novel of the Future* she speculated that fiction probably developed when people could not present certain emotional truths as fact.

Unsent letters teach a writer flexibility. Addressing a variety of different audiences allows you to experience how whom you write to determines both what you say and how you say it. And dialogue, of course, is the basis for writing conversation in plays and other forms of fiction. From the diary dialogue you also learn to maintain more than one point of view at a time, a technique on which creative expression often depends.

After keeping a diary for a while you will be able to see your own creative strengths. A particular affinity for a certain diary device may suggest further creative pursuits. For example, if you write dialogues with a certain flair, this naturally evolved ability may lead you to try your hand at writing a play. Or you might apply a facility for description and portraits to writing a novel. Or taking pleasure in guided imagery and free-intuitive writing may lead you into poetry. Because you have become familiar with the tools of the creative process, you will bring to any other creative form you try the ease and individuality of style you have developed spontaneously in the diary.

A Treasure Trove of Creative Inspiration

In addition, you will often find within the diary the inspiration for a creative work. I carried this book in my diary long before I knew I would actually write it. Over a seven-year period I made entries about my own process and about my reflections on other diaries, without considering to what use I might later put them. And I asked myself questions about journal writing, to which at first I didn't have answers. Gradually I began to see the answers to those questions evolving on the pages of my journals. The concept for this book developed organically and effortlessly out of my personal diary, and many other projects have come from it as well.

You, too, may wish to turn to your diary for creative material. You might discover a continuing interest in a particular subject, a political or environmental issue, a mythological or psychological theme that you might wish to develop as an article to communicate to others. You might discover "found poems" by selecting and combining lines and images scattered throughout the diary—perhaps from dreams or fantasies, perhaps from descriptions. You might find stories that have begun to tell themselves within the journal, characters that could be used for a play, or a dream that could be expanded into a poem, a song, or a story.

Wanting to write a short story several years ago, I turned to my diary and found the initial inspiration in a childhood dream, earlier recalled and recorded. One of the settings came from the description of a girlfriend's unusual apartment, and the characters were formed from a synthesis of real and imaginary people whose portraits I had written. The story seemed to lift itself right out of the diary. Like the origin of a living cell, all the separate elements found connection with each other simply because I had placed them within the fertile pool of the diary.

Creative people in many fields have traditionally kept journals because the form encourages the creative process. The journal provides a place to deposit the first flash of creative inspiration or impression. It allows you to capture the essence of the moment while it is still vivid and fresh in your mind.

One man went on vacation with his wife to her hometown, a settlement of Greek and Italian miners. He was intrigued with the differences in vocabulary, the characters he met, the jokes he heard. Without knowing exactly how he would use these impressions, he captured them in his journal so that they would be preserved for an eventual exchange of humor or for a speech or a story he might one day write. In this way the diary provides you with your own hoard of creative material. The photographer makes a note, "An interesting image as I got off the freeway at Silverlake"; the architect jots down, "I'd like to experiment with solar reflectors on the side of the hill"; another person records fleeting thoughts on home improvements, "A loft would make a lot more space," and "I'd love to have a teahouse in the backyard like the one we saw outside Tokyo"; and the writer speculates, "It might be interesting to write a book about women's periodic cycles."

These imaginings and impulses are the beginnings of the creative process—a process that is often slow and complex and in which the final product may be unclear for a long time. Rather than getting lost in a wasteland of forgetfulness such fragile, undeveloped inspirations are held in the diary like eggs in a nest, until you have time to nurture them to completion.

All inspirations seem at the moment of conception to be genuine, but it takes time to tell which will be fertile. In the diary the collected inspirations for a book, poem, painting, film, sculpture, musical composition, or any other creative work lie side by side in incubation. Some seem to augment their meaning in relationship to others; some seem to drop away as irrelevant; some merge into larger, more comprehensive ideas.

The Creative Project Journal

Some diarists include creative inspirations and related impressions along with daily concerns and dreams inside the personal diary. Others keep a separate notebook specifically for creative ideas. In either case, once you have decided to pursue a particular project most people find it helpful to use a separate "creative project" journal. For example, once I decided to write this book I made a list of the possible chapter headings in a separate notebook. To develop the project I chose a three-ring binder because it would be convenient to rearrange pages. I inserted dividers, each with the title of one of the chapters. Then I simply filed the ideas as they came to me within the already established sections of the special journal. As I came to writing a new chapter I had notes waiting for me in their appropriate sections. I could evaluate these and then proceed with rearranging and rewriting.

This same method can be used for writing your autobiography. A simple list such as the stepping-stones of your life could be the chapter headings. You could then create sections in a three-ring binder so that specific memories could be filed in the appropriate time period.

A novelist friend of mine uses a slightly different, less structured, method to develop his novels. His method can be adapted to any creative endeavor. You simply make consecutive dated entries in a blank book, just as you do in a personal diary—except that each entry in the creative project journal relates directly or indirectly to the concept you wish to develop. You follow your intuitions chronologically, as in the personal diary, recording bits of information, hunches, or seemingly unrelated images that may or may not actually find use.

The novelist might first experiment with different plot ideas, asking questions beginning, "What if ... ?" or "Why not ....?" Answers may not come immediately. As in the personal diary the writer must be patient with the process. Everything at this stage of development is tentative. At first you may come up with clichés, but by pushing forward you move beyond them. Problems in the work eventually find solutions.

Whatever format you choose for your creative project journal, certain principal themes recur and combine simply from permitting the possibilities to accumulate. Dreams from your personal diary that seem to relate to material in the project journal can be included at any point. When you are thinking about a particular project you may automatically have (or you can invoke) dreams that will carry the creative process forward.

This process of filing bits and pieces of ideas and gradually developing and elaborating on them could be used effectively by an architect designing an office building or a teacher developing a grant proposal. It can also be a welcome solution to a conflict between practicality and the creative impulse for people whose demanding lives or jobs do not permit much creative expression. You can keep a creative project journal in a kitchen drawer or in an office desk, carry it in the car and record notes for it on a tape cassette. When an inspiration comes you can record it quickly and go on with your other activities. In this way you can develop a cookbook, a novel, or a ship design, a landscape for a Japanese garden, a screenplay, or a comic routine while working full-time or taking care of a family.

When you have time (for the working person that may mean on weekends) you can read over and evaluate the notes you have accumulated. Some may no longer seem valid, and others will leap out at you as just right. Those that seem right can be developed further. You will notice patterns that will begin to shape the work. By the time you are ready to execute the project it will already have formed itself in the creative journal through the free play of ideas.

The Diary as Creative Midwife

The familiar processes of writing or drawing spontaneously and reviewing the entries for patterns can go on within the protective womb of the journal. But the last steps involved in the creative process—execution, revision, and polishing—force the actual birth of the work, and this can be painful. Yet even here the diary can be helpful—as a figurative midwife.

The actual construction of a house, originally designed and developed in the journal, or the actual writing of a novel, outlined and sketched in a journal, exposes you to external considerations and challenges. At this final stage of the creative process, diary and creative product become quite distinct from each other. The prepared creative product—whether it be a garden, a novel, or a painting—takes on an independent life with its own dynamics. The personal diary or creative project journal, however, remains untransmuted process.

Yet communication between the separate creative work and the journal can be invaluable in nurturing the work to completion. In the diary you can complain or rejoice in the progress of the work, let off steam, continue to pose questions, comfort and advise yourself. In your diary you overcome blocks to creativity by adapting any of the techniques suggested in Chapter 10. You can write dialogues with the Internal Critic, who frequently functions as a valuable consultant or editor in the final revision of a work. You can dialogue with the various characters in a fictional work-in-progress to learn more about them. For example, one novelist was writing about a group of Aztec Indians in the period immediately following the Spanish conquest. She felt the need to know more about their way of life, so she dialogued with one of her characters, Star-Jaguar:

> **Jane**
> I need to understand you. I feel so far away.
> **Star-Jaguar**
> You should visualize us as we walk in file with the
> burdens on our backs. Watch our legs, our feet. Watch
> the way we spread our toes out on the dirt,carefully,
> avoiding the sharp stones. Watch us as we set our
> burdens down and prop them with the sticks. Watch
> the way we sit. Each of us sits differently.

You could even dialogue with a color in a painting. The dialogue device is helpful in making decisions or finding new solutions throughout any creative process.

It is also extremely valuable to write dialogues with the creative work itself. Because the novel or painting or design has a developing spirit of its own, you can consult with it and communicate with it. You simply pose whatever anxiety, dilemma, fear, or confusion you feel, and you allow the work to speak to you with the knowledge it seems to have of its own nature, its own internal coherence and rules of development.

When I was working on the second draft of this book I became frustrated and discouraged because the task of rewriting seemed interminable and new ideas were still entering and reshaping the work. Yet when I dialogued with the developing book in my personal diary, the work offered me the patience I needed to continue:

Me
Sometimes I feel that you are eating me alive, that you've taken over too much of my life and my energy.
Work
I have to make sense, and the only way I'm going to make sense is through completion. Remember the story you loved as a child, the rennet-custard story? It was about a gatekeeper who dropped a golden key into a deep moat. He had to dive into the water to retrieve it, swim way to the bottom. It was very hard, he was never sure he would make it, it was such a long distance, but he kept his eye on the key.
I'm afraid you are still diving, but the key will open many doors.
Me
I don't want to resent you.
Work
Then don't make things worse than they are. Don't exaggerate.
Me
What is this anxiety?
Work
Impatience. Part of the process. All to be expected.

And when I finished writing the book, instead of the joy I expected to feel, I began to have a terrible anxiety—worse than that which had gone before. I wrote another dialogue with the work in my diary, and it told me that I was actually afraid of the final separation, and again offered me the solace I needed:

Work
The sorrow of separation you have is like that described by women who have carried a child for nine months and have finally given birth.

Me
Yes. Don't leave me.
Work
I won't. I'm only freeing you to grow and have another child. You can talk to me here any time. And you will be able to go to your bookshelf and find me.
Me
But what will come next?
Work
I can't tell you that. But I know that you already have the seeds for the next work within you, and if you are patient the conception will come.

The Diary as an Aid to Professional Writers

As a protected place in which to refresh your spirit, keeping a diary can be an important aid for the professional writer. It also serves the writer as a place to "work out" regularly. Anaïs Nin recommended in *The Novel of the Future,* "Writing . . . as one practices the piano every day keeps one nimble, and then when the great moments of inspiration come, one is in good form, supple and smooth."

For those taking the first steps toward publication, the diary can provide a familiar, sheltered place to write the first draft of short pieces. For example, a friend of mine had tried unsuccessfully many times to write a short story about the birth of her first child. Each time she became self-conscious and hypercritical before she could complete a first draft. Finally she decided to write the story in the diary, where she had become accustomed to writing with complete spontaneity and immunity from premature criticism. The story flowed without any problem. Afterward she reflected in the diary:

> I am delighted that I don't feel the revulsion that usually erupts immediately after finishing a piece. A function of having written this story in the diary. I didn't bind myself with a "sense of the literary." And I think I came

closer to touching how I, as a woman, experienced the event—which is probably the reason I am more content with my results.

Having developed a natural writing style in the diary it was easy for her to extend it to her first structured writing project.

At the opposite end of the spectrum many commercial and professional writers need the diary as a sustained line to the self. Without the personal diary they are in danger of becoming so "objective" or so "commercial" that they lose the ability to be subjective. In a class I taught with Anaïs Nin on diary and fiction writing, at least half of the prospective students who wanted to concentrate exclusively on diary writing were already professional writers making a good living in journalism, commercial or technical writing. When I asked them why they wanted to take a writing class, they explained that in learning how to write commercially they had either neglected to develop the capacity to write for themselves or had forgotten how to do it. Most of them said that they couldn't write in the first person nor use their own experience and feelings as material, and they felt cut off from themselves when they wrote.

These writers believed that before they could write anything of lasting quality they had to be able to write in their own voice, and they knew intuitively that writing a diary would be the fastest, surest way to discover that personal voice. The women also sensed that their commercial writing had unsexed them. They felt that when they wrote professionally they generally wrote to please a male audience. In a diary they would write as women, because they could write for themselves.

For both men and women the diary provides a counterbalance to the demands of the writer's marketplace. It develops flexibility, naturalness, and originality of style and subject matter. In the diary you become attuned with the true self that cannot lie, and writing which evolves from that source is recognizably genuine.

The Diary as a Source for Further Autobiographical Writing

Autobiography differs from diary writing because it is a view of one's life reevaluated from a later perspective in time. However, notes kept in a personal diary are invaluable source material for your autobiography. In recent years writing autobiography has fast become a popular leisure and retirement activity. It was once assumed that only statesmen and the distinguished had the privilege of writing their memoirs, just as it was once assumed that only "bluebloods" should trace their ancestral roots. But a new consciousness is arising about autobiography—that it belongs to everyone, just as creativity belongs to everyone. Women and men are writing autobiography and family history for their children and grandchildren as a way to create a new and honest base of family cohesion. Others are writing autobiography as a way of bringing their lives into focus, to see the meaning and continuity for themselves, to tie together the loose ends, or simply to achieve a sense of personal completion.

Even the most externally "typical" life has running within it a deep underground river of inner significance that may be reached when one has the leisure and desire to search it out. A diary can be the principal source for an autobiography, along with collected personal letters, photographs, and other aids to remembrance.

The Natural Diary as a Source for an Edited Diary

A few diarists will find in rereading their journals sufficient internal coherence to consider editing them, either for family and friends or for publication. The true diary remains the untransmuted original, a work of process that belongs to the creator alone. But it may become a literary work when crystalized, refined and edited from the unifying perspective of a later time, with an eye to the informational needs of an external reader.

In editing you omit what is unimportant, trivial, or repetitious and look for underlying themes that run through the whole. You retain and polish the entries that carry your themes, such as a theme of a maturing mother–daughter relationship or the theme of discovering a new vocation. You delete entries that seem entirely unrelated to any of your central themes. If you have written many lists or dialogues or experimented with free-intuitive writing and guided imagery, you may wish to delete these for the sake of readability. And you may wish to make the point of view consistent if you have used altered point of view. You also have the ethical responsibility to delete whatever would be potentially harmful, hurtful, or scandalous if revealed about another.

In editing a natural diary you may find it necessary to write transitional entries or explanations to lead from one subject to the next or to fill in missing periods of time. But if there is too much rewriting the diary loses its unique quality of immediacy and becomes autobiography or even fiction. The diary is as related to random collage as it is to these other literary forms, so don't expect to impose absolute thematic unity on it. A reader expects to feel some of life's chaos in a diary. The fragments make up a pattern from their chance interrelationships.

Those who have attempted to edit their diaries have found it to be an extremely intense experience. As when you reread your diary, feelings from the past seem to flood into the present. And at this stage of the creative process you must be very careful to remain objective.

The satisfaction of editing a diary lies in discovering a hidden order and meaning in your life and bringing it into focus. It is like the microphotographer's art of capturing a snowflake on film—seeing and preserving the intricate pattern of nature in the instant before it disappears. Similarly, in the revelation of inherent patterns, the edited diary allows people to feel, wonder at, and share the mystery and beauty of a human life.

Postscript

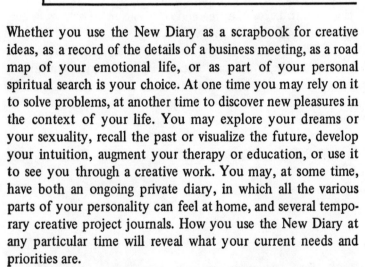

Whether you use the New Diary as a scrapbook for creative ideas, as a record of the details of a business meeting, as a road map of your emotional life, or as part of your personal spiritual search is your choice. At one time you may rely on it to solve problems, at another time to discover new pleasures in the context of your life. You may explore your dreams or your sexuality, recall the past or visualize the future, develop your intuition, augment your therapy or education, or use it to see you through a creative work. You may, at some time, have both an ongoing private diary, in which all the various parts of your personality can feel at home, and several temporary creative project journals. How you use the New Diary at any particular time will reveal what your current needs and priorities are.

You cannot know where the diary will take you or what will ultimately evolve from it. Unpredictability, mutability, and adaptability characterize the form. One woman's diary began as a record of household expenses and expanded into a saga of her ancestors in the nineteenth century. One man's diary began as a punching bag for his anger and became a haven where he opened up the poet and the songwriter in himself. The diary is a never-ending process of search and discovery. It changes as you change; and by acting as a mirror to the self it encourages personal transformation.

It is, in fact, precisely the qualities of mutability and adaptability that have kept the diary alive for so many centuries. It served our ancestors in their earliest attempts to learn to write; it became a form for poetic expression in ancient Japan and was there transformed into the first novel; it absorbed the magic of pagan witchcraft in the West, the self-improvement of Puritanism, the self-reliance of Transcendentalism, the mutual support of women's shared self-knowledge, the insights of psychology, and the boundless experimentation of modern literature. The diary is now shedding its old skin of guilt, shame, secrecy, and unnecessary isolation to become a free and open means of achieving deep intimacy with the self and with others.

What I have called the New Diary will continue to evolve, change, and re-create itself. For the diary, so intimately linked to time, is ever renewed and cannot be outdated. The diary has always recorded the present as a gesture of faith in the future.

Readings of Interest to Diarists

The following published diaries may be of interest to readers of this book. I have also included some supplementary works in psychology, literature, and philosophy that helped to formulate my approach to the New Diary.

(In addition, if you are interested in diaries as creative source books, you might wish to look at the published notebooks and diaries of Leonardo da Vinci, Franz Kafka, Charles Darwin, Leo Tolstoy, Fedor Dostoyevsky, Eugène Delacroix, Paul Gauguin, Gertrude Stein, Françoise du Maurier, John Steinbeck, and William Gibson.)

Akeret, Dr. Robert U. **Photoanalysis.** Edited by Thomas Humber. New York: Simon and Schuster, 1975. The body language of snapshots.

Ashton-Warner, Sylvia. **Myself.** New York: Simon and Schuster, 1967. The conflict between obligations to her family and the pull of writing and teaching; also how she found "a room of her own."

Atwood, Margaret. **The Journals of Susanna Moodie: Poems.** Toronto: Oxford University Press, 1970. Poetry inspired by the journal of Susanna Moodie (1805–1885), who emigrated from England to Canada in 1832 and wrote **Roughing It in the Bush,** a classic account of pioneering in Canada.

Avakian, Elizabeth. **To Deliver Me of My Dreams.** Millbrae, Calif.: Celestial Arts, 1975. Diary of a young woman trying to find a synthesis between love and freedom.

Baldwin, Christina. **One to One: Self-Understanding through Journal Writing.** New York: M. Evans, 1977. A beautifully written account of Baldwin's experience writing a journal and conducting journal workshops.

Barreno, M. J.; M. T. Horta; and M. V. de Costa. **The Three Marias: New Portuguese Letters.** Translated by Helen Lane. New York: Doubleday, 1973. An important example of a collective diary. All three writers were imprisoned for publishing this work, which contains passages of genuine female eroticism.

Bashkirtseff, Marie. **Marie Bashkirtseff: The Journal of a Young Artist.** Translated by Mary J. Serrano. New York: E. P. Dutton, 1923. Every young girl at the turn of the century read this diary, as they read Anne Frank's in the 1950s. Bashkirtseff, who began writing her diary at the age of fourteen and died at twenty-two, had a premonition of her early death and was determined to become famous through her diary in defiance of time and mortality.

Begos, Jane DuPree. **Annotated Bibliography of Published Women's Diaries.** A complete bibliography that is a work of love. Available by writing directly to Jane DuPree Begos, P.O. Box 41, Pound Ridge, N.Y. 10576.

Browning, Elizabeth Barrett. **Diary by E. B. B.** Edited by Philip Kelley and Ronald Hudson. Athens, Ohio: Ohio University Press, 1969. An insight into the life of Victorian England and how "other-directed" women of the time were. Elizabeth doesn't write to herself but to an older man she admired.

Burney, Frances (Fanny). **The Journals and Letters of Fanny Burney (Madame D'Arblay).** Edited by Joyce Hemlow, with Curtis D. Cecil and Althea Douglas. Oxford: Clarendon Press,

1972. A novelist and lifetime diarist, Fanny Burney portrays the literary and social life of eighteenth-century England.

Carlyle, Jane Baillie. **Letters and Memorials of Jane Welsh Carlyle,** 3 vols. Prepared for publication by Thomas Carlyle. Edited by James Anthony Froude. London: Longmans, Green, 1883. Some of Jane Carlyle's diaries were destroyed by her husband, Thomas Carlyle, when he first found them; others she destroyed. Those that remain are sharp and witty.

de Beauvoir, Simone. **The Second Sex.** New York: Random House, 1974. The theory of existentialism as applied to women.

Dostoyevsky, Anna Grigor'evna (Snitkina). **Dostoyevsky Portrayed by His Wife, The Diary and Reminiscences of Mme. Dostoyevsky,** Edited by S. S. Koteliansky and translated from the Russian. New York: E. P. Dutton, 1926. Dostoyevsky dictated his novels to his wife. Her sympathetic portrait of him as a compulsive gambler shows she had literary talents of her own.

Dunaway, Philip and Mel Evans, eds. **A Treasury of the World's Great Diaries.** Garden City, N.Y.: Doubleday, 1957. An anthology of famous diaries.

Durrell, Lawrence. **The Black Book.** New York: E. P. Dutton, 1963. Like Maude Hutchin's **Diary of Love,** this is a nonfiction novel that resembles the diary in structure.

Evans, Elizabeth. **Weathering the Storm, Women of the American Revolution.** New York: Scribner's, 1975. An anthology of women's diaries.

Falk, Ruth. **Women Loving. A Journey toward Becoming an Independent Woman.** New York: Random House/Bookworks, 1975. A feminist handbook for exploring one's feelings and sharing them with others. Includes the author's intimate diary.

Faraday, Ann. **Dream Power.** New York: Coward, McCann and Geoghegan, 1973. A good basic text for no-nonsense dream work.

Field, Joanna. **A Life of One's Own.** London: Chatto and Windus, 1936. A superb book on diary writing, far ahead of its time (presently out of print).

Fiennes, Celia. **Through England on a Side-Saddle, in the Time of William and Mary.** London: Field and Tuer, 1888. The diary of an independent tradeswoman who traveled for her business on horseback. As vivid a picture of Restoration England as that seen through Samuel Pepys's diary.

Forten, Charlotte. **The Journal of Charlotte L. Forten: Free Negro in the Slave Era.** Edited by Ray Allen Billington. London: Collier-Macmillan, 1969. Charlotte Forten came from one of the few wealthy black families before the American Civil War. Her diary is a good example of the Puritan self-disciplinary journal.

Frank, Anne. **Anne Frank: The Diary of a Young Girl.** New York: Doubleday, 1952. Look especially at "Kitty's" role as audience in Anne's diary.

Garfield, Patricia. **Creative Dreaming.** New York: Simon and Schuster, 1974. More information on dream control: how to choose and guide your dreams.

Gide, André. **The Journals of André Gide.** New York: Alfred A. Knopf, 1947. At eighteen Gide began keeping his first journal with the intent of becoming a writer. They are a classic example of the *journal intime* kept by most French men and women of letters.

Hamilton-Merritt, Jane. **A Meditator's Diary. A Western Woman's Unique Experiences in Thailand Temples.** New York: Harper and Row, 1976. An example of the diary for spiritual growth.

Harris, Thomas A. **I'm OK—You're OK**. New York: Harper and Row, 1967. A good introduction to Transactional Analysis.

Horney, Karen. **Self-Analysis**. New York: Norton, 1942. Horney, a psychiatrist, explains that self-analysis is possible and desirable.

Hutchins, Maude. **A Diary of Love**. New York: New Directions, 1950. Like the early Japanese diaries, a work somewhere between fact and fiction.

Isherwood, Christopher. **Kathleen and Frank**. New York: Simon and Schuster, 1971. Using his mother's diaries and his own memory, Isherwood tells of his early family life. Mainly covers the period between 1883–1919, with some later excerpts.

———. **Berlin Stories**. Set in Germany before World War II, this is a nonfiction novel that resembles a diary.

Izumi Shikibu. **The Izumi Shikibu Diary: A Romance of the Heian Court**. Translated with an introduction by Edwin A. Cranston. Cambridge, Mass.: Harvard University Press, 1969. Includes poems exchanged with her lover.

James, Alice. **The Diary of Alice James**. Edited by Leon Edel. New York: Dodd, Mead, 1964. Unlike her famous brothers, Henry and William, Alice never found an outlet for her abundant intellect and energy—except in her diary. In it she faces death with wry wit and graceful philosophy.

Jung, C. G. **Memories, Dreams, Reflections**. Edited by Aniela Jaffé. New York: Random House, 1961. Jung's autobiography.

———. **Synchronicity: An Acausal Connecting Principle**. Princeton, N.J.: Princeton University Press, 1960. The first book on meaningful coincidences.

Koestler, Arthur. **The Act of Creation: A Study of the Conscious and Unconscious in Science and Art.** New York: Dell, 1964. Presents creativity as a process of synthesis.

Lessing, Doris. **The Golden Notebook.** New York: Simon and Schuster, 1962. A great novel about modern woman's consciousness. A hybrid of diary and conventional novel form that transcends the limitations in point of view of each.

McKee, Ruth Karr. **Mary Richardson Walker: Her Book.** Caldwell, Idaho: Caxton Printers, 1945. A pioneer woman who kept a strong, honest journal.

Mansfield, Katherine. **The Journal of Katherine Mansfield.** Edited by J. M. Murry. London: Constable, 1954. Covers the period of 1904–1922. Contains examples of altered point of view and incidents she used later in her exquisite short stories.

Martin, Martha of Alaska (pseud.). **O, Rugged Land of Gold.** New York: Macmillan, 1953. Diary of a female Robinson Crusoe, who gave birth to her first child alone in the Alaskan wilds.

Masters, Robert, and Jean Houston. **Mind Games.** New York: Dell, 1973. Progressive exercises in guided imagery.

Miller, Henry. **Tropic of Cancer.** New York: Grove Press, 1961. A semi-autobiographical novel with all the free-form spontaneity of the diary.

Miner, Earl. **The Japanese Poetic Diary.** Berkeley and Los Angeles: University of California Press, 1969. An anthology of early Japanese diaries with an excellent critical introduction that shows how the early evolution of the diary in Japan has influenced the Japanese theory of literature to this day.

Mitchell, Suzanne (pseud.). **My Own Woman: The Diary of an Analysis.** New York: Horizon Press, 1973. Diary of a woman trying to find herself and her sexual feelings through two analysts and a long marriage.

Moffat, Mary Jane, and Charlotte Painter, eds. **Revelations: Diaries of Women.** New York: Random House, 1974. A first-rate anthology of women's diaries.

Munby, Arthur J. **Munby: Man of Two Worlds.** Boston: Gambit, 1972. The private diary of Munby—barrister, poet, and friend of Ruskin and Browning. He reveals his lifelong obsession with female manual workers and the fact that his secret wife for twenty-five years was a charwoman.

Murasaki, Shikibu (Lady). **The Tale of Genji,** 2 vols. Translated from the Japanese by Arthur Waley. Boston: Houghton Mifflin, 1935. This is the first Japanese novel. Murasaki was also a diarist.

Nichols, Susan Claire. **The Personal Journal: A Mental Health Proposal.** Unpublished Ph.D. dissertation. Ann Arbor, Mich.: University Microfilms International, 1973. Presents supporting research for the theraupeutic benefits of diary writing.

Nijinsky, Vaslav. **The Diary of Vaslav Nijinsky.** London: Jonathan Cape Ltd., 1963. Nijinsky wrote this diary as a last stand against encroaching madness. Had his doctors known how to interpret his diary, he probably could have been helped.

Nin, Anaïs. **A Woman Speaks: The Lectures, Seminars, and Interviews of Anais Nin.** Edited with an introduction by Evelyn J. Hinz. Chicago: Swallow Press, 1975. Nin examines and answers many questions about diary writing.

———. **The Diary, Volumes 1 through VI.** New York: Harcourt, Brace and World: 1966, 1967, 1969, 1971, 1974, 1976. The self-told story of the woman-artist's evolution of consciousness. Simultaneously the history of the avant-garde in Europe and the U.S. from 1931-1977. Read in conjunction with the diaries, Nin's novels—**Under a Glass Bell, Ladders to Fire, Children of the Albatross, The Four-Chambered Heart, A Spy in the House of Love,** and **Seduction of the Minotaur,** in **Cities of the Interior** (Chicago: Swallow Press, 1959, 1974)—fill in the missing pieces to give the full picture of her emotional life. Like diaries, the novels are "continuous," without beginnings or ends. The same characters weave in and out of the ongoing "emotional algebra."

Omori, Annie Shepley (trans.), and Kochi Doi. **Diaries of Court Ladies of Old Japan.** Boston: Houghton Mifflin, 1920. A delightful collection of early Japanese diaries.

Ornstein, Robert E. **The Psychology of Consciousness.** New York: Viking, 1973. A good foundation for understanding right brain—left brain theory.

Pepys, Samuel. **The Diary of Samuel Pepys,** vol. 8. Edited by Robert Latham and William Mathews. Los Angeles: University of California Press, 1973. Written in the most colloquial prose of the seventeenth century, but in a secret code understood only by English gentlemen of the Restoration. When the code was cracked, the diary became famous overnight.

Perls, Frederick S. **Gestalt Therapy Verbatim.** Lafayette, Calif.: Real People Press, 1969. A foundation for understanding Gestalt techniques.

Priestly, J. B. **Man and Time.** New York: Dell, 1964. A good overview for those interested in the subject of time.

Progoff, Ira. **At a Journal Workshop.** New York: Dialogue House Library, 1975. The basic text for using the INTENSIVE JOURNAL.

———. **Jung, Synchronicity, and Human Destiny: Noncausal Dimensions of Human Experience.** New York: Dell, 1973. Expounds on Jung's theories of meaningful coincidences.

Rich, Adrienne. **Charleston in the Eighteen-Sixties: Poems: Selected and New.** New York: Norton, 1975. Poetry inspired by another woman's diary.

Riedesel, Frederika Charlotte Louise. **Baroness von Riedesel and the American Revolution: Journal and Correspondence of a Tour of Duty, 1776–1783.** Edited by Marvin L. Brown, Jr., and Marta Huth. Chapel Hill, N.C.: University of North Carolina Press, 1976. The most detailed recording of the Revolution by a woman.

Rossi, Ernest Lawrence. **Dreams and the Growth of Personality.** New York: Pergamon Press, 1972. A case study of how dreams lead the individual to psychic healing and growth.

Sand, George (pseud. for Amandine Aurore Lucie Dupin). **The Intimate Journal of George Sand.** Translated with notes by Marie Jenny Howe. London: Williams and Norgate, 1929. In her journals Sand wrote what were perhaps the first Gestalt dialogues.

Sarashina, Lady. **As I Crossed the Bridge of Dreams: Recollections of a Woman in Eleventh-Century Japan.** Translated by Ivan Morris. New York: Dial, 1971. A charming diary in which fact and fiction interweave. A woman adopts a stray cat that turns out to be the reincarnation of a Japanese princess.

Sarton, May. **Journal of a Solitude.** New York: Norton, 1973. Account of a woman's seeking to find herself during a year alone on a New England farm.

Scott-Maxwell, Florida. **The Measure of My Days.** New York: Knopf, 1975. The record of her strong reactions to being old and her feelings of being at variance with the times.

Sei Shōnagon. **The Pillow Book of Sei Shōnagon,** 2 vols. Translated and edited by Ivan Morris. New York: Columbia University Press, 1967. The observations of an intelligent, complicated, well-informed woman during the ten-year period

314 THE NEW DIARY

she served at court. A collage of anecdotes, portraits, descriptions, and lists.

Shelley, Mary Wollstonecraft. **Mary Shelley's Journal.** Edited by Frederick L. Jones. Norman, Okla.: University of Oklahoma Press, 1947. Written as an unsent letter to Shelley when he died.

Spencer, Sharon. **Time, Space, and Structure in the Modern Novel.** Chicago: Swallow Press, 1973. Shows the relationship between diary writing and the newest novels.

Thoreau, Henry. **The Journal.** Chicago: University of Chicago Press, 1976. Shows Thoreau's value of spontaneity and attunement to one's inner wisdom. (Both Thoreau and Emerson were, according to Anaïs Nin, strong influences on her own diary writing.)

Waldman, Anne. **Journals and Dreams.** New York: Stonehill, 1976. Poetry based on journal writing, journal reading, and dreams.

Warhol, Andy. **The Philosophy of Andy Warhol (From A to B and Back Again).** Transcribed and edited by Paul Warhol. New York: Harcourt Brace Jovanovich, 1975. A tape-recorded journal of a notorious artist.

Woolf, Virginia. **A Room of One's Own.** New York: Harcourt, Brace, and World, 1957. A brilliant essay that helps explain the historical development of the Internal Critics and Censors that plague women writers.

–––. **The Diary of Virginia Woolf: Volume I, 1915–1919.** Edited by Anne Oliver Bell. New York: Harcourt Brace Jovanovich, 1977. Woolf wrote to herself at sixty. Shows that in their diaries even the greatest writers worry about shabby furniture or a new dress.

Wordsworth, Dorothy. **The Journals of Dorothy Wordsworth,** 2 vols. Edited by E. de Selincourt. New York: Macmillan, 1941. Entries from this lovely diary were used by her brother William Wordsworth and their friend Samuel Taylor Coleridge for their poetry.

Index